Avoiding Prison
and Other Noble
Vacation Goals

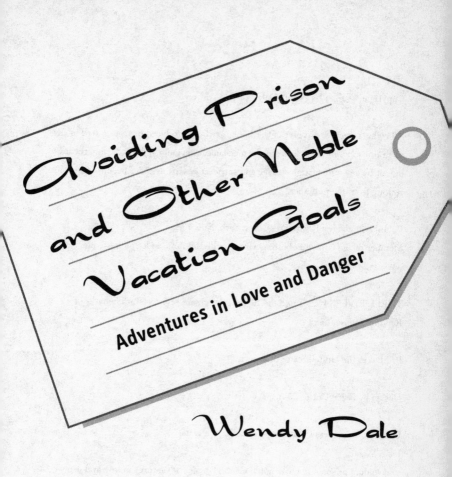

Avoiding Prison and Other Noble Vacation Goals

Adventures in Love and Danger

Wendy Dale

 THREE RIVERS PRESS · NEW YORK

Published by Three Rivers Press, New York, New York
Member of the Crown Publishing Group, a division of Random House, Inc.
www.randomhouse.com

THREE RIVERS PRESS and the Tugboat design are registered trademarks of
Random House, Inc.

Printed in the United States of America

Design by Fearn Cutler deVicq

Library of Congress Cataloging-in-Publication Data
Dale, Wendy.
   Avoiding prison and other noble vacation goals : adventures in love and danger /
Wendy Dale.—1st ed.
     1. Dale, Wendy—Journeys. 2. Voyages and travels. I. Title.
G465 .D347 2003
910.4—dc 21   2003002164
ISBN 0-609-80983-0

10   9   8   7   6   5   4   3   2   1

First Edition

For my mom.

For La Troje and those that are a part of it.

And for Douglas Adams.

So long and thanks for the inspiration.

Disclaimers, Claimers, and Acknowledgments

This is a book about my travels, but it is also a memoir, and trying to describe a life on paper has its limitations. This is because life is a complex event, full of contradictions and inconsistencies, but literature requires a thesis and so a writer is forced to pick out the patterns, making sense of a seemingly random series of events and, in effect, oversimplifying what actually happened.

In this book, I have been faced with the difficult choice of providing a literal account of conversations and events as they transpired or with offering a sense of the "truth" of these occurrences, while slightly altering the details. In theory, I could have done both: recounted events nearly exactly as they occurred and still been true to the themes of my life, but "in theory" does not get anyone very far in the real world of publishing. Although I tried to convince my editor of the virtues of a seventeen-hundred-page work, she successfully countered by elaborating on the virtues of actually making a profit on this project, and guess who sided with the money. (For the answer to that question, see footnote below.)

In the interest of space (and in keeping my book advance), I have taken liberties with time as well as the order of events, and I have occasionally combined two trips into one. I have also changed sev-

---

Answer: Wendy Dale, Wendy Dale's creditors.

eral names and identifying details to protect the identities of CIA agents, convicts, and anyone else who doesn't need the publicity. Many of the remarks made by my family members are recorded here exactly as originally uttered—for years, I have been taking notes of interesting lines for future use. In other instances, where memory failed, I did my best to express the main intent of the conversation that occurred, punching it up whenever it suited me. Besides that, the only other license I've taken is to make myself appear far more intelligent and wittier that I am in real life.

Finally, a few thank yous. There were so many people in the course of my travels who showed up when I most needed and least expected them: Farzana Abdullah, Lena Calla, Ron Combs, Clark Cardoza, Manfred Hirsch, Gerty Holmer, Jaime Salinas, Saúl Sarabia, Antonio "Tuco"Vargas, Michael Warner, and Sharon Warner. My apologies for not being able to fit all of you into the pages that follow.

Thanks also to Peter Saiers for countless favors and adventures over the course of our fifteen-year friendship, to Lisa McPherson for her unwavering belief in this book during some pretty daunting times, and to Michael Cathey for his neverending supply of stories and Jack Daniels.

My gratitude to Felipe Rossell, Carloncho, and their *tio* Jorge for their determined attempts to help me locate a Macintosh-compatible printer in Bolivia.

My appreciation to my family for being a gold mine of good material and for the graciousness to allow me to share their eccentricities with the world, and to my Uncle Mitch whose name isn't mentioned in this book but deserves to be.

To Arvli Ward, whose advice more than a decade ago gave me the courage to pursue writing as a career; Liz Spears, for teaching me where the commas go; Chuck Blore, writer extraordinaire and mentor, who was kind enough to pay me while training me in my craft; Dennis Naumick and Marta Stowe, the best editors gratitude can buy. (And since Marta's name is mentioned in the text of this book, Dennis' name bears repeating here: Dennis, Dennis, Dennis. Thanks, Big D.)

To Steph-O-Rama (her other clients probably know her by the much more formal moniker, Stephanie Lee), my agent, literary guide, and friend. To Dorianne Steele, an intrepid editor who let me know it was okay to break the rules. And to the warm and wonderful people at Crown, especially those I was fortunate enough to meet personally: Brian Belfiglio, Jill Flaxman, Pete Fornatale, Melissa Kaplan, Annik LaFarge, and Philip Patrick. My appreciation also to Laura Duffy for her creative cover design and to Fearn Cutler DeVico for her interior design.

And most of all, my thanks to Miguel Yaksic for finally showing up, even though it took him 28 years.

Travel Plans

Anything you can do is boring and old and perfectly okay. You're safe because you're so trapped inside your culture. Anything you can conceive of is fine *because you can conceive of it.* You can't imagine any way to escape. There's no way to get out.

—Chuck Palahniuk in *Invisible Monsters*

I like to think that I'm a typical traveler, that my idea of a good trip is pretty much the same as the next guy's, but every once in a while something happens to make me suspect this isn't really the case.

The first time this occurred was on a flight leaving Cuba when the Italian in the adjacent seat (literally, the next guy) began swapping stories with me about Havana.

"Museum of the Revolution," he announced. "Very worthwhile."

I hadn't made it.

"La Bodeguita del Medio, that bar that Hemingway used to hang out in?"

No. No time.

"So, what beaches did you go to?"

The idea that a person could go to a body of land completely surrounded by water and not make it to the beach was a little more than the sun-soaked tourists on my flight could take. Conversation momentarily stopped while passengers leaned over one another, trying to get a peek at my face.

"But it's an island," the Italian next to me accused.

Where *had* my time in Cuba gone? I'd met a lot of prostitutes, shopped on the black market, drunk contraband rum, and desperately sought out a place to rendezvous with a Cuban man who could not legally enter my hotel room. This hadn't left a lot of time to get a tan.

In Costa Rica, the conversations were even more difficult. Determined travelers touring Central America always found time to hike a handful of mountains, take dozens of photos, and swim in both the Caribbean and the Pacific in the course of just two weeks. And when they discovered that I had spent months in the country, they would gush over with enthusiasm, happy to have met someone who could finally relate to their experiences.

They had visited jungles and beaches and volcanoes, and as it slowly dawned on them that I had seen none of these places, they would curiously pry, "So what have you been doing the whole time you've been in Costa Rica?"

"I've been hanging out with my boyfriend."

"Well, that must be nice."

"It was till he got arrested. Now I've been spending most of my time hanging out at the jail."

After enough chats like these, I started to suspect that my concept of a good time was a bit different than other people's and perhaps I was missing out on the really worthwhile things there were to do in these countries. The problem was, going to beaches and mountains would require some sort of advance planning (whereas having my boyfriend snatched away from me one day by a carload of Costa Rican federal agents required no forethought whatsoever). That was the difference between these other travelers and me: they all organized their trips ahead of time.

For a brief while, I considered the possibility of becoming a "planner" instead of (what would the opposite be? Oh yes . . .) a "fun person," but in the end I realized that a structured itinerary would probably only get me to monuments and tourist traps, and these were not the kinds of trips I wanted to be taking.

But my life hadn't always been this spontaneous. I didn't arrive at lightheartedness until late in my youth when I first got up the courage to travel seriously. Something happened at that point—it would be easy to explain if someone had died or a relationship had ended—but what occurred was subtler, more profound. It was as if I had woken up one day with a sudden realization: My life begins now.

Up until that point, my life had felt more like a dress rehearsal than the actual performance. For twenty-five years, it was as if I had been waiting for the good part to start. I liked time passing. To me, each year was an investment, something that would be useful later on but that had yet to do me any good. I had tried life on, but had yet to grow into it. My life had been a triple-A training bra.

I survived this dull and tiresome existence for more than two decades by constantly convincing myself that the future would be better. I pictured my impending adulthood as one endless cocktail party after another—at least this was how it was described in the books I devoured (until I got to *Slaughterhouse Five* and then I thought being a grown-up had something to do with traveling in time).

I persuaded myself that all I had to do was get through adolescence and then everything would be easy. I did all of the right things. First it was a high school record that was a college admission counselor's dream. Then it was a move on my own to Los Angeles and four years at UCLA, while I worked three jobs to put myself through college. And finally adulthood arrived with a real career, a position as a corporate writer at Hughes Aircraft, sitting in front of a computer creating employee newsletters. But where were the cocktail parties? Where was the time travel?

I spent my days surrounded by a group of middle-aged engineers whose energy had long since been drained away. They shuffled along the halls like a herd of elderly elephants, dragging their weight along slowly, their arms dangling limply at their sides. (The only exception to this continual display of lethargy occurred on days when free T-shirts were being given out in the auditorium, in which case the plantsite became the scene of a chaotic stampede.)

I had nothing to say to the people I passed by in the halls. They talked about kids and IRAs and 401(k)s. Even their attempts to be lighthearted grew old because the aeronautical engineers' repertoire always included the same tired joke: "Wow, you'd have to be a rocket scientist to be able to do this."

I felt so out of place around my colleagues that when lunchtime came, instead of going to the cafeteria with my boss, I'd drive down to the residential neighborhood nearby, park on the street, and eat alone in my car. I had given away my youth for *this*?

My life was nothing like my childhood fantasies of what adulthood would be. Sure, Zelda and F. Scott could run around drinking Manhattans at noon—but that was because they had money. They did not have to spend their days interviewing aerospace engineers and writing things for the employee newsletter that went like this:

Cafeteria Offers a Menu to Love

Invite your valentine to a special meal in the cafeteria Monday, February 14.

Win that special person's heart with breast of chicken d'amour, lover's rice, sweet peas, roll and butter, and a small beverage, all for $2.00. Finish off the meal with a Valentine's cookie, free with any purchase.

Live music will complete the mood, and door prizes will be given out every 15 minutes.

It was during the worst of these days that I devoted myself to the ultimate irresponsibility fantasy. Staring out the window of my tiny cluttered office, I imagined leaving work at lunchtime and never coming back. In my daydream, I simply hopped in my car, raced toward the 405 freeway, and made a beeline for the airport. At LAX, I would breathlessly enter whichever terminal struck my fancy and hop on the next available international flight, free to begin over again in a new country whose inhabitants had never heard of bills or student loans or deadlines.

Of course, this was just a fantasy. Real people didn't do things like this. Real life was about responsibility. Or so I thought—until one day my parents casually informed me that they were selling everything they owned in Tempe, Arizona (basically the car, the house, and anything else that could be considered their children's future inheritance), and were taking my brother and two suitcases and moving to the Third World. It was the kind of radical idea that had the potential to change everything.

Chapter One

Will Honduras
Endure Us?

Moving to a Third World nation with no job and no concrete plans for the future was an interesting plan, the kind that could seem reasonable under certain circumstances—like when you've reached the part of the tequila bottle when you're faced with the decision of eating the worm. At this point, a lot of insane ideas could occur to you. You have a round, ribbed invertebrate in your mouth: moving to one of the poorest countries in the Western Hemisphere with a kid, maybe even two, could seem like a really good idea.

However, my mother didn't drink. So as we discussed her imminent plans to flee the United States with my father, I leaned against the kitchen counter in my parent's middle-class suburban Phoenix home, amazed that I was staring at a completely sober individual. After all, that was half my gene pool standing in front of me—not even *one* of those genes drove her to consume alcohol?

My mother happily gnawed away on a piece of red licorice and explained that she had limited their choices down to two potential areas: Asia and Latin America. Each of these places had its benefits and drawbacks. For instance, India would be the cheapest place, but it had the most frightening diseases. Did I have any opinion on this?

"I think you should avoid leprosy at all costs, Mom."

"Good point," she said, drawing a line through half a dozen countries. "Anything else?"

"Guerrilla warfare—also not a good thing."

"Hmmm. How about Guatemala?"

"Too soon after the era of peasant disappearances."

"El Salvador?"

"Mother, please."

"Nicaragua?"

"The beginning of democracy after years of socialism—not a stable political climate."

"You're not making this easy. Do you have any suggestions?"

"How about Italy?"

My mother shook her head vehemently.

"What's the matter with Italy? Red wine, pasta, hazelnut gelato. No one could possibly object to a nice place like Venice, Rome, or Florence."

"No, no, no! Do you know the percentage of homes with running water there? We could never afford a First World country."

As if the idea should have been obvious to me from the beginning, my mother took a frustrated sigh and stressed that the goal was to choose a poor country where their funds would stretch the furthest. In certain Central American nations, a thousand dollars a month would pay for a luxurious four-bedroom house, living expenses, even cover the costs of a full-time maid. This was the whole reason they were planning to leave the United States in the first place. If they found a favorable exchange rate, they could live off their savings and would never have to work again.

"Well, where are you going to go?" I asked.

"There's one place left."

As my mother said the word "Honduras," the other half of my gene pool asked me to go to the fridge and get him a stiff drink.

Fleeing to a new place and leaving one's problems behind was a proud family tradition. My mother had grown up this way, having been raised by army parents who roamed all over the world and finally retired in Mexico. And there was an alarming indication of it on my father's side as well. My grandma Barb had managed to live in Arizona for thirty years, took a vacation to Hawaii one day, returned home long enough to pick up a few things, kissed her husband good-bye, and moved to Honolulu.

My uncle Bob was the only one in the family who hadn't quite come to terms with the concept of travel as a means of escape. His work as an international photojournalist had taken him out of the country often enough, though he'd always wound up in nations with even more problems than the ones he was trying to avoid. In an attempt to elude his ex-wife, he'd fled to Central America in the eighties, though after a few years of running from guerrillas, the governments of crazed dictators, and paramilitary forces out to kill him, the idea of being chased by a diminutive blond woman started to seem pretty damn appealing. He returned to the States, vowed never to set foot in a Third World region again, and locked himself away in a private manicured neighborhood in suburban West Virginia, where the majority of his time was spent reading gourmet cookbooks and consuming expensive foods and wines with Italian names.

A typical conversation with him would go something like this: "It's not pen pasta. It's pen-eh. And whatever you do, if you ever decide to travel, make sure you go to Europe."

He was the most vocal opponent of my parents' impending move, but the pesto-stained letters that arrived in their mailbox with the message "Don't do it" did little to deter my folks. They were used to picking up and heading off to exotic places. They had taught us kids early on that distancing yourself from your problems was as easy as calling up the moving company. The Dale family members dialed the toll-free number for Allied Movers as if it were a crisis hotline.

By the time I was sixteen, my dad's mining engineering jobs had taken us to Arizona, California, Tennessee, South Carolina,

Minnesota, Montana, and Peru—and this nomadic lifestyle was something I never considered a hardship. Whenever times got rough at school (which they inevitably did for the new girl who spent her free time in the library reading about the latest scientific discoveries in *Discover* magazine), I knew that all I had to do was endure the barbs of the kids for a little while, because soon we'd be leaving.

I approached all of our impending departures with unwavering optimism. Each time, I convinced myself that this move had to be the one that would take me to that scholastic utopia I was seeking, a place where the students got together during their free time for fun and informative didactic chats, where they met up after school happily exchanging useful tips on the periodic table, evolution, and relativity.

In South Carolina, the kids just called me booger-picker because they were ignorant—everybody said "over yonder" and "young 'uns"; I became convinced that all we had to do was move to a place where they didn't speak this way. In the northern part of the United States, I was sure eighth-graders sat around debating the finer points of quantum mechanics.

When I was thirteen, and my mother came into my room yet again to explain that my father had a new job, there was only one thing I needed to know about our future destination of Minnesota: "Mom, do they say 'you guys' there instead of 'y'all'?" (The answer to this question was yes; however, for anyone who has never been to Minnesota, I feel the need to tell you that the eighth-graders do not in fact sit around discussing particle physics over lunch. Apparently there is still some distance between the phrase "you guys" and the phrase "Newton's corpuscular theory of light failed to adequately explain why the empirically measured entropy of pure substances at equilibrium tends toward zero as the absolute temperature decreases toward zero.")

Growing up, moving had never been a big deal for any of us, and now that my folks planned to go to Honduras without even visiting the place beforehand, no one in my family was entirely shocked. My mother explained that this was the best thing for my father—he needed a change of pace, a more relaxed existence, and I couldn't possibly object to something that was supposed to do my father good.

Everyone in my family was slightly in awe of my dad. All the good attributes came from his side of the family—he had wound up with brains *and* looks. When I was twenty-three and got diagnosed with gallbladder disease (the same thing had happened to him a decade earlier), he guiltily said, "I promise, it's the only bad gene I gave you." And it was true.

But high intelligence wasn't necessarily the key to a contented existence. My dad had traded personal happiness for the material comfort of his family, giving most of his adult life away to mining engineering work he had hated. Every two to three years, he'd find a better paying job in a new state, but in the end he'd always wind up where he began—spending his days in an office feeling like his life was pointless.

But this time the move was going to be different. My dad wasn't going to Honduras because he had a new job; he was headed there because he'd never have to work again. For once, he'd get the chance to stop and smell the roses—or at least the banana plants.

My sister Heather and I were going to be mostly unaffected by our parents' departure—we were both living on our own—but there were still two kids at home. A month before leaving, my folks gave my seventeen-year-old sister Catherine two options: okay, you can come with us to the poorest country in Central America or you can spend your senior year of high school without any adult supervision. It was not a hard choice.

Before they had time to change their minds, Catherine quickly found herself a nearby apartment in Tempe with another senior who had also chosen to be guardianless for the year.* And like jubilant

---

*I never did learn why Catherine's friend moved out of her parents' so young—but I suspect that it was not because her folks were moving to the Third World in order to save on household expenses.

Price Is Right grand-prize champions, the two of them set about filling up their new place with my parents' television, couch, stereo, VCR, computer, and dining room set that Mom and Dad would be leaving behind in the States.

My eleven-year-old brother, Richard, was not so lucky. He was going to have to whittle his possessions down to the contents of one piece of luggage. This was not too difficult; what was a problem was that most of the items he had chosen to take with him were forbidden by all international airline carriers. Years ago as a precocious eight year old, Richard had decided that his future lay ahead of him in the ever-growing field of weapons design so what he considered essential items were contraband in most developed nations.

"But Mom, why?" he cried as my mother pulled another offending item out of his suitcase.

"You will not be bringing nitroglycerine to Honduras."

"Okay, but let me keep the gunpowder. Pleeeeease."

Rich didn't understand why his parents were dragging him off to the Third World. After all, none of his other friends had to spend their Saturdays getting yellow-fever vaccinations. They were eating soft-serve dairy-based frozen food products, playing video games, and surfing the Internet. But I told him to look at the bright side: He wanted to be blowing things up, and it sure was going to be a hell of a lot easier in Central America.

"So, what do your parents do?"

In the past, this question had never caused me to hesitate. I had always been able to provide a simple one-word answer, a title like "engineer" or "geologist" in my father's case and the label "housewife" to describe my mother's role. But after my folks headed down to Central America, coming up with a response suddenly wasn't so easy. I sought in vain through my dictionary, my thesaurus, and any other reference materials I was able to get my hands on and finally resigned myself to the fact that there wasn't a term that expressed the concept: "They sold their house, their car, and their furniture and took my brother and two suitcases to Honduras."

"Wow, what are they doing there?" people would respond, intrigued.

I was led to the dictionary again, searching for a way to describe what it was my parents actually did in Honduras and remarkably enough, this term did exist. The word was "nothing."

However, saying that you do nothing is a difficult concept for most Americans to grasp, I knew; I had had the do-nothing conversation many times before.

"What did you do today?"

"Nothing."

"You couldn't have just done nothing. Come on, what did you do all afternoon?"

"You're right. Actually, I lay on my bed and stared at the ceiling."

A brief moment of silence would follow, after which the other person would condescendingly respond: "Oh, you mean you really did *nothing*."

Of course, it was much more complicated if you were a writer because there were days that you lay on your bed and stared at the ceiling and it was called working. But this was a difficult concept for most nonartist types to grasp.

My sister Heather was getting asked these types of questions as well, but she was the only one clever enough to derive advantage from my parents' move to Honduras. She was at Vassar on a full scholarship, one of a handful of middle-class kids at an otherwise elite school. There, like at any other Seven Sisters or Ivy League college, "doing nothing" was synonymous with trust fund or was code for sitting on a yacht, playing golf, and attending charity luncheons. So Heather actually looked forward to being asked about her parents. She would lean back in her chair, cross her legs, and answer, "They're abroad." And everyone would be quite impressed when she added, "Doing nothing."

• • •

Even though we often lived in geographically distant places, the six members of my immediate family had always gotten together at Christmas. According to my parents, there was simply no plausible excuse for not showing up, not "Mom, I'm sick" or "Dad, I have to work" or even "Sorry, but you guys live twenty-four hundred miles away in a Central American country."

This year, we were going to be spending our first holiday season in Honduras. To avoid any potential reticence on the part of her daughters, my mother sent a letter explaining that she and my dad were springing for the airplane tickets—not that her children really needed any convincing when it came to hopping aboard an airplane. I was in desperate need of a trip abroad—it would bring some much needed excitement to my dull existence of employee newsletter writing, and for several weeks prior to departing, the high point of my workday was witnessing the puzzled look on the aeronautical engineers' faces after they innocently inquired into my plans for the holidays.

Did I plan to go home?

"Sort of."

Where was home?

"This year it's Tegucigalpa."

Tegucigalpa?

"Yes, you know, the capital of Honduras."

They weren't sure if I was kidding, but since the exchange had already used up several minutes of valuable rocket-making time, they would smile uncertainly and quickly excuse themselves to go back to the safety of their secret labs and soundproof rooms. Alone in my office, I would chuckle happily at the private joke they had not understood, reassured in the fact that I was not one of them after all.

• • •

a week before Christmas, landing at the airport in the capital of Honduras, I was struck by a twinge of nostalgia. The plane came careening down, barely avoiding the mountains beneath us, and made a bumpy landing on a runway much too short, which was compensated for by the pilot who frantically slammed down on the brakes and swerved to the left, skillfully avoiding the airport in front of us. Ah, Latin America. It hadn't changed a bit in the past twenty years.

One of my father's mining engineering jobs had taken us to Peru when I was four years old, and as a kid for a while I really had believed I was a Latina. I switched between English and Spanish without effort, wandered about in an alpaca poncho, and hung out with our maid, Ana, who taught me words in Quechua and took me up into the Andes where we ate beef-heart shish kabob (called *anti-cuchos*) surrounded by a herd of llamas.

Needless to say, I returned to the States a pretty weird kid. I was the only third-grader in my class who had never tasted a Big Mac, had no idea who this Grover guy was (was it true that he was blue?), and was completely baffled by the machine that you put a quarter into (which coin was the quarter?) and got a soda can out of. In Peru, soda did not come from machines, and it definitely didn't come in a can.

Eventually, my images of Peru faded to that dreamlike state reserved for childhood memories. I learned how to play Atari and I realized that American girls got a lot more mileage begging for ponies instead of pet llamas. But there was always a part of me that longed to return, to see that mysterious country that had given me the ability to pronounce strange-sounding words in an accent that always made my friends in Tennessee laugh, the place where my daily happiness had been as certain as the fact that summer arrived each December.

I walked down the stairs that they had rolled out to the plane, feeling strangely like a kid again. The scent of dust in the air triggered images of my childhood and all around me were the familiar sounds of a language I could nearly make out but not quite understand. It was eerie—I could imitate the words I heard with the flawless accent of a native speaker, but I had no idea how to string them together to make a coherent sentence.

In a slight daze, I crossed the dry pavement and entered the dilapidated airport filled with cigarette smoke, wondering where I would meet up with my parents. Looking around the tiny building, I realized there weren't too many possibilities: first, the entire building consisted of one gate, which left very little room for confusion, and second, while standing in line at immigration, I heard the familiar, high-pitched voice of my mother, indistinguishable even in Spanish, saying, "*Permiso. Perdón. Permiso.*" Before I had time to count to *tres,* the entire room turned to view a lively, loud, platinum-blond woman completely ignoring the Do Not Enter sign, climbing over a rope, waving past a security guard, and joining me at my side, welcoming me to the country with an emotional scream and a bear hug.

This was a typical Cathie Dale maneuver. Years ago, after discovering that the Rosarito Beach Hotel in Baja California was all booked up, she'd tried to sneak us into the pool anyway, which she had assured us would be as simple as lying about the room number on the sign-in sheet at the entrance. Unfortunately, the number she wrote down belonged to a single, and since it was unlikely that a family of six was going to be sharing a double bed, the manager had come over to politely ask us to take our lying asses to another establishment. "But I don't want to leave!" my eight-year-old brother shouted as my parents dragged him out of the pool.

At the Tegucigalpa airport, this behavior was repeating itself. Smothered in her embrace, I couldn't help but comment, "You know, no one else's mother met them at immigration."

"Yeah, but only because it's not allowed."

"But you—"

"I have connections," she proudly announced. "My Embassy Friend is outside."

Apparently those connections were not enough to ensure that everything would run smoothly at the airport. At baggage claim, the roped-off area into which suitcases were tossed by a man into the center of the room, we failed to find my maroon Samsonite. While I had arrived safe and sound in Tegucigalpa, it seemed that my suitcase was enjoying a three-day stay in Houston, courtesy of Continental Airlines.

"I'm sorry, but there has been a problem with the luggage," the airline representative at the counter informed us.

"What kind of problem?" I asked.

"It will remain in Houston until we have space available on the plane to retrieve it."

"You mean, my clean underwear, my deodorant, my toothbrush, my socks, and all my other personal belongings are going to be delayed indefinitely?"

"I'm afraid so."

Unintentionally, I let out a small yelp of joy. For the first time in my life, I had had the foresight to purchase a traveler's insurance policy. It had been a simple financial decision really: A month's health coverage had turned out to be cheaper than getting the recommended hepatitis, cholera, and yellow-fever shots. And unlike spending a day in a vaccination clinic after which I would have nothing to show for myself other than a few track marks, my traveler's insurance policy came with a delayed luggage clause. They would reimburse me up to two hundred dollars for necessary expenses. And here I was, in need of a couple hundred dollars worth of personal-care items.

"So what's the first thing you want to see in Honduras?" my mother asked me, excitedly rushing toward the more restrained half of my parental unit who was patiently waiting outside the airport.

"The Estée Lauder counter!" I shouted.

•   •   •

For me, travel was the real-world version of falling down a rabbit hole. In a foreign country, everything was slightly off: the smell, the sounds, the view. Now I knew why everyone made such a big deal when it came to the phrase "treading on foreign soil"—on the other side of an international border even walking across the ground felt new. It was like a drug-induced high, only better—with travel, the next morning when you woke up, you were still there.

On the ride to my parents' house, chauffeured by the woman I still knew only as "Mother's Embassy Friend," I stared out the window of the car, struck by the strangeness of the place. The vehicles racing alongside us were familiar to me in that they had four wheels, a steering column, and were covered in metal, but here they seemed to operate on a different set of principles. Vehicles that long ago would have been relegated to the junkyard in the United States tentatively puttered along here, held together with bungee cords and electrician's tape, as if no one had bothered to inform them of Newton's laws of motion. And the cows and pigs we passed by were different too. Personally not an expert when it comes to farm animals (to this day my father's greatest disappointment has been raising four children, none of whom shares his enthusiasm for livestock), I am not competent to describe the exact nature of their dissimilarity, but they felt foreign to me. They were unmistakably Honduran.

But the strangest sight of all were the signs that appeared along the road. Even after I painstakingly translated one of them with the help of a Spanish dictionary, its meaning still eluded me: "Don't leave your rocks on the highway." This kind of warning just didn't appear along the California freeways. There were Slippery when Wet, Dangerous Curves Ahead, even the occasional Falling Rocks signs, but never before had I come across any request to kindly leave my stones elsewhere.

I turned to my father who was seated next to me in the backseat, figuring that after having lived in the country for nearly a year, he'd be able to help me make sense of the signs, but my mother was quick to interrupt.

"Honey, they put them up because so many people have been leaving their rocks on the highway," she explained. I waited for my mother to complete her explanation, but clarity was not her strong point.

"Dad," I said, turning to my Mensan parent, "Why is everyone going around carrying rocks and leaving them on the highway?"

"When their cars break down, which they do a lot, instead of using triangles or flares to divert other cars, they pile rocks in the road so that traffic swerves out of the path of their vehicle. But a lot of people get their cars fixed and leave the rocks. Hence the request—"

"Please don't leave your rocks on the highway."

"Exactly."

Twenty minutes later, successfully having avoided all the rocks in our path, we arrived in my parents' neighborhood, the ritziest area in town, where a two-story, three-bedroom Spanish colonial-style house ran my parents four hundred dollars a month, a price way out of reach of all but the wealthiest Hondurans. My younger sisters ran out to greet me, and after a round of gleeful screams and boisterous hugs my father insisted on having us all go inside so that he could show me around the place. Heather and Catherine, who had already taken this tour upon their separate arrivals, had found it so amusing they insisted on going one more time.

"Wait till he explains about the toilet," Heather whispered to me as we huddled around the amenity, the first time I could remember that four Dales had entered the bathroom at the same time.

Other than being forest green, it looked like any normal toilet to me. "Toilet paper is the great enemy of Honduran plumbing," my father explained, launching into a lengthy description of the septic system of the house. This was like poetry to my dad, and when it came to explaining any scientific process, he could ramble on for hours and hours. As children, he had inculcated us in the finer details of plate tectonics, ensured we could spot fake trilobite fossils at a glance, and trained us never to leave home without our emergency bottle of hydrochloric acid, in the event that an innocent bike ride would result in the immediate need to determine the chemical composition of a mineral sample picked up along the way.

His motto was that if you understood, you'd never have to memorize. You didn't learn the periodic table by rote; you comprehended it. Ag stood for silver because argentum meant silver in Latin, which was where Argentina got its name. Ask him to pass the sugar at the breakfast table and he'd end up explaining the entire fermentation process for you.

As a consequence, our "why phase" as children lasted only a matter of days. Other kids got the pleasure of watching their parents roll their eyes, throw up their hands, and plead, "Just quit asking questions!" But by the time we were three, we actually knew why grass was green (a result of the chlorophyll), how come the sky was blue (the cones in our retina respond most strongly to the short blue wavelength of the color spectrum), and the reasons birds flew (a column of decreased air pressure created by the movement of their wings).

This tutelage continued even as adults, and today we weren't going to get out of the bathroom until we learned the workings of the entire plumbing system in the house. By the time he'd finished and we all knew how to fix the sink in the event that a meteorite came crashing down on it, I couldn't quite remember what the point was.

"Don't throw any paper in the toilet," Catherine summed up. Instead, we were supposed to dispose of our used bits of tissue in the wastebasket, a rule in force in the bathrooms throughout Central America.

Now that we were on the subject of strange Latin American habits, there was one other issue I needed clearing up immediately.

"Do they ever switch their soda from bottles to cans?" I asked anxiously, wondering if anything had changed in the two decades I'd been gone.

"No," my father said, happy to continue today's lesson. "They drink it out of plastic bags."

This was something even my sisters had a hard time buying. "What—you go to the store and buy yourself a little baggie of Coke?" Heather asked.

"Or Pepsi," my dad added, launching into a lengthy explanation of the raw materials of Honduras that might have been titled:

"The Scarcity of Raw Materials Combined with a Limited Economy and the Resulting Cultural Anomalies Among the Honduran Population"

Author's note: For reasons of length, the full text has been omitted. See abstract below.

Abstract: In Honduras, it's cheaper to drink soda out of a bag.

To get a sense of what Honduras was like, you have to know a little bit about its history, which has had a lot more to do with bananas than any sane country is likely to consider prudent. Beginning in the early 1900s, this yellow innocuous-looking fruit has been the source of civil unrest, military occupation, strategic alliances, and, of course, potassium.

In the early twentieth century, Honduras became the epitome of a banana republic—and not the kind selling high-quality cotton shirts at the mall. This was a poor nation that relinquished its national hold on its own interests in the pursuance of a higher good: money. Like a poor kid who invites his unpleasant rich neighbor to his birthday party in the hopes of scoring a Game Boy, Honduras welcomed U.S. investment in the region and in return offered to sing the tune "Happy Birthday" in English.* In exchange for the con-

---

*Strangely enough, this actually happens in most of Latin America—for some reason, people always sing "Happy Birthday" in English (granted, it comes out sounding like "Hoppy Burtday").

struction of roads and railroads, Honduras handed over its fertile farmland to American banana companies, which in the end turned out to be like getting the cartridges for free while having to rent the Game Boy.

For the next sixty years, the United States exerted its imperialist hold on the region, doing everything from applying stern diplomatic pressure to financing government overthrows, while Honduras went through the normal phases of development for a Latin American country: the oral stage, in which it paid lip service to U.S. demands; the anal stage, in which it became obsessive and detail-oriented in complying with these demands; the phallic stage, in which it realized that the United States was a lot bigger than it was; and the genital stage, which led the country to the conclusion that it was completely screwed.

Within a few years of the arrival of the American fruit companies, the true power of the banana had begun to surface. In the past, its capacity to transform three scoops of ice cream into a mighty dessert had been common knowledge; however, it soon became evident that its metamorphic powers stretched to the Honduran political climate as well. Banana companies began placing their employees in local government positions, offering kickbacks to sympathetic politicians, and funding insurgent military groups to topple noncooperative presidents.

In the 1980s, while the United States saw the advent of Cabbage Patch Kids, parachute pants, Strawberry Shortcake, and the Smurfs, Central America too went through tremendous changes. The majority of inhabitants in the region were sick of being poor, sick of being mistreated, sick of the United States, and sick to death of bananas. Honduras' rebel neighbors, the Sandinistas in Nicaragua, figured that Marxism had nothing to do with any of this unpleasantness and with the help of Cuba and the Soviet Union, launched a successful guerrilla campaign that eventually overthrew the right-wing Anastasio Somoza dictatorship.

This did not make Ronald Reagan very happy. With all the changes going on in this part of the world, his address book was too small to keep crossing out the name of the current leader of Nicaragua, and, besides, this Soviet-Cuban alliance was beginning to reek of communism.

If there was one thing he had learned from U.S. history, it was that presidents were not above the law, but Hollywood celebrities generally were. Hoping that his past as an actor would sway a jury, he illegally sold arms to the Iranians and used these funds to covertly fund the *Contras,* the right-wing Nicaraguan guerrillas determined to defeat the left-wing Sandinista regime.* And since Honduras was right next door and practically a U.S. colony, it provided an ideal *Contra* training base.

Eventually the war ended, the threat of communism dissipated, and the U.S. presence in the region waned. Honduras entered a stage of fledgling democracy but remained one of the poorest Latin American nations.

These days, Uncle Sam's influence basically consisted of international aid and a strong diplomatic presence in the region, but my mother still held out hope that there was some secret agenda. In fact, now that Rosa, the underpaid Honduran maid, had taken charge of mopping the floor, scrubbing the bathroom, washing dishes, and ironing the clothes, my mother was devoting the majority of her time to trying to figure out who was CIA among all her new embassy pals.

Based on a string of dubious clues and rampant rumors, my

---

*For the record, it wasn't actually Reagan but rather Lieutenant Colonel Oliver North who conducted the transaction with the Iranians. Based on circumstantial evidence, it's likely that Reagan was aware of the proceedings but there has been no conclusive proof.

mother had pieced together a list of those she was positive were agents. And whenever one of the embassy people invited her to dinner or a luncheon social, she was sure to attend, trying to gather as much information as possible on what she was convinced was the U.S. secret plan for Central America.

As it turned out, she hadn't been all wrong. My sisters and I couldn't help but giggle when Mom explained that in spite of all her digging and prying, a real CIA agent had been sitting right under her nose. In an attempt to sort out the rumors about James McPherson being a spook, one day she had set her best friend, Maggie, down for chocolate-chip cookies and a heart-to-heart interrogation.

"All this CIA stuff that everyone is talking about. Maggie, I just know it has to be true."

"Cathie, you really can't tell anyone. This is serious."

"Oh, I won't. I promise."

"Besides, my job—it's nothing that important. I just take down messages."

"Oh my gosh!" my mother screamed. "*You* are an agent?"

"You said you knew," poor Maggie said aghast, realizing she had just entrusted one of the nation's secrets to a woman who would from then on refer to her as "my best friend, the CIA agent."

Of course the magic word was "ambassador," and any time the word got brought up my mother was quick to remind us that she had been invited to the American ambassador's house on not one, but two, occasions. And although she had never met the man personally, she had had tea with his wife. My mother had turned into a Third World socialite.

While she was off eating finger sandwiches and teacakes, my brother had painstakingly downloaded *The Anarchist's Cookbook* on a disturbingly slow Central American Internet connection and had set about to turning himself into an anarchist chef—which actually did have its bright side. Because my mother refused to buy the ingredients he needed for his experiments, he had been forced to learn Spanish on his own and when it came to chemicals and fireworks, he had become quite fluent. Now he was able to complain about his life in two languages: "Honduras is a pit. When are we going to move to a country where I can actually get a DSL line?" he would gripe, in between blowing up small portions of the country.

Meanwhile, my father had been busy with a project of his own. "Jalapeño chili peppers," my mother explained. "Your father has become a jalapeño-chili-pepper farmer in Honduras."

Most people, upon hearing such news, would have reacted with some surprise. I, however, did not come from a typical family. "Again?" I asked.

My mother rolled her eyes. "Again," she said.

My father had tried farming once before. For years as a mining engineer, he had felt something was missing from his life: poverty, we assumed, because he rashly quit his well-paying job in Peru and moved his wife and three daughters to the backwoods of Tennessee. We were all to take part in his dream of self-subsistence—though when we first got there, there hadn't been much to subsist on. I was only seven years old, but it didn't take me long to notice that we didn't have a house to live in. "Quit complaining," my dad scolded me. "Look at the bright side. We have a car."

And the bright side was, it was a big car—one of those 1970s station wagons whose seats fold back—which was very convenient when a family of five (Richard hadn't been born yet) was going to sleep in one of them.

My mother had her doubts about the whole project, but my father remained upbeat.

"Dick, you've never been a farmer before. How will you know where to begin?"

"Don't worry, pookie," my father answered in the same tone of voice that had gotten my mother to agree to the whole scheme in the first place. "I have a lot of books on the subject."

The sight of my father sprawled out on the grass in front of our station wagon reading about agriculture caused a great deal of laughter among our neighbors. After all, they were real farmers. Their farms had animals, unlike ours, which just consisted of two hundred acres of vacant land, half of which was a forest infested with wild boars. But within two months, my father had planted an orchard, bought us a trailer, built us a greenhouse, and had become a major source of information for the farmers who now timidly trekked over to our land to ask my dad's opinion on pesticides, planting times, and harvesting seasons.

My dad's farm only lasted as long as my mother could stand the project. Concerned that her daughters were developing a taste for wild squirrel and that we would think lice shampoo was what everyone used to wash their hair, she convinced my father that open-pit mining wasn't such a bad way to spend his days, and within a year we were back in the real world, in a real house, with real beds to sleep in. But those eleven months of my childhood left their mark, and from time to time I remembered that it was my father who taught me that it didn't matter what the neighbors thought, that it was okay to sleep in a station wagon as long as you had a dream.

𝕴n the four days I'd been in Honduras, we hadn't really done much of anything. We'd basically just lounged around the living room laughing and joking while eating the food made by the maid: chow mein (her last job had been with a Chinese family) and refried beans, the only two items she seemed to know how to prepare. My brother would ditch us in favor of his best friends, a set of American twins living down the street, and the rest of us would sprawl out on the floor, cracking each other up with embarrassing stories about the members of our family.

There wasn't a lot of material on most of us: Heather at age nineteen was blond, boisterous, and bubbly, an antiacademic with an academic's résumé——she was at the top of her class and she kept piling up grants and awards. Catherine was quieter, darker, and introspective, qualities at odds with her stunning good looks——but these traits weren't exactly incriminating. Dad was always cloning blueberries or cacti in a climate-controlled lab that he had set up for himself in the house, which would have made for a few good jokes, but we tended to see his eccentricities as endearing. That left my mother. Her grasp on reality was so far removed that we could spend hours on end making fun of it.

She was always doing airheaded things like picking us up at the airport and expecting us to remember where she had parked the car. And there were her inappropriate comments during otherwise coherent conversations, something that came to be known as a Mom sequitur. There was the time that she was so busy talking to my father that she accidentally followed him into the men's rest room. Seeing a guy in there, she chided him, "Excuse me, is this a unisex bathroom?" And there was the whole moving story told to me by my sisters (I was already living in Los Angeles when this notorious relocation occurred), when my family caravaned from Montana to Phoenix in three separate cars, one driven by my father, one by my mother, the other by fifteen-year-old Heather who had learned how to operate a motor vehicle just weeks earlier. My father had insisted that everyone make two signs out of poster board: Bathroom Break and Food Break. And my sisters ended up making a third sign, just for Mom: Turn off Turn Signal.

People outside my family saw our joking as cruel, though it was my mother who always laughed the hardest, enjoying constantly being the center of attention. "Don't say a word while I'm gone!" she'd insist, not wanting to miss anything during her bathroom break.

At the end of the night, our favorite activity was to read from Mom's diaries, which I had insisted she give me when she had been tossing out everything else in preparation for their trip to Honduras.

Reading the events of her adolescent life inevitably had us rolling on the floor, especially the June 14, 1964, entry:

Dear Diary,   June 14, 1964

    I've got just oodles to tell you!!

    Well, today I was diving down at the pool & I met so many cute boys. They were giving me all these unneeded instructions on the art of diving. (phooey!) When I got at the end of the line, they put me all the way in the front. (such gentlemen!)

    The other night, my mother & Mrs. Howe were discussing whether teenagers ever think deep. Of course we do! Why right now Im wondering what I'll be, who I'll marry, about religion, & life in general. But people just think that were delinquents, (so that we can't express our deepest feelings.)

    I just measured my face & here is the comparison between a perfect oval & my face!

Flat measurements

Oval		*Mine*
5	across forehead	(5.2 in.)
5½	under eyes	(5⅝) almost!
4½	under nose	(5⅞) heck!
3¼	under lips	(4½) waa!
7½	from chin to hairline	(about 6 something)

Well, I've got a round face!

    I'm going to try a new hair style tomorrow (not tonight because it's too late.) It's called "Offbeat Bubble."

    You know when I get married I want to have a daughter, & if I do, I hope that we'll be close & she'll be able to confide in me. & if she ever says that I just "don't understand," (like I say to my mom) I'll just pull out this diary & let her take a peak! ooh la la!

It was that last paragraph that always made me sad because she had almost been right. In thirty-one years, she hadn't really changed. She was a taller, plumper version of that fourteen-year-old girl, and true to her word she had never turned into a stern authority figure like her mother.

My mom had raised us to be her playmates. As a kid, I was her buddy, both of us living on a diet of ice cream and macaroni and cheese that I had learned how to cook by reading the package. She'd take me to R-rated movies, giggling at the fact that she could get me in, since she was my legal guardian. And she bought me a pink canopy bed, the kind her mother had always denied her as a kid.

It would have been an ideal childhood had there been an adult to take care of us. In Peru, we'd had the maid to clean up our messes and prepare our food, but when we moved to my father's dream farm in the backwoods of Tennessee, the responsibility shifted to me. Now living in a sparse trailer, her favorite joke had become: "We don't need a dishwasher. We have one. It's called Wendy."

Up until then, the most difficult challenge I had faced in my life had been choosing between apple pie or coconut cream, but at seven years of age, what had formerly been done by the maid now fell to me. At night it was the kitchen: I'd slide a chair up against the sink so that I could reach the dishes, the counters, and the stove. On the weekends it was the bathroom and my room. And in the mornings, while my mother slept in, I began getting myself off to school alone. It was a two-and-a-half-hour bus ride to Rickman Elementary so I'd be outside waiting at five-thirty after I'd cooked my favorite breakfast, fried hotdogs on sliced bread with ketchup.

At five in the evening, the bus would drop me off outside our trailer, where I'd turn on our black-and-white television, engrossed with American entertainment, which I was seeing for the very first time. I would watch *Wonder Woman* and the *Six Million Dollar Man,* doing my chores during the commercial breaks.

When we moved from Tennessee to South Carolina, my father began working long hours—he'd leave before I got up in the morning and would come home too exhausted to do anything other than watch television or fall asleep—so my mother began relying on me for other things as well. There was "Wendy, Heather talked back to me today. How should I punish her?" and "Wendy, Catherine's arm looks kind of funny. Should we take her to the doctor?" And then there was her concern when she took four-year-old Heather to the dentist for the first time, after having teethed her on licorice. "Wendy, what are we going to do? Heather has nineteen cavities."

To her, she was just the biggest of a bunch of kids having a good time, and she intended to teach us that adolescence could go on indefinitely. And for her, it did. She was carefree and fun, flitting away her time on soap operas and junk food while I grew into a somber, bookish, responsible teenager—if only to prove that all children eventually rebel from their mothers.

These days, my mother still turned to me for advice on everything from which dress to buy to the problems she was having with her friends while I kept the important details of my life hidden, sharing them only with my younger sisters. I was five years older than Heather, seven years older than Catherine, and I still remembered the years I had longed for them to hurry up and become adults. Now the three of us were inseparable, getting together any time we could, always leaving a trail of secrets, empty wine bottles, and broken hearts behind us.

This Christmas vacation had been slightly different though. In the five days we'd been in Honduras, we'd basically just sat around the house, trapped by lack of transportation and not knowing our way around. My mother, whose strongest maternal instinct was to fill her children with food, spent her time baking brownies and lemon squares while my father whiled away hours polishing minerals in his shop. But my sisters and I were getting restless. Even Rich was desperate to get out of the house.

"Mom, isn't there anything to do in this town?" Catherine pleaded.

"We could go for a drive," my mother said.

"You guys don't have a car," Heather reminded her.

"How about a bus ride?" my mother suggested.

We'd all seen *Romancing the Stone.* A bus ride in Tegucigalpa—it had to be interesting.

All six of us walked down the hill out of my parents' posh neighborhood and into a slightly more modest area where we hailed the first bus that came by. Climbing aboard, I was struck with a severe case of déjà vu—this wasn't a Honduran bus; it was an old Bluebird school bus imported from the United States. It could have been the very same vehicle that carried me to Rickman Elementary so long ago, assuming that the bus had been pelted by rocks and baseball bats, dragged through a river, and subsequently left to rust and decay. Lots of the seats were missing cushions, most of the windows didn't open and there was a small hole in the floor through which we could see the street below.

"No fighting, horseplay, or loud talking," I mock-scolded my sisters, reading from the rules in English that still hung in the front of the bus. "And even though it's not on the list, I hope everyone understands that no one will be placing their feet through the hole in the floor."

We'd only been outside of my parents' house for a matter of minutes and we were already having fun. A simple bus ride through Tegucigalpa was in itself a cultural experience. Rickety cars spewed fumes out into the street. Street vendors hawked fried plantains, *pupusas,* and fruit drinks. Pedestrians bumped into one another on the street, their arms loaded with purchases. Music and dust competed for space in the air.

Like most Third World cities, Tegucigalpa had imported lots of modern conveniences but had been ineffective at completely blocking nature out. There were computer stores, Benetton shops, and a Pizza Hut, but outside of downtown, many residential streets still remained unpaved, the cries of chickens and dogs filled the air, and majestic green mountains loomed in the distance, making a city of nearly a million seem provincial and friendly.

Just as a "rock-free highway" sign had first clued me in on the foreignness of the place where I found myself, the most revealing part of our bus trip consisted of the strange and funny signs I kept seeing outside. "A friendly reminder for you, Dad," I said, pointing out the government billboard put up in the interest of bettering the population, reminding them "A woman is a companion, not a slave." And in the same spirit of honesty was a sign for Flor de Caña, a popular brand of rum billing itself as "Your happiness and old friend."

The popular pastry manufacturer Bambino promised, "You won't get cholera with our bread," while its main competitor was a line of bread products called Bimbo, which claimed to be "always soft, always fresh."

And driving by the hospital, I couldn't help but point out that there were three signs: one for emergencies, one for general admittance, and a special entrance just for cholera patients.

We were laughing so hard that our stomachs hurt, but I couldn't help but prolong the pain.

"Dad, have you seen any other funny signs?" I asked my father as we were nearing the end of our ride.

"Please don't burn the trees."

What's so funny about that?

"Well, your brother went on a Boy Scout camping trip through the park El Tigre here in town. The kids really wanted to make a campfire but they didn't want to go against the rules."

"So what'd they do?"

"They burned the sign."

$\mathcal{I}t$ was a unique holiday season, to say the least.

My sisters and I had already counted on not having any snow, but learning that we were also to be deprived of a Christmas tree came as a bit of a shock. This had nothing to do with any stinginess on the part of my parents—it was because it was impossible to buy real Christmas trees in Honduras (due to government laws designed to protect the forests) and you couldn't buy fake ones either (due to what I can only assume were government laws protecting plastic)

"Dad, does this mean we won't have a Christmas tree this year?" my youngest sister asked, concerned.

"It's just a different kind of tree," my dad answered.

This different kind of tree was called branches.

Although it was illegal to cut down pine trees in the country, for some reason it wasn't against the law to go around yanking off the branches. So around Christmastime, vendors would set up places along the road where you could go and pick out your cuttings.

Filled with holiday cheer, the six of us headed out of the house to the nearest stand but once we were there, we stood perplexed, wondering how to pick out a good branch. When selecting a nice tree, I knew that you tried to find one without any naked areas, in other words, one that wasn't missing any branches, but this suddenly wasn't an issue. You couldn't pick out a branch that was missing a branch. Branches didn't *have* branches; they *were* branches, for God's sake!

"How many should we get?" Catherine asked. "Is the price per branch or is there a package deal?" Christmas had never presented these kinds of challenges before.

After a bit of discussion, we decided that we would take three home. However, once we were back at the house, we looked at our purchase, unsure exactly what to do.

"It's just like having a tree—without the inconvenience of dealing with a trunk," I said.

"Yeah, maybe later we can sing, 'O Christmas branch, O Christmas branch . . .'" Heather added.

"Maybe we should have bought a stand or something," Catherine commented.

We tried to rest the branches up against the wall in the living room, but they kept falling over. After several failed attempts, we realized we were going to have to think up something better.

"What if we plant it?" Catherine suggested. "You know, we put it in a pot of dirt."

It was the best idea anyone had come up with. We stuck our branches in a pot and stood back to admire our work.

Next came the hard part: decorating. We had to find the delicate equilibrium of our Christmas branches. My sisters and I took turns cautiously placing each decoration on, waiting to see if this was going to be the one to tip the branch over again. And after an hour of frustration, we had finally succeeded in deducing the plant's limits: Three branches could endure the weight of exactly six ornaments.

"It's like the Charlie Brown Christmas tree," Heather said gleefully as we watched another ornament topple off and roll along the floor.

Christmas came and went, and while my sisters packed up and headed back to school, I had a few more days in the country, which my mother insisted would be a great opportunity to go to the dentist. I had a few qualms about the whole thing—after all, a country whose leaders put up public-interest signs with the messages "Where there is electricity, there is progress" and "Let's help eradicate dengue" wasn't exactly the ideal place to be shopping around for highly specialized medical treatment. The mere thought of going to a dentist in Honduras filled my head with images of unsterilized needles, old-fashioned drills, and inadequately trained staff.

"But you're only looking at the negative!" my mother scolded me.

"And the bright side would be?"

"This second-rate health care—"

"Yes?"

"It's really really cheap. The other day I went to the gynecologist. Two dollars, I paid! I'm going to start going more often."

I reread my travel insurance brochure carefully and as there was nothing in it that allowed me to go to the dentist in the event that my luggage had been delayed for three days, I politely declined.

"Just a checkup," my mother pleaded. "No one can screw up a cleaning."

Maybe she was right. How much damage could a little fluoride do? And that was how my dental odyssey began.

"What time is my appointment?" I asked my mother the next day.

"You don't need an appointment, you just show up."

"Like Supercuts, you mean?" I asked as I flashed back to the time my mother talked me into going with her to get a haircut and the month that followed of tying my hair back in a bun. "What's the dentist going to do to me? Just shave a little enamel off the sides?"

"Don't be so negative. She's very nice."

"Nice is important for restaurant staff, airline attendants, and veterinarians. I don't want her to be nice. I want to know that she's not going to start inhaling nitrous oxide, go loony on me, and begin drilling all my teeth."

As it turned out, she didn't need the nitrous oxide. (I, on the other hand, found myself longing for some, especially after hearing her verdict on the shameful state of my mouth.) The woman must have had bionic vision because she had found cavities in places I didn't even knew I possessed teeth.

Now in the United States, a dentist would present you with this news and then give you a few days to get used to the idea that you were going to have sit for hours with your jaws open while she jabbed needles, drills, and metal utensils into your mouth. You went to the first visit because you knew it was just going to be the cleaning. Not here. This was the do-it-now-before-the-Sandinistas-invade part of the world. And as Dr. Silvia asked me to open up, just as she would on the next six visits, I found myself silently cursing the Reagan years.

I don't recall if I ever did get a cleaning, but most of my whole dental experience has been mercifully repressed by my subconscious. I remember big needles, whiny drills, and days of not being able to eat. My gums swelled up, my cheeks turned into round, little balls, and finally, when I thought it was all over and I had been assured that it was my last visit, I got home and felt a suspicious hole in one of my teeth.

"How can you feel a hole in your tooth?" my mother asked. "You told me yesterday that you still hadn't regained the feeling in your tongue."

She had a point. So, I ran my finger over the surface of what remained of the upper part of my mouth, and sure enough, there was a Tic Tac–sized opening in one of my upper molars.

Reluctantly, I showed up at the dentist's office one additional time.

"Dr. Silvia," I mumbled with as much articulation as possible given the altered shape of my mouth. "I think there is a hole in one of my teeth."

She had me open my mouth and took a look inside.

"Is that what you're worried about?" she asked as she inserted a hook-like metal instrument into my exposed upper tooth.

I screamed in pain. "That's the one."

"That's nothing to worry about."

"It's not?"

"No, I just forgot to put in the filling."

I had always sort of believed that we were your typical dysfunctional American family, but the fallacy of this logic began to dawn on me on my last day in Honduras as I watched my mother making cookies with her best friend, the CIA agent. This was not a normal thing to do. Normal parents resided in the suburbs, watched game shows on television, and had jobs. They didn't hang around the kitchen, baking with spies.

But try telling this to my folks. My parents moved to a country they had never even visited and sold everything they owned to do it. My mother, who lived her life with as little synaptic interference as possible, had figured it would be tons of fun, but my dad had thought the plan through. In typical Richard Dale fashion, he had read a stack of books, pored through magazine articles, and after some final calculations he realized exactly what he would be giving up: middle age spent between the office and the television set, a life of sameness, of growing old with nothing but a résumé and a manicured lawn to show for it. Suburban Tempe was nothing but going to work, buying things, and going to bed. My father had wanted to escape. And he had wanted his children to understand why.

All those years of plate tectonics and fossils and chemistry—as a kid, I had naively believed the lessons were about science—when all along my dad had been talking about life. In forbidding me to memorize and forcing me to think, he had been ensuring that I'd never coast along on autopilot, that I would only adhere to beliefs I had fully thought through. He had made me question everything, giving me permission to pursue life on my own terms.

As I watched my mother and the government official in our kitchen form the cookie dough into little round balls, my dad bounded into the kitchen, anxious to show me the latest batch of opals he had just polished up in his shop. He couldn't wait to extol the virtues of his new diamond-tipped lapidary sander, one of his new projects now that he had eliminated the annoying working-for-a-living part of his life—my father now *lived* for a living.

It seemed so simple, yet few people were ever able to accomplish it. Was the secret to happiness as simple as buying a ticket to Honduras? If that were the case, surely American Airlines would have taken advantage of this in its advertising campaign. ("We are your ticket to happiness. Low one-way fares to Tegucigalpa.") Perhaps it was that my parents had had the courage to make unconventional choices, to discard what didn't matter, separating out what was expected of them from what was really essential.

As my father laid the specimens out on the table for me to peruse, I couldn't help but imagine myself at his age. When I was fifty years old, would I look back on what I had done and regret that I had traded happiness for stability? I had already let my childhood pass me by. Would I give up my early adulthood just as easily?

I had been so content for the past two weeks in Honduras. I had had fun with my family. We'd all been so distracted by the newness of the place that we hadn't had time to remember all the old resentments and gripes.

All it took was this simple realization to completely turn my life around. After all, happiness was like alcoholism—it began with a single sip.

Chapter Two

The Only American Tourist in Beirut

Back at home in Los Angeles while I contemplated the sorry state of my life from the safety of my bed, it occurred to me that if there was anyone who could teach me to lighten up and have fun, it had to be my friend Peter. For the past eight years, he had been showing up at my apartment in L.A. whenever I needed a few laughs. In general, his levity-inducing methods were mild, but on occasions when I was particularly resistant to his charm, he wasn't above resorting to force. When necessary, he would shove me into my walk-in closet, follow me in with a fifth of tequila, and assure me that my freedom could be obtained as soon as I had consumed two shots. I would squeal and plead, realize that I had no chance of overpowering my six-foot-two-inch captor, and finally accept his terms, reluctantly downing one drink and then another.

Peter always kept his word—after I took the recommended dose of alcohol, he would graciously open the door, but by then the tequila would begin taking effect and whatever productive activity I had been consumed with an hour earlier would seem trivial compared with my duty to the closet and my responsibility to continue, um, consuming.

Peter's good-natured efforts on my behalf had gone on for years, something I attributed to affection as well as force of habit. We had met as high school foreign exchange students in what was then West

Germany, and from the very beginning I had admired the effortless way Peter always managed to have a good time. I had never met anyone like him, someone who could be smart and popular too. In the tiny towns I had grown up in, making the fatal mistake of letting a word like "onomatopoeia" slip out just one time was enough to get you relegated to the geek table forever.

I had liked Peter immediately, but I was also somewhat in awe of the way he took hold of his whole foreign-exchange experience. I was a shy and insecure sixteen year old, a result of years of torment at the hands of my American peers, but Peter seemed unintimidated by anyone or anything, even when presented with an entirely new culture. Unlike myself, who very courteously spoke to her host parents in the German formal *Sie,* Peter sat his parents down, explained that he was going to be living in their house for a while, and he would be damned if he wasn't going to call them by the familiar *du.*

He handled his teachers in much the same way. When they began to complain that he rarely showed up for school, he explained that it was merely a misunderstanding on their part, that he was receiving no high school credit for his year abroad, and that instead of harping on his absences, they should consider it extra credit every time he decided to show up in a classroom.

Before I met him, my biggest entertainment had been sitting alone in my bedroom making strange guttural noises that in any other country would have been a sure symptom of demonic possession (in Germany, this was merely called "practicing your consonant sounds"). But Pete insisted I have some real fun. There was a spontaneous journey to Copenhagen, a week spent in Sweden, and a stay in West Berlin, where I ran my hands across an ominous wall that would come tumbling down a year later.

After Peter and I parted ways in Germany, we met up again in California, first in Peter's hometown of Stockton and later in Los Angeles. While I was going to UCLA, Pete was alternating his time among Santa Monica College, San Diego State, and Berkeley, doing his part to contribute to California's entire higher educational system without playing favorites. ("I've dropped out of some of the best schools in this country," he was fond of saying.) He was never more than a six-hour drive away and he'd always find some excuse to come see me in Los Angeles.

Our visits usually ended at the international terminal of the L.A. airport—Peter was continually jet-setting to some foreign destination, taking advantage of his in-between-colleges time by traveling to whatever country was offering cheap tickets. There had been several visits to Germany, a trip to see his aunt and uncle in Mexico, a week in (what was then) Czechoslovakia, even a last minute flight to Poland.

The last time I had seen him, he had been waving good-bye to me out the window of an Amtrak train, the beginning of a journey he planned to take by land to the farthest tip of South America. From what I understood, he got as far as Guatemala, had a revelation that more or less dealt with how much he disliked squeezing into overcrowded buses filled with livestock, sped to the nearest international airport, and hopped on the next flight to Europe. From there, my knowledge of events gets kind of confused, but there was something about reading a Middle Eastern guidebook in a bookstore in Germany, Peter's subsequent journey to Jordan, and finally a trip to Lebanon—a place he had yet to return from.

He had been living in Beirut for the past three years, which made it a lot tougher for him to drive over to my apartment any time he suspected I was in need of a good time, so he had resorted to calling me up every few months or so and insisting I come and see him. I had continually rejected the idea, not because I was against it on principle—I was as fun-loving as the next twenty-five-year-old subscriber to *Scientific American*—it was just that as a person paying her own way through college (subsequently followed by being a person paying her own way out of student-loan debt), my financial circumstances had ruled out jet-setting as a potential lifestyle choice.

"When are you coming to visit?" he'd ask at the end of every phone conversation. By now, the question had become so routine that he put it to me more out of habit than in the hopes of receiving a sincere reply.

"No time, no money," I'd automatically answer.

But this time when the phone rang, just weeks after my return from Honduras, for the first time I gave Pete's query some actual contemplation. Going to Lebanon—what would that mean? I imagined myself sitting in a Middle Eastern café, sipping thick coffee, gazing out over the Mediterranean and picking the tabbouleh out of my teeth, gracefully sliding my chair out of the way of any wayward bombs. Later, we'd ride camels through the desert (I'd call my camel Sandy), the wind blowing through our hair, our billowing white tunics flowing behind us. We'd camp with a group of nomads. We'd eat dates we collected ourselves. It would be glamorous, exciting, and just a bit risky—exactly the qualities that were discouraged among the employees of Hughes Aircraft.

There was just one obstacle. If I remembered correctly, Peter had once mentioned that visiting Lebanon was sort of illegal. When I asked him about this, he explained that this was true only if you were the kind of person who happened to take seriously the advice of the U.S. State Department, and given the disdainful way Peter spoke this phrase I was sure this was the type of individual that I definitely didn't want to be.

There were ways around these restrictions, he insisted. The U.S. government didn't have to *find out* I was traveling to Beirut. I'd buy my ticket in London and the Lebs (as Peter affectionately referred to them) would be more than happy to allow me into the country. All I had to do was go to the Lebanese consulate in Los Angeles and bring along some official-looking papers (that Pete would provide me with) that declared I had legitimate business to conduct.

"And if that doesn't work," Peter advised me over international phone lines, "just flirt your way in."

Peter was from a respected upper-middle-class family. His father was a judge, for God's sake. If Peter said it was okay to break the law, I had to believe him. So armed with several passport photos and a few documents in Arabic that Peter had faxed to me, I made my way to the Lebanese consulate wearing a .short dress and a big smile, feeling for the first time gleefully dangerous.

My conversation with the man behind the counter went something like this:

WENDY: I'd like to get a visa.

LEBANESE VISA GUY: May I see your passport? *[Wendy hands over passport, makes eye contact. Smiles seductively. Man notices it's an American passport.]* Americans aren't allowed to go to Lebanon.

WENDY: Yes, but I'm a writer. *[Then, in as sexy a voice as it is possible to use when uttering words like "The documentation that I am providing attests to the fact that the Lebanese Ministry of Tourism has hired me to write some brochures," Wendy says:]* The documentation that I am providing attests to the fact that the Lebanese Ministry of Tourism has hired me to write some brochures.

LEBANESE VISA GUY: *[Man looks at documentation suspiciously, looks at Wendy. Big smile from Wendy. A small wink. Man thinks a moment. Then:]* No problem, beautiful lady. You want some coffee?*

[Wendy spends the rest of the afternoon drinking coffee at the consulate's office chatting about what a lovely time of year it is for visiting Lebanon.]

One of the disadvantages of vacationing in Beirut is that it deprives you of one of the greatest pleasures of taking a trip in the first

---

*Flirting is currently unnecessary for anyone wishing to visit Beirut. A year after I made my trip there, the State Department removed Lebanon from its list of nations that Americans are prohibited from visiting.

place: the jealousy of your friends. I realized this a week before my departure when not one of the people I knew expressed the slightest tinge of envy at my impending visit. As I emphasized the phrases "international trip," "vacation abroad," and "on the coast of the Mediterranean," they looked at me with a mix of fear and concern and mentioned something about bombs. (The good news, as I would learn later, was that they were small bombs. "Very small bombs," as my Lebanese friend Hadi would helpfully point out.)

Even my guidebook seemed less than optimistic. On the subject of the country I was soon to visit, it had these words to say: "If God created a training ground for the Armageddon, Beirut would be the stage. . . . Populated and run by tribes of fanatical gangs, the realities of Beirut would challenge even the most creative scriptwriter. Religion, drugs, war, love, and death all interact in this biblical epic of death and destruction." This was not encouraging advice, but neither was the title of the book I was holding. Unable to find Lebanon listed in *Let's Go* or *Lonely Planet,* the guide I had resorted to was called *The World's Most Dangerous Places.*

On the bright side, the book had devoted an entire chapter to the country, including lots of important travel tips such as: "Kidnapping is a fine art in Beirut. . . . Have a driver meet you at the airport with a prearranged signal or sign. If not, take the official airport taxis. If you take a taxi, officials will write down your name and destination so the news media can get it right after you're abducted."

Of course I wouldn't be faced with such problems. I had Peter, a guide who spoke fluent Arabic, owned his own car, knew his way through Hamra and Achrafieh the way I navigated around Hollywood and Santa Monica. I had nothing to worry about—except maybe Peter. On my first day in Lebanon just hours after I had descended from my plane, before I even had a chance to adapt to the contradictory sights that bombarded my senses, intricately beautiful Byzantine arches side by side with decaying buildings that had been hollowed out by bombs, Peter informed me what he wanted to do: go sightseeing—in southern Lebanon.

There was something ominous about this suggestion. In fact, during our phone conversation several weeks earlier when I had expressed a slight concern over my safety, Peter had gone out of his way to explain that violence in the country tended to be concentrated around certain areas, that all we had to do was avoid perilous places like the border between Lebanon and Israel, and everything would be okay.

But now this was exactly where we were headed. I couldn't help but be concerned. "Pete, aren't we in danger of the shelling going on there?"

"Don't worry, Wend. They usually only shell in the morning," my friend said with a maniacal grin.

The southern border of Lebanon was not a warm, fuzzy place to be. It was like a huge dodgeball field—though instead of avoiding the path of a red rubber ball, today's task would be to drive out of the trajectory of any shells pelted at us from the Israeli army on one side, Hezbollah guerrillas on the other.

It sounded terrifying, but I had decided to say yes to the possibility of excitement and danger. I was determined to take life less seriously.

"So why is it that everyone wants to kill us?" I asked Peter, trying to sound as nonchalant as possible as we began our trip through the hilly and dusty brush-covered terrain.

"They don't want to kill us, silly," Pete said, consoling me. "They want to kill each other. We just happen to be driving down the middle of their firing zone."

This was not the Lebanon of thirty years ago. Several decades earlier, Lebanon had been one of the Middle East's success stories, a nation where Christian, Muslim, and Druze* families lived side by

---

*The Druze are a religious group whose teachings are so secret that only an elite group of Druze is let in on them.

side in relative peace and harmony. Beirut was "the Paris of the Middle East," a thriving adult playground on the shores of the Mediterranean filled with exotic restaurants, expensive nightclubs, and international shopping centers.

Shopping lost a lot of its allure in 1975 when civil war broke out. Initially, the Muslims had felt they weren't adequately represented in the government, and it was a war between Muslims and Maronite Christians, but after a while the situation got so complicated and the alliances so tenuous that it was nearly impossible to remember who was against whom at any given time. One day it would be Sunni Muslims against Christians; the next week, it would be Sunni Muslims allied with Christians against Shiites. And then the alliances would shift all over again, like a game of musical chairs.

These days, the country's internal religious conflicts had simmered down, making Beirut a relatively safe city—so Pete had wanted to drag me down to the southern border of Lebanon, where a different but equally complex conflict was taking place: Hezbollah guerrillas were fighting against Israel.*

I was at one of the world's most notoriously dangerous borders, one of the hotspots in the ongoing conflict between Muslims and Jews. But my friend and tour guide made it sound as if we were just taking a ride through Disney's Small World attraction.

"On the right-hand side, you'll notice the Israeli bunkers, the mounds of earth on the horizon, and on the left, don't forget to snap a photo of the Hezbollah flag."

He was right—a real black and yellow Hezbollah flag was waving in the wind right in front of me. I couldn't believe my eyes. I wanted to grab the flag and take it home, the ultimate travel souvenir, but contented myself with snapping a quick photo.

As Peter sped up the car and drove on through the dust, I won-

---

*Israeli forces withdrew from Lebanon in May 2000, ending twenty-two years of occupation.

dered if my friend was right—maybe this was no big deal. Maybe there was nothing to be afraid of.

"And coming up ahead," Peter continued, "those men with camouflage gear and machine guns—those would have to be soldiers."

I knew from all my reading that a Hezbollah soldier encountering an American basically took one of three actions: (1) killed the American, (2) kidnapped the American, or (3) screamed, "Welcome to my country. Would you like some coffee?" In Lebanon, you really had no idea which of these actions was most likely to take place, because guerrilla logic on the subject seemed to be open to some debate. Some felt that Americans were Israeli allies and therefore the enemy. Others thought that since the United States was generally considered a Christian country, it should be left out of this religious bickering. And then there was the ever-popular international view that Americans were to blame for all the world's problems.

Maybe this excursion hadn't been such a good idea after all. The men up ahead were brandishing huge firearms. Just the sight of these weapons terrified me.

We stopped in front of a barbed-wire fence that had been strung across the road and a grim-faced soldier peered into Peter's car. I held my breath and tried to look as Muslim as possible.

"You speak English?" he asked in a strange accent.

Peter nodded.

"That's a real spot of luck. We do too. We're from Ireland," the soldier said.

These were not Hezbollah guerrillas; they were UN troops and this was one of their checkpoints. This didn't quite put us in the clear. After all, we were in the country illegally. What did the United Nations have to say about that?

"Welcome to Lebanon!" the soldier said, extending his hand for Peter to shake. Then they cheerily raised the bar blocking the road and waved us on through.

I spent the rest of the day awed and amazed. We steadily made our way through a barren and monotonous landscape with few people, few structures, and very little to see. Had this been the Sonoran Desert, I would have been apathetic and bored, but this was Lebanon. I was driving through thousands of years of history; not only that, my life was in peril. Nothing of note was going on outside, but there was the constant threat that this calm could be disrupted at any moment. In Lebanon, life could be changed in an instant.

Visit a friend abroad and it's nearly a given that at some point you will take part in an expatriate gathering. This highly ritualized event consists of you sitting in a room with lots of alcohol with people who all grew up speaking English (although most of them speak it with a funny-sounding foreign accent). The conversation always includes the same three topics: (1) international politics, (2) sex, and (3) boy, you sure got the wrong end of the deal when you had to be born an American.

The night always starts out with Topic Number 3. The first thing all the Brits have to do (believe me, there will always be at least one or two Brits) is imitate your accent. "Golly gee whiz guys" and "like totally awesome" are the two phrases that invariably will be chosen to demonstrate the fact you do not speak English, you speak American.

After you've cleared this hurdle, they will ask if you have ever met any movie stars and, if so, do you have any gossip to tell? After racking your brain for sordid tales about the people you watch on the screens in dark movie theaters and brush elbows with occasionally as they're walking down the streets of Los Angeles, your host Michael (well, he won't always be named Michael) will then top your stories with "real dirt." For instance, if you come up with a story about a famous male artist who has sex with boyish looking twenty-year-olds while they're wearing football uniforms, Michael will give you an in-the-know, step-by-step, detailed account of the sex act in question, right down to the number on the uniform.

Then it's on to international politics, which tends to overlap a bit with the "America sure is a lousy country" category. We begin with "America sure has a lousy foreign policy," move on to "America sure has a lousy president," and top the topic off with "Americans sure have a lousy knowledge of other countries' affairs." Which is just the point you've been waiting for all evening. Now is your chance to strike.

You dazzle the guests by quoting verbatim from the latest tome by Chomsky, drone on intelligently about a recent editorial in the *New York Times,* and roll off subjects like Sinn Fein peace talks and the possible opening up of Cuba when the room becomes encompassed in an awe-filled silence. After paying their respects, your host Michael (he won't always be named Michael) will inevitably break the quiet with the following compliment: "Wow. You really aren't dumb like most Americans."

By this point in the conversation, the Brits will have gotten pretty drunk (and the Americans will have gotten pretty offended), so it's time to move back to the subject of sex. On this particular evening five days into my visit to Beirut, sitting in the comfortable and cozy living room of Peter's friend Michael (okay, so it's possible that he *will* always be named Michael), the category is dominated primarily by Giles, who has an awful lot to say on the subject of orgasms, especially for a person who doesn't have them. This is because orgasms are unhealthy, he informs us. He has embarked on the Taoist journey, which encompasses many beliefs none of us really wants to hear about; we want to talk about Giles' not having orgasms.

It's not that he doesn't ever do the dirty, he explains. In fact, he does it rather well. He goes for hours, but he just doesn't finish the job. Not for himself anyway. Penetration is fine, he tells us, it's just the loss of those vital fluids—wouldn't want to sap his psychic energy, you know. I tell him I completely understand and quietly slip him my phone number under the table.

This segues brilliantly into our next topic of conversation: the fact that Michael's sister strategically places bowls of water in her hallways to help the cosmic energy flow more evenly throughout the house.

At this point, I decide it's really about time to be hanging out with some more Lebanese.

Five days of my ten-day trip had already been eaten up, and Peter felt terrible about having to go into work. As we ate a breakfast of flatbread, yogurt, and fresh fruit on his balcony, I tried to convince him that I'd be fine in his absence.

"Are you sure? I promise we'll go out for dinner this evening," he said.

"Of course, I'll be okay," I insisted, stuffing a fig in my mouth.

Peter had mentioned his job to me once over the phone. I remembered that it had something to do with journalism. What was it exactly?

"I'm the anchor for the English news."

No, that wasn't it. He wrote some kind of newsletter or something. What was it?

"That was my old job. Now I'm on TV every night. I sit in a studio in front of a live camera and read off the teleprompter."

This information came as kind of a shock. The man who used to measure out tequila as if it were NyQuil, handing it to me with the concerned look of a mother tending to her sick child, now put on a suit and tie and provided the nation's international citizens with their daily dose of news. I had never imagined seeing Peter on the news before—in the same way that I hadn't counted on opening up my closet and running into Dan Rather or Tom Brokaw. There were people you saw on television and there were people you saw in your closet. When these lines got blurred, the whole world stopped making sense.

However, Peter explained to me that this was the job he had always wanted: He got to apply his vast knowledge of Middle Eastern politics, he put his journalism experience to use, and no one was trying to kill him. At his last job, on his first day, the coffee boy had come up and introduced himself to Peter by saying, "You American? I hate American. I kill American. New Jersey kill my brother." It had not been an auspicious start to his new position (but on the bright side, it was the excuse Peter needed to finally give up that nasty addiction to coffee).

"You can watch me tonight," Peter explained. "When you and Hadi get home."

Hadi was Peter's roommate, a good-natured Beiruti who seemed excited at the prospect of playing tour guide for an American visitor. Later that morning, he began tirelessly dragging me from one attraction to another.

While I was amazed at the devastation that surrounded us, Hadi was determined to show me the best the city had to offer. As we headed toward downtown in his tiny dinged-up car, Arabic music blaring out of the radio (to my embarrassment, the one song I chose to compliment turned out to be an advertising jingle), I pointed to a five-story structure that had been gutted out by bombs, and to my surprise, Hadi acted as if he was embarrassed. He tried to distract my attention by motioning toward the building next door, a beautiful marble high-rise in the final stages of construction.

The rest of the ride, our conversation centered around the same basic theme. "Wow, Hadi, check out the death and destruction on the left!" I would enthusiastically remark, which would cause my well-meaning tour guide to defensively respond, "Yes, but look at the life and renovation on the other side of the street."

What he didn't understand—and what I hadn't realized either until that point—was that it was the death and destruction that I had come to see. Part of the allure of going to a foreign place is that even the problems are foreign. The hollowed-out buildings all around us didn't apply to me. If I was going to continue traveling, it wasn't going to be Club Med, the kind of place that allowed you to forget your worries for a week. No, I needed to head to the dark corners of the world, where my problems would seem insignificant by comparison.

Hadi parked the car and turned off the engine. As we exited the vehicle, I was baffled when we suddenly began walking toward one of the decaying structures that Hadi had made such an effort to shield me from. As I stared up at the top stories of the building that had been destroyed, true to form, Hadi drew my attention to the ground floor, which I hadn't noticed before. It had been completely preserved. Painted titanium white and garnished with shiny brass trim, this was where we were headed.

Just minutes ago, we had been driving through a maze of traffic, surrounded by the remnants of devastation and swirling dust and suddenly we had entered a spotless café, where a white-suited waiter was accompanying us to a table with a smile and a menu.

"Where's the no-smoking section?" I asked Hadi as we were suddenly engulfed by a thick black haze.

"That would be East Beirut."

I had initially assumed that religion was what separated the two sectors of the city, but talking to Hadi, I began to understand that it was more a matter of vices. In Christian East Beirut, drinking was the pastime of choice. However, in West Beirut, where Mohammed's advice was heeded in place of the surgeon general's, alcohol was a big no-no. The Koran had issued strict admonitions against the dangers of wine, tequila, and peach schnapps—though it had neglected to insert that little warning about nicotine, birth defects, reproductive harm, and so forth. So in West Beirut, they went about smoking anything they could set fire to.

I had never heard of a hookah (this was before they became trendy), so as I gazed around the room, I became convinced that we had walked into an opium den. I tried to be as self-possessed as possible and ignore the fact that nearly every table was equipped with a sophisticated-looking bong adding smoke to the black haze that already engulfed the room.

"Do you want to try?" Hadi asked, as I tried to make myself comfortable at the table.

Hell, I'd been to college. "Sure," I said.

Hadi called the waiter over to the table and ordered something in Arabic that sounded horribly menacing. I wasn't sure I really wanted to know what it was, but I timidly asked him anyway.

"Strawberry," he replied.

This sounded like what you'd order at an ice-cream parlor instead of an opium den. "No, I meant the bong thing."

"The *nargeileh*."

"Yeah. Did you order us one of those?"

"Yes. Strawberry."

This had to be code for something.

"Hadi, strawberry opium?"

"It's not opium. Whoever heard of strawberry opium? This is normal, everyday strawberry-flavored tobacco."

I felt rather foolish at my mistake, but things only got worse when the waiter returned with our order. He was carrying the *nargeileh,* a vase-shaped glass filled with water and equipped with a three-foot-long hose. He skillfully plugged the upper end of the gadget with a metal tray, added a chunk of tobacco, and placed a disk of red-hot charcoal on top. The tobacco began to burn and Hadi handed me the hose, gallantly insisting that I begin.

I wasn't sure exactly how to maneuver this apparatus. Normally, whenever I found myself in any awkward social situation, I watched the other people at my table to figure out which fork I was supposed to be wielding, but here I was in the land of Middle Eastern hospitality, where the Lebanese graciously waited for you to start, insisting that guests always go first.

Pete had already told me about the difficult situation this same custom had once placed him in at an elegant party in Beirut when the hostess bounded upon him with a tray full of roasted pigeon. Pete was not really in the mood for roasted pigeon and never had been, but a refusal would have been seen as a grave insult to the woman of the house, who had devoted hours to basting and cooking the birds, not to mention the amount of time she must have spent rounding them up at the park. He was going to have to eat one and what was worse, he was the center of attention; they were all waiting for the guest to begin, and he didn't know whether you picked pigeon up with your fingers chicken style or used a fork. He timidly reached for a small bird and plopped it into his mouth, crunching on the tiny bones and trying to swallow it out of his life as quickly as possible.

Now I was in a similar situation. I had never smoked out of a hose before, but I sportingly placed the tube to my lips and took a deep breath, as self-conscious as an adolescent Arabic girl taking her first inhale out of a *nargeileh* in her high school bathroom.

Other than the fact that there was a tube in my mouth, it was like smoking a cigarette—a berry-flavored one. Nicotine flooded my brain, sped up my heart rate, and made my head spin. But this was just the beginning. Lebanese tradition demanded that smoking a *nargeileh* go on for an entire afternoon. I passed Hadi the hose, took a sip of my coffee, and decided it wasn't such a bad country after all.

On my last weekend in Beirut, I was all for the idea of running off to yet another smoke-filled café, but Peter had a better idea: detox. Although he was a staunch supporter of the virtues of alcohol, like a true Californian he was an adamant antismoker and had every intention of ridding me of the nicotine addiction that Hadi had spent the past few days carefully cultivating.

"We're going to get you some fresh air," he said, pushing me into his car.

This didn't sound nearly as entertaining as inhaling smoke. "Couldn't we just pick up some muscle relaxants at the drugstore?"

Peter rolled his eyes and started the engine. He was determined to show me another face of Lebanon, an ancient side, and for the rest of the afternoon we wandered about the ruins of one bygone civilization after another.

Our first stop was the Phoenician port city of Sidon, where we roamed through a thirteenth-century Crusader sea castle. The structure wasn't much bigger than a typical house in Beverly Hills, but it was made entirely of stone and appeared to be rising out of the sea. It sat on a tiny island connected to the mainland by a short bridge.

Then, it was onto Tyre, a three-thousand-year-old city that had been conquered by big name headliners such as Alexander the Great and King Nebuchadnezzar. Just feet away from the blue waters of the Mediterranean, Peter and I strolled between the colonnades that had once formed part of an impressive city.

But this was just foreplay. The real deal was another two hours away, the ancient Roman city of Baalbeck. So far I'd been having a good time, but when you got right down to it, ruins were just one rundown building after another. Not Baalbeck. As Peter and I got out of the car, I could see the tremendous structures in the distance, the largest Roman temples ever constructed.

The temple of Jupiter was the most gigantic of all. I got vertigo looking up at its seventy-foot-high columns, imagining what this city must have been like in its day. All around us was what I decided to call "temple dandruff," huge chunks of rubble that had broken off and fallen to the ground. These colossal blocks of beautifully carved stone contained the ornate moldings of leaves and lion heads. Peter and I couldn't resist climbing over them in spite of their size. Like energetic preschoolers, we pulled ourselves up using both hands and ascended the slanted rock hunched over so that we could quickly grab hold of the stone in the event of losing our balance.

There were three other structures to see so we headed over to the temple of Bacchus, which was the most impressive, simply because it had been so well preserved. It was like pictures I had seen of the Parthenon—a rectangular structure surrounded by columns—and its size was staggering.

"Three hundred years they spent building this place," Peter informed me, walking up the temple steps. "And they never finished."

"Talk about a bad case of procrastination."

"Tell me about it. You know, there are ruins in Beirut too."

"I know. Hadi and I go to cafés in them."

"Not the ruins of the war. Ancient ruins."

"Oh."

"They've been trying to rebuild downtown Beirut, but half the time, when they begin excavating, they unearth another set of Roman ruins. For them, it's a real pain. They give the archeologists a couple of months to scavenge what they can and then they bulldoze it all."

"Damn Roman ruins. What an inconvenience."

Late that afternoon, both of us famished from a long day of walking, we stopped at a restaurant along the highway for *mezze,* which could be roughly translated as "lunch, a whole lot of it." It always began with a series of appetizers (hummus, tabbouleh, baba ghanoush, plain yogurt, and flat Arabic bread), moved onto main dishes (lamb, chicken, or beef), and ended with fruit and sweets. Food was fun enough, but my favorite part of the meal was the traditional drink *arrack,* a licorice-flavored liquor that turned milky white when served over ice cubes and mixed with chilled water.

Sitting in the outdoor patio of the restaurant watching the other patrons, I couldn't help but think how calm they all seemed. They were, after all, Lebanese. They woke up in a war-torn country, ate lunch surrounded by strife and civil unrest, and lived with the threat of bombs all day. Yet here they were laughing over glasses of *arrack,* asking their family members to kindly pass the flatbread.

These were the moments I had not counted on in Beirut. I had been prepared for guns and bombs and destruction. But this was also a place where people got on with their lives. They got up in the morning, read the paper, headed to work, and returned to have dinner with their families.

After an emotional good-bye, I boarded a flight leaving Lebanon the next day. It was a short journey to Cyprus, then another flight to London, and finally onto Washington, D.C., where I arrived exhausted and jet lagged. From there, I took what Southwest Airlines would refer to as a direct flight to Los Angeles (meaning two obligatory stops at Nashville and Phoenix).

It was during a layover at the Phoenix airport, sitting at the gate waiting for my flight that I began to feel the effect of travel on my outlook. In my own time zone for the first time in weeks, I was having a hard time. It wasn't the fact that my neck ached, my head hurt, my feet were sore, or that my body clock was set ten hours ahead. It was that after Beirut, everything around me seemed so trivial. The conversation going on across from me went something like this:

"Have you had those new lattes?" an overweight woman with feathered and frosted hair asked her friend, pronouncing the word "latte" to rhyme with "batty."

"You like lattes? Cappuccinos are better. Or you can have them with chocolate. That's called a mocha."

"How about café au laits? You like those?"

"I don't know. I never had one."

I was tempted to walk up to them and tell them it was coffee for God's sake—it was some grounds, some water, and some milk, and it really didn't matter. What mattered was the fact that their houses weren't being bombed, that half the people they knew hadn't been killed, that they could sleep at night, not worried that the roof above their heads would soon be lying on their chests.

But I kept it to myself. I sat in my chair, watching the planes take off and land, quietly smiling, thinking that my friends truly did have something to be jealous of, after all.

Chapter Three

Cuba Libre, Muy Libre

All of the boring people I knew—the ones who led lives I didn't want mine to turn out like—they had one thing in common: they all had jobs. I realized this on an especially dreary Monday morning at Hughes Aircraft. Days earlier, I had been fleeing bombs and sniper fire in Beirut, sipping *arrack,* and inhaling the smoke from a *nargeileh,* but now I was back where I had started, looking out at the world through the window in my office. The change I'd undergone in Beirut had been fleeting thanks to a little fun damperer called work.

The monotony was worse than it had been before because now I had a different frame of reference. I had memories of warm flatbread topped with oregano and other spices, dribbled with olive oil and oozing melted cheese. The engineers around me had never tasted freshly heated *mankoushi,* which is why they were able to sit there day after day leading productive, fulfilled, flatbread-free lives—because they had no idea what they were missing out on.

The work itself wasn't what bothered me, rather, it was the predictability of it all. Every day at 8 A.M., the same freeway, the same office, the same boring business attire. The days of my life stretched out in front of me, one after the other, no surprises in store. I wanted my life to matter, to mean something, not just to get used up and discarded like a roll of disposable towels.

Quitting my job would have been easy if it weren't for the simple matter of supporting myself. I had no idea how to get out of working and still earn a living. Had I had some sage guidance from, say, an eloquent and wise mentor or, lacking that, a really good Magic 8 Ball, I might have been able to get some valuable insight into what was soon to occur, a conversation such as the following:

WENDY: Will I have the same job in three months?
MAGIC 8 BALL: No.
WENDY: Will I be broke in three months?
MAGIC 8 BALL: No.
WENDY: What is to become of my life?
MAGIC 8 BALL: Your future is inexplicably intertwined with that of Wink Martindale.*

Since I never did get my hands on that Magic 8 Ball (meaning that the preceding conversation never actually took place) when I met Wink Martindale three months later, needless to say, it came as a complete surprise to me.

My life changed with a phone call. When I received it, I had been at my wit's end, wondering how I was going to pay my rent and the stack of bills that kept piling up while I survived on Top Ramen and adrenaline. The division of Hughes Aircraft where I had worked for the past two years had quit on me (before I got the pleasure of quitting on it), recently having transferred its operations to Arizona, so I had been struggling with the new reality of living without a regular paycheck.

If I had ever been in need of good news, it was certainly that night sitting outside on my porch, nursing a Manhattan, staring at

---

*Wink Martindale was the most famous game show host of my childhood, whose list of credits includes *Tic Tac Dough* and *Joker's Wild*.

what was left in my glass and realizing that it was my last cocktail; there wasn't money left to spend on any more sweet vermouth. I heard the dim ring of the phone and fiddled with the latch on my door, racing to get inside in time. It was a friend from college, which was nice enough news in itself, but better yet she was calling to tell me that she'd just gotten hired at the *Advocate,* a gay and lesbian newsmagazine, and that the editors were looking for someone to write profiles on celebrities. It would only be sporadic work, but I figured that any income was better than what I was subsisting on now and it turned out to be relatively easy. My job consisted of basically going around and asking famous actors how they felt about gay people. (In case you're wondering, Billy Crystal said he liked them, Jane Hamilton said she liked them, and John Lithgow said he liked them but not nearly as much as he liked dressing up in a skirt and pearls.)

It was a good beginning, but it was still a tenuous existence. For the next few months, I just had enough to pay my bills, assuming I never ate out and was careful at the grocery store. I needed to augment my income with another freelance client, but I had no idea how to go about it. I tried everything I could think of—I walked around my apartment practicing saying I was a journalist, I bought myself a supply of spiral-bound notebooks and Uniball Deluxe pens—but these preliminary attempts were futile. What else could I do? I figured it wouldn't hurt to sit outside my friend Lisa's building with a laptop attempting to look writerly. Fortunately, this managed to do the trick.

One day as I literally sat on her front steps, her neighbor Bill walked by. I had spoken to him many times before, but I had never managed to grasp how he afforded the rent on his sixteen-hundred-dollar apartment while earning his living as a writer. He had occasionally thrown out clues, referring to his past in New York advertising and his subsequent move to Los Angeles to work in the film industry. Once, I had gone up to his place to take a peek at his ad copywriting portfolio and had noticed that his living room was full of scripts, but how did a writer go about getting such jobs?

Bill's life bore no resemblance to my own. He drove a brand-new Saab convertible and got free tickets to exclusive Hollywood screenings. And he had just gotten a job writing a brand new sitcom, or so he informed me as I sat on the steps with my clunky out-of-date laptop. Speaking of which, would I have any interest in interviewing for the ad copywriting position he was leaving behind? It paid five hundred dollars a day.

He was so casual about it. It was the job he was discarding—to him, it was just leftover material. But five hundred dollars? A day? That would put me in the same league as engineers, doctors, lawyers, and prostitutes. All I had to do was go in for an interview and convince the ad agency owner, Chuck Blore, that I was the writer he was looking for.

Bill acted as if it was no big deal, but I knew that Chuck was a powerful man. He had worked with Hollywood celebrities. He was friends with TV network presidents. He had personally produced all the radio spots for AT&T's "Reach out and touch someone" campaign. What could he possibly see in an ex-corporate writer like myself?

A few days later as I nervously trudged my way up the stairs to his Hollywood office, my chances were actually a lot better than I suspected. Chuck had a personality trait that was about to work in my favor: he prided himself on making brave choices. He had hired Drew Barrymore before anyone had even heard the phrase "E.T. phone home." He had been taping Christina Applegate's voice since she was a baby. Chuck loved being able to spot new talent. He took chances on people, paved the way for their success, and watched as they moved on to bigger and better things.

The first time I walked into his office, he seemed genuinely happy to see me, treating me like the guest of honor at a dinner party. He had me take a seat, and before there was time to introduce myself or exchange a few words of chitchat, he enthusiastically popped a cassette into his stereo. "These are some of the radio spots I've written," he announced grandly, pressing play on the machine.

He listened to the tape as if hearing it for the first time. He laughed at the jokes, acted surprised by the endings. His pride was that of a little kid, a joyous five-year-old who shouts out to his mother, "Look what I can do!" I found him completely endearing.

I wondered what I could say to convince him that I was the writer he needed, but once the tape had finished, Chuck seemed uninterested in discussing my experience, a lucky break for me considering there wasn't much of it to discuss. He instantly hired me on a trial basis based simply on a gut instinct he had about these things.

Fortunately, I was a quick learner. After turning in a few mediocre scripts, three days later I came in with a radio spot that had him laughing out loud and he immediately upgraded my trial-basis status to that of a full-fledged writer.

As if the entire experience hadn't been ludicrously lucky enough, the good fortune that followed was the stuff of freelance writing legend. Chuck had been trying to get a television project off the ground for thirty years—one week after he hired me on, the deal finally came through. I arrived in his office just moments after he received the news. Giddy with excitement, he raced over to me and gave me a warm embrace. "Ever-Lovely," he said, using the nickname that he would call me from that day forward, "now that you're my writer, I have a new challenge for you. Have you ever thought about writing for television? I want you to help me script a TV program."

A week later the executive producer of the program walked into Chuck's office for the first time. It was none other than Wink Martindale in the flesh.

While other people slaved away at their jobs, trapped by convention and an oppressive sense of impotence, at age twenty-five, I had found the secret trapdoor out. I felt like Jim Carrey finally fleeing *The Truman Show*. I was like the bubble boy inhaling his first breath of mountain air. It was incredible. I had stepped into the life I had always imagined.

The glee was a little bit hard to take. It was such a novel sensation for me that I wasn't quite sure how to behave. I didn't know the norms for happiness. What did happy people do? How did they behave? For God's sake, where did they shop?

If I was having a tough time getting used to my newly prosperous existence, my ATM was even slower to be convinced. Several months into my freelance writing career, I had tried to deposit a check totaling more than eight thousand dollars, but even the normally agreeable Wells Fargo machine seemed to have a hard time buying it.

I had begun the normal transaction process by keying in the total amount of my check. "You have entered eight thousand dollars. Is this correct?" I hit the OK button, figuring the next step would be to insert my deposit envelope—but it was as if this ATM machine had known me personally: "You have entered eight thousand dollars! Are you sure this is the correct amount of your deposit?" This screen had never come up in the past. I didn't even know this screen existed. I had never been worthy of the incredulity screen before. With a big grin, I hit the OK button one last time, realizing that I had finally joined that small rank of people who enter eight thousand dollars on the automatic teller key pad: the wealthy and the dyslexic.

For a while, the idea of having money was more fun than spending it. In my mind, I squandered my entire wealth dozens of time, reveling in pretending to empty my bank account more than actually going through with it. I could buy six hundred bottles of Absolut vodka, I imagined, picturing a whole side of my living room suddenly transformed into a wall of crystal. Or I could purchase a dozen Macintoshes, two for every room of the house. Or I could go to my favorite Goodwill, and like a millionaire let loose on a capricious shopping spree I could clean out the store's entire inventory.

Of course this was all just a good-natured game. I was never really in danger of relinquishing my entire net worth to the Absolut bottling company. I had already spent the past year planning what I would do if I ever got my hands on a significant chunk of dough: I was going to buy irresponsibility.

Unlike happiness, which seemed to be a result of wisdom, acquired experience, or a lifetime spent in the self-help section of Barnes and Noble, irresponsibility could only be purchased. It was the ultimate luxury item. Poor people never got to be irresponsible without suffering for it. If they didn't get their student-loan application in on time, no college for them. If they decided to have one more margarita and ended up an hour late for work the next morning, no job for them. But all of a sudden, these rules didn't apply to me.

My new freelance existence had the capacity to transform my life. I was just twenty-five years old yet I was already going to avoid all those years of drudgery and office work endured for decades by my father. I wanted life to be spontaneous. I needed freedom the way other people craved money or fame, and my recently acquired wealth suddenly made this possible. "I think I'll go to Cuba next week," I said with the same ease that other Americans used when they made plans to visit the supermarket.

This didn't gel particularly well with many of the people I knew. Even my travel agent seemed to need some sort of justification for my whimsical decision to flee the country. Was it a vacation? Was I going with some sort of political group? No, I explained, no reason. I simply figured Cuba would be the ideal place to pick up the things that were missing from my life: I lacked rum, I lacked cigars, and having been out of college for several years now, I missed having communist friends. (See, this really was just like a trip to the grocery store—I even had a shopping list.)

Had I given the trip more forethought, I might have gotten nervous about the prospect of going. Twenty-five-year-old women didn't just hop on international flights to Cuba by themselves. I would be traveling alone in a part of the world where it was unthinkable for women to do such things, but I was determined to be brave. It wasn't like I was going to a completely unknown place. Latin American culture was familiar to me. Cuba would be like Honduras—with the addition of communists and salsa music.

The fact that it was illegal to go there was slightly more worrisome. Even though I had experience in this particular area (Lebanon didn't exactly top the State Department's list of recommended vacation destinations), in Beirut I'd had a friend picking me up at the airport. And had something bad happened to me there, say for instance, losing my passport, Peter would have found some plausible way out—such as sneaking me across the border to Jordan where we would have entered the U.S. embassy in Amman and smiled up innocently at the officials, explaining that we were two American kids backpacking through the Middle East in need of a replacement passport—and by the way, did they know the way to the nearest international youth hostel? (For your information, the answer to that question is "Go north forty-three hundred miles and when you hit Europe, hang a left.")

But Cuba didn't have friendly bordering countries such as Jordan. Cuba's nearest neighbor was well, us, and we weren't considered exactly friendly.

The State Department's official policy has been that the embargo we have against Cuba is economic. Therefore, it wasn't illegal to visit the island—it was just illegal to spend money there. This didn't make a great deal of sense to me, but the man who continually supported this paradoxical legislation was the same man who had gotten himself mixed up in a lawsuit, in which he went to great lengths to explain that although a White House intern had provided him with a few oral favors, this, however, did not constitute a sexual relationship—which sort of put the whole Cuba logic into clear perspective.

However, it was common knowledge that Cubans welcomed

American tourists to the country. All I had to do was jet down to Mexico and pick one of several flights headed to Havana each day.

$\mathcal{T}$here are a few tricks for getting into Cuba that any American visiting the country illegally should know. The first challenge is successfully passing the luggage inspection. Now every country has those questions on their customs forms that everyone giggles about, no one takes seriously, and to which you dutifully check off "no" on the cards they hand out on airplanes. Those are the questions about whether you're bringing in livestock, carrying arms, smuggling narcotics, and so forth. Of course there are the trickier decisions such as deciding whether to declare your liquor when you have exceeded the allowance by say, a dozen or so bottles, but in general the questions are pretty straightforward (except on my recent trip when I'd been handed the card printed in Arabic).

Unfortunately, customs officials in Cuba take their jobs a little more seriously than those of other nations where a sense of humor is still legal. I had placed a neat little row of X's down the "no" line of the customs form (after all, I had come to Cuba to buy contraband merchandise; I wasn't bringing any in), so I was a little surprised when the guard standing watch over the X-ray machine spotted something suspicious looking on the monitor as my bags made their way through the conveyor belt.

"You may enter Cuba," he said pulling the offending item out of my luggage, "but not with this."

It was an apple. A nice big red juicy apple. The officers would let a capitalist-bred American illegally into a communist country but not if she wanted to bring in things like produce. So that was my choice: some of the world's best rum, cigars, and salsa music or one-fifth of the recommended daily allowance of fiber.

"No problem," I said to the guard, adding my apple to the trash can overflowing with illicit peaches, grapes, and bananas.

"No agricultural products," he explained apologetically.

"I thought you were talking about things like sheep."

Then it was onto immigration, which was a simple enough process. While all the Dutch, German, and French tourists added a Cuba stamp to the back pages of their passports, I had the guard kindly place the stamp on my visa, a little white card stapled to my passport that had been issued to me by my Guadalajaran travel agent.

And that was it. I uttered an enthusiastic "*Gracias*" and officially entered Cuba.

Umberto was a thirty-something businessman from Mexico City, and when I learned that this was his twelfth visit to Havana, I figured it wouldn't be a bad idea to tag along with him. Of course, it actually was a bad idea, a real doosey of a bad idea, but hindsight always comes into focus after the fact.

Meeting him had been a strange coincidence. We had casually struck up a conversation at the Guadalajara airport where we discovered that we were both departing on the same flight to Mexico City. Then we found out we were sharing the same plane to Cuba and that we even had reservations at the same hotel in Havana.

It turned out that we had a lot in common: I was going to Cuba because I had nothing better to do; he was going to Cuba because he was divorcing his wife and had no one better to do. But he wasn't into *gringas,* he informed me on the taxi ride to our hotel. Or smart women, he added, rolling his eyes at what I assumed was my intellect.

Luckily, I had ruled him out as a potential romantic partner already. It had happened sometime after we had met and sometime before he began yelling "Death to all Americans!" out the window of the cab. One minute we were driving along discussing Cuban food and beaches and the next minute, he was shouting with his fist in the air, "*Yanquis* go home!"

Needless to say, his outburst had come as a bit of a surprise.

Luckily, he noticed my startled expression and quickly explained himself. "Don't worry, I don't think that way at all. I was just reading that sign over there." I looked over and caught a glimpse of the writing on the wall: a spray-painted anti-American slogan.

"I'm Mexican," he continued. "And we like Americans. It's just the Cubans who are against you. It was just a sign. There, you feel better now?"

"Umberto, what country did we just leave?"

"Mexico."

"And what country are we in now?"

"Cuba."

"Do you really think I feel better now?"

At that moment, I suspected that hanging out with Umberto was going to be one irritating incident after another. Sure enough, by that evening, this premonition had been confirmed: It was annoying talking to him, it was annoying being with him, and it was annoying having to hang out with so many hookers.

Umberto had insisted on an authentic Italian meal. And my first night in Havana, there definitely was a pizza on the table, but with all the prostitutes in front of me competing for a place on Umberto's lap, it was hard to concentrate on picking off my anchovies.

Umberto grinned over at me, happy as a boy in a Nintendo factory.

"Which one do you think?" he whispered over at me as a peroxide blonde in a tight orange dress ruffled his hair.

"So many to choose from—difficult, isn't it?"

"Yes. I'm so glad you understand. A Latin woman would never understand. Take my wife, for instance. She would never be sitting where you're sitting now."

"I imagine she wouldn't."

"Are you having a good time? I want you to be having a good time, you know."

"Umberto, if it makes you feel better, I'll tell you that I've never had more fun surrounded by prostitutes and anchovies than I'm having right now."

By the time I had gotten rid of all *my* unwanted toppings, Umberto had whittled the women on his lap down to just one. One was fine. I could deal with one. I just didn't want to have to deal with her alone.

"Be right back. Have to go to the bathroom. You girls sit and chat."

So there I was: eating pizza in an Italian restaurant trying to find something in common with a fifteen-year-old prostitute from Havana. But it turned out she liked anchovies so she filled the remaining time (and her mouth) by plopping one hairy fish after another in between her well-defined lips.

Prostitution is a sad and inevitable fact of living in Cuba. A woman can make more in a single night using her body than a Cuban doctor can make in a whole year, which means that many women simply can't afford *not* to do it. Or as Umberto pointed out with a roll of his eyes, "I've managed to find the only two women in Havana who won't sleep with me for money. And one of them is an American."

The other one was Mayra, a lovely, pale twenty-eight-year-old Cuban physician we had befriended while strolling through the streets of Havana on our second day in the country. She represented yet another of Umberto's failed pickups. This was a peculiar habit of my Mexican acquaintance: Instead of discarding women when they refused his advances, Umberto simply accepted the rejection and had them tag along and join us as platonic companions. But that's not to say he was happy about it.

"How come all I ever meet are intelligent women?" he growled that evening over drinks at a posh hotel bar when Mayra and I attempted to include him in our conversation on U.S.-Cuban relations.

Even the previous night had ended without success by Umberto's standards. Every woman in the pizza place had either been too tall or too young or too lacking in passion. So he'd sent them away one by one, cursing his luck and consoling himself by glaring at me and adding, "Don't look so smug. You're not getting any either."

Perhaps I can forgive my Spanish dictionary for failing to include the words "vagina" and "penis"; however, neglecting to insert a translation for "hangover" seems to me a great omission in a book that boasts over seventy-thousand entries. Nor is there a listing for the phrase "to have sex." To the dictionary's credit, it does include "to make love to," which is translated as *"tener afición a,"* but somehow telling a red-blooded Cuban that I want to have an affection (or was it an infection?) for him didn't seem like it was going to get me very far.

Luckily, getting laid in Cuba is easy, a lot easier than making tacos. (On one of my ventures out of my hotel room in Guadalajara, I had walked past a restaurant with a sign in the window that said: "Taco maker wanted. Experience necessary.") And finding a bed buddy is especially easy if you are either a man with lots of money (I hear it helps if you're not named Umberto) or a woman with two arms, two legs, and a head.

Considering that I possessed all the essential limbs and (in spite of his unfortunate name) Umberto was well endowed in the wallet department, he and I left the hotel bar with Mayra and headed out to explore Cuban nightlife.

In a packed club blaring salsa music, I realized that the moment had finally come—I was actually going to get my hands on some real Cuban rum. However, I had not planned on the political dilemma I would face at the bar. What I wanted was a rum and Coke, called a Cuba Libre in most of Latin America, but as I thought it over, I wondered whether this name ("free Cuba") was in fact the rest of the world's ironic jab at the communist nation where I currently found myself. I remembered that one Latino acquaintance of mine laughed every time he heard someone order that drink. "Well, in Honduras," he claimed, "we call it a Cuba Oppressed."

Not wanting to create any problems for myself, I asked for a "rum and some Coke," which reminded me of the days of alcoholic ignorance years ago when not knowing what the different cocktails were called, I used to order all of my drinks by their ingredients instead of their names. Instead of a Bay Breeze, I'd ask for vodka and cranberry; in place of a Greyhound, I'd ask for vodka and grapefruit juice; instead of a gin and tonic, I'd order—well, that one hadn't changed any.

Halfway through my first drink, a thin Cuban man suddenly appeared at my side and asked me with a timid smile if I would like to dance. I gave Umberto a rather large, victorious smirk.

"I'm sorry, were you two together?" the man asked, watching Umberto glare at me. "Do you mind?"

"You don't have to ask me, *compañero,*" Umberto answered. "You just might have to ask your government." Then he added in a loud whisper, "Death to all Americans! *Yanquis* go home!"

I ignored him and walked onto the dance floor, overwhelmed by the bigger problem in front of me, namely my feet. Salsa is very difficult to master, but when done well it is a mesmerizingly sensual dance. When done poorly it looks—okay, so it looks the way I did it.

As we found an open space among the crowd, I struggled to follow my dance partner's lead. For me it was still a challenge to combine the essential hip movement with the simple forward-back step. As if to highlight the contrast between his abilities and my own, in between spins, to my great humiliation, my partner would do back flips across the dance floor as people stood back and applauded. Fortunately, within less than an hour, I became a little too drunk to care.

Alcohol, the friend of inhibited dancers everywhere, had come to my aid just in time. The man I was with (I had learned that his name was Alberto) had snuck a bottle of rum into the club so every few songs, we'd creep off to a dark corner and take several swigs, which was having a beneficial effect. My ability to gyrate my hips was consistently increasing while his ability to do acrobatics was rapidly decreasing so in just a short while, our dancing talents were beginning to even out.

During our dance breaks, I had managed to learn a few details about him. He was twenty-seven, had just graduated from college as a civil engineer, and while he looked for a job (how one went about this in a communist country was a concept I didn't completely grasp), he worked as a supervisor on the bus lines.

He was a few inches taller than me with nice features, a bit on the skinny side but otherwise attractive. He looked like a regular guy—he had short hair and wore a T-shirt and jeans. Like many Cubans, he was light-skinned with green eyes. But it wasn't his appearance that drew me to him; there was something erotic about him—not in that overboard, sleazy, male swagger kind of way— rather, he wasn't aware of his power, which made it all the more effective.

During a slow dance, standing provocatively close to each other, it occurred to me that there was an advantage to travel that I hadn't considered before—the possibility of a vacation fling with no strings attached. Travel would allow me to savor the heart-pounding adrenaline rush of a new romance without having to stick around for the hard part, the predictable part, the "we have to talk" part. Besides, most of the men I had met in my life had proven themselves so good at refusing to commit. I figured that any woman capable of it was just helping to even the score.

• • •

Consider this a public service announcement broadcast in the interest of American women everywhere, but there is a Latin lover myth that I think needs to be cleared up before I go any further. In an extensive study I would conduct much too late to do myself any good, I now present my findings in the hopes of benefiting others.

Using the criteria of (1) duration and type of foreplay, (2) duration of intercourse, and (3) probability of subject's staying the night, Latin men consistently scored lower than all other groups in the first two areas.

"Slam, bam, thank you ma'am" was the phrase characteristic of most participants, with several subjects occasionally falling into the "slam, bam bam, thank you ma'am" category. Though one "bam" was by far the most frequently encountered.

Several subjects did show some signs of recognition of the concept of foreplay, but even the most highly advanced in this area had never put the idea into practice and had discarded it as a theory with about as much validity as the Lamarckian concept of evolution.

To the subjects' credit, Latin men continually scored higher in the third category than any other group; however, given their consistently low performance in the first two areas, who the hell wanted them to spend the night?

I woke up the next morning in a foul mood. I was still exhausted from the previous evening and the amount of effort it had taken trying to get Alberto into my room—not because I had found an unwilling partner (after all, I had made sure he was pretty liquored up by the time we left the club) but because of the strange law that forbade any Cubans from staying in my hotel.

It had been a ridiculous scene. Earlier that evening, we had persuaded the hotel manager to let Alberto join me for a drink in the restaurant on the fifth floor, on the condition that he didn't accompany me back to my room. But as the empty glasses piled up and the image of the wall in front of us became more and more blurred, so too did our understanding of the Cuban government's logic.

Laws, as I saw them, were good for things like preventing robbers from entering my house, stopping gang members from shooting my neighbors, and keeping shirtless people from being served in restaurants. The law, however, was not supposed to infringe on my innocent attempt to have a good time.

Besides, how hard could it be to sneak Alberto in? All we had to do was quietly pay the bill and saunter out, go down one flight of stairs, and turn the corner. Who would have the nerve to follow us? It was a question I would repeat five minutes later as we headed toward my room.

"Who would have the nerve to follow us?" I asked again, this time not rhetorically. Someone was definitely trailing us.

"I don't know him."

"Should we run?"

"I think we should run."

So we sped up our pace and continued out of breath until I slammed the door of my room shut behind us, slightly aware of how ridiculous it was to be twenty-five years old and still trying to sneak men into my room. What could they possibly do to me? Ground me? Deprive me of Cuban TV for a month (not much of a punishment, I might add)? They couldn't take away my drinking rights, could they?

There was a pounding at the door that left Alberto and me unsure what to do. The knocking came again. We looked at each other and with a deep sigh, I realized that the moment of truth had come. Now my mom was gonna call his mom and they were going to talk about the condom they found in the backseat of the Plymouth Voyager—wait, I wasn't a teenager anymore. I was a grown woman leaving condoms in the back of Plymouth Voyagers. No one could do a damn thing about it—except maybe that guy pounding on the other side of our door.

Feeling like an adult forced to confront the high school principal, reluctantly I removed the bolt and looked out into the hall. The hotel manager was there, looking very communist.

Alberto muttered some excuse about having come up to explain to me the finer points of Castro's agricultural plan and then with his head facing toward the ground, he quietly allowed himself to be led out of the hotel into the early morning rays of a humid Havana morning.

The rules at the hotel where I was staying were pretty much in force throughout Cuba. Hotels, restaurants, and shops that admitted tourists wouldn't allow in Cubans and vice versa, a result of the double economy that functioned on the island. Visitors had to purchase everything in dollars; Cubans patronized stores and restaurants that only accepted pesos and where the tab was about twenty times less than what a tourist would pay, which made me start to rethink this sneaking-around-hotels thing. If one of us was going to be entering every establishment clandestinely, we might as well be sneaking me into Cuban places, where our bill was going to be one-twentieth of the price. I wouldn't have to change my dollars on the black market—I'd get the best exchange rate on the island by handing all my money to Alberto and having him pay for everything.

The plan worked brilliantly. My former thirty-five-dollar dinner bill got reduced to two bucks; instead of buying liquor in the expensive tourist stores, we'd get a liter of homemade rum on the black market for a couple of dollars. This fortuitous turn of events came about none too soon. I was running out of money and there wasn't a Wells Fargo anywhere in sight.

My account was full of money, but suddenly I didn't have access to it. Given the economic embargo, Cuba had no links to any U.S. banks, making my ATM card about as useful as Vicodin past its expiration date. I thought I had arrived in the country with plenty of cash; however, things in Cuba had turned out to be far more expensive than I had expected. I was staying in a rundown hovel with no hot water in a bad part of town that was running me forty-five dollars a night (this same place would have cost two dollars in Honduras).

Luckily, though, in addition to making the switch from dollars to pesos, Alberto moved us both into a private home where they charged just twenty-five dollars for a room. I was slightly curious as to why Alberto didn't just offer to let me stay with him at his place, but a few days later when he invited me over for the first time, the reason became painfully clear. It was on my fourth day in Cuba when we stumbled in around two in the morning after a long night of drinking.

"Take a seat," Alberto said, turning on the lights and the music.

I would have loved to, but there didn't seem to be any space. Everywhere I looked, sleeping people were lying all over the living room.

"Wake up, guys," Alberto said. "We have company. Wendy, I'd like you to meet my relatives."

As if this sort of thing happened all the time, Alberto introduced me to his half-awake cousin, her husband, and their two-year-old son, who were visiting from out of town. Hearing all the ruckus, his aunt Mercedes came out of her bedroom and I wondered how many other people this tiny house held. Alberto hadn't told me he didn't live alone.

I was feeling terribly self-conscious about the scene we had created and was expecting a shouting match to begin at any moment, but I was the only one in the room who seemed to think anything strange was going on. In a matter of minutes everyone was up, shaking my hand, drinking coffee, and acting like it was a privilege to be woken up in the middle of the night to sit around with a foreign guest. And within an hour, we'd pulled out the bottle of rum and were sitting around laughing, joking, and telling stories.

My new Cuban friends explained the matter to me: Why sleep when you could be having fun?

•   •   •

a week into my ten-day trip and my favorite thing to do in Havana was to sit around drinking rum and smoking strong Cuban cigarettes with Alberto's aunt Mercedes—my Cuban mother, as I jokingly called her. This was my kind of authority figure—she spoiled me rotten, was nurturing and kind, and was always ready to slug another shot of rum at any opportunity.

In fact, she was so entertaining that I didn't even miss Alberto while he was off dealing with his relationship drama. His ex-girlfriend had found out about me, and in an attempt to get Alberto's attention she had downed a bottle of pills. Now she was recovering at home in a weakened state, while Alberto was racked with guilt and remorse, nursing her back to health.

Alberto would show up distracted and distant at night and we'd engage in a total of about ten minutes worth of lousy sex before falling asleep. I wanted to attribute this to Alberto's anxiety-ridden state, but the truth was, he had been a selfish lover from the beginning. I would have kicked him out, but I kept hoping that things would get better. Besides, I didn't want to jeopardize the friendship I was forming with his aunt.

I spent hour after hour with her, never getting bored. Sometimes we'd talk politics, a subject she loved to educate me on, but she never mentioned Fidel Castro by name. Fearing that a neighbor would hear and report the slightest criticism, she would simply mouth the words "the bearded one." Other times, we'd discuss mundane things like the color she thought I would look best in or her plans to do my astrological chart.

One morning, Mercedes even got it into her head that she was going to teach me how to dance. Loosened up a little by an early glass of rum, she turned on the sounds of Celia Cruz and my first salsa lesson officially began.

It was all in the hips, she explained, somehow managing to move her large flanks with grace to the complicated drumbeat. I watched in awe as my sixty-year-old friend, heavyset and wearing a polyester muumuu, still managed to move to the rhythm like a young girl. I tried in vain to imitate her steps while Mercedes continued swaying to the music, succeeding in lowering her body to within inches of the floor.

"Is that legal?" I asked her, astounded.

"*Querida,* everything is legal in Cuba. Except, of course, for drugs, prostitution, leaving the country, buying Nike tennis shoes, criticizing the government, staying in *Yanqui* hotels, drinking home-made rum, buying eggs on the black market, and making fake cigars. But dancing is 100 percent legal. Unless, of course, you do it on Sunday."

"What?"

"Just kidding. You can do anything you want on Sunday."

"You can?"

"Yeah, because being religious is illegal!"

Then she slapped me on the back and let out an uproarious laugh, guffawing as she rolled her head around in circles.

English wasn't exactly the most popular language in Cuba so I was forced to rely on my mediocre Spanish. I still struggled with the subjunctive, which was a verb tense we had all but edged out of our own tongue centuries ago at a time when we were busy incorporating lots of other tidbits from Romance languages, and it was a difficult concept to grasp.

In Spanish, there was a whole verb tense devoted to the concept of maybe. For example, when *cuando* vengo *a tu fiesta*—"when I show up at your party"—was converted to the subjunctive, *cuando* venga *a tu fiesta,* it was more like saying, "Maybe I'll come to your party" and you understood that this person was going to try and make it but was excusing himself in the eventuality of being hit by a bus, being mugged on the way there, or finding out that a much cooler party with more expensive booze was going on next door.

This seemed to express a weakness of character to me, and as I once explained to a teacher of mine in high school, I was philo-sophically opposed to a verb tense that expressed doubt. Of course, I just said this to get out of learning the subjunctive and now ten years later I was forced to deal with it on a daily basis.

It went right along with another view I had problems with: the whole Spanish concept of time. *Ahora,* usually translated in English as "now" meant "in five minutes" as well as "in an hour," "in a day," "in a week," or "next month." Tell people to show up at your house *ahora* and they might come next Friday, long after the cleaning you'd just given the place had had time to degenerate into a sinkful of dishes and a fresh layer of dust on the floor.

But having spent time in Central America, Mexico, and a whole week now in Cuba, I was finally starting to master all of these con-cepts. Every time I successfully used the subjunctive, I would raise my arms up in the air in a sign of victory, like a soccer player who has just made the winning goal in the World Cup, and would say to an unimpressed Alberto, "Yes! Subjunctive!"

I think this began to grate on his nerves after a while so I asked him as much, to which he said no, managing to complete the sen-tence in the subjunctive.

Two days before I was supposed to leave, Alberto bailed, never to be seen again, with a sappy note explaining that he wouldn't be able to make it to the airport, that he was secretly married to the suicide-prone girl but that he intended to file papers to get a divorce so that he and I could be together. He really believed we had a chance and hoped I would return so that he could prove it to me, blah, blah, blah.

Had this happened in real life, it would have been painful, enough to zap me out of commission for a couple of weeks, but as I folded up his note and packed it away in my suitcase next to my other souvenirs, I realized that this wasn't real life—this was *travel-*

ing. In Los Angeles, I had to live with the consequences of my actions, but every time I showed up at a travel agency, I was buying myself another ticket to irresponsibility. No matter what happened to me in a foreign country, it was all over when I got on the departing flight.

Had Alberto turned out to be someone who really mattered, the end result was still the same: Two days from now, our romance would have been over anyway. And like it or not, I was even going to have to say good-bye to my good buddy Mercedes.

Realizing that I didn't have much time left, I headed over to her house and timidly offered up the note. She shook her head and cursed Alberto's name.

"Don't worry, *querida,* your Cuban mother will go with you to the airport," she said, giving me a big hug.

And then the morning was just like any other. We chatted over coffee and rum as she gave me her drunken version of everything from communism to getting the best deal on groceries.

"Let's go to the market," she said that afternoon after managing to intimidate me with yet another complicated salsa move.

"Sure. Did you have a specific market in mind?"

"Yes. The black one."

Grocery list in hand, Mercedes and I headed out toward the street. "Just how far do we have to go?" I wanted to know.

"The black market is everywhere and nowhere at the same time," she confided to me with a wink.

Cubans were issued a *libreta,* which was a card that entitled them to a monthly ration of goods. Being a somewhat progressive country, "essential goods" also included cigarettes, coffee, and rum. However, there were always shortages in the government stores and so a thriving black market had sprung up, providing everything from shrimp to toilet paper.

The vendors hung out on street corners quietly whispering what they had to offer: meats, cheese, rice, exotic fruits. We made our way down the street (that is to say, I walked, she danced salsa in a forward motion), and when something interested Mercedes, we'd walk off with the salesperson, slink around the corner, and make the deal in a quiet corner or in the person's house.

We finally arrived at her house, both of us aglow with the thrill of the black market: She was happy because she had managed to come home with her arms full of groceries, and I was amused at the fact that by simply buying bread, cheese, and mangos I had managed to violate the laws of two nations.

It was the last full day I was going to be able to spend with Mercedes so we celebrated with a large lunch, a bottle of rum, and a leisurely afternoon spent looking at photos of her family. After perusing five albums and several stacks of loose pictures, she asked if I would like to see the video of her son and his family in Miami.

"Of course, I don't have a VCR, but I'll show it to you anyway," she explained.

I didn't understand the concept of watching a tape without a tape player until she pulled out the cassette and handed it to me.

"See?"

Yes, now I had seen the video.

There are several ways to leave Cuba, none of which is particularly convenient if you happen to be Cuban. There's the popular "*balsero* route," which is the Caribbean equivalent of rafting down the Mississippi (but which doesn't always end happily with a reunion with Aunt Polly—the most frequent conclusion is an unpleasant confrontation with Uncle Sam). The journey is full of risks and tragically enough most Cubans I met had a tearful story to tell me of some family member who didn't survive the trip. (Mercedes had lost several nephews; Alberto had lost his father.)

My trip home was going to be a bit simpler. All I had to do was get to the airport, hop on a plane, and fly directly to any country that wasn't the United States. (In this case, Mexico was the closest and most convenient.)

I packed up the last of my things, fought with the zipper on my suitcase, and struggled with my thoughts about the island nation I was leaving. I had come here illegally, ironically enough against the law of the United States, a country that didn't want its citizens having anything to do with a place where the people were denied freedom. And Cubans were not free by American standards: They couldn't say what they wanted, they couldn't buy what they wanted, they couldn't even walk down the street without the constant fear of being watched. Yet they were liberated at the same time. They revealed their skin as if it were nothing to be ashamed of and moved their hips to a pounding salsa beat without ever feeling self-conscious.

Havana was full of life and desperation at the same time. Surrounded by tropical heat, the beat of island music, dilapidated architecture, and the constant presence of sex, in Cuba I had had the constant feeling that something was just about to occur—because in a place so full of uncertainty the only thing that was for sure was that something inevitably *would* happen.

It took me a while looking out the window of the plane on the runway of the José Martí International Airport to realize that I had completely failed in acquiring the things I had come to Cuba to get. A last-minute fear of customs officials had made me decide against the box of Cohibas at the airport and I had handed my last bottle of rum to Mercedes as a thank-you gesture.

So that was the situation: I had gone illegally to a communist country and had nothing to show for it. I would be coming home empty-handed: no rum, no cigars, no bringing along my new Cuban friend. But as I thought I distinguished Mercedes waving at me through the glass of the airport, I realized that it was okay. Because now I would have a good reason to come back.

Chapter Four

Sex, Lies, and Tapeworms

Costa Rica was not a fitting place for a traveler intent on adventure. It was nicknamed the Switzerland of Central America. It was full of rosy-cheeked tourists and shops with signs in English that proclaimed, "Come inside. We love Americans." It was *so* legal to go there, I didn't even need a visa. And it was the only country in the Western Hemisphere without a national army. Eliminate the possibility of war and what lure could a nation possibly hold for me?

However, the place had one important thing going for it—namely, it was not Honduras. Freshly back from my Cuba trip, I was visiting Tegucigalpa for the second Christmas in a row, and since my sisters hadn't yet arrived, being trapped at my parents' house with no transportation and nothing to do was beginning to wear on me. What I needed was a little rest from my vacation and there seemed to be a simple solution: a couple of weeks in Costa Rica would cost me next to nothing, it was just two days away by bus, and I'd be back at my folks' in time to open presents.

My mother, who was always supportive of her children's international attempts to ditch their problems, filled my backpack with homemade brownies and sensing my misgivings about the boring country I was about to visit consoled me, "I'm sure you'll make your own fun." As it turned out, she was right. Within three week's time, I was going to have made headlines in the papers, visited a prison, and been interrogated by Costa Rican federal agents.

• • •

Seated on a surprisingly plush air-conditioned bus nearing the Costa Rican capital, I decided to peruse my guidebook, which offered this disconcerting piece of information: "Whenever traveling in Costa Rica, always always plan ahead and always always make reservations in advance." Of course, they always hid these types of warnings in the body of the book, kind of pointless for me now that I'd gotten in the habit of not even opening my guidebook until I had nearly arrived at my destination.

I would just have to make do. Arriving at sundown in the dirty congested chaos of San José, I had no idea where I would be spending the night, but I quickly deduced that the bus terminal was not my first choice. The taxi driver who picked me up spoke of a vacancy at Hotel Venecia, which sounded like an elegant and continental place, but the only thing it turned out to have in common with Venice was that turning on the shower converted the entire bedroom into one giant canal. Water gushed from the showerhead, water flowed from the knobs on the wall, and a noisy drip even came out of the handle on the toilet.

The sign outside had advertised hot showers, which was completely true. What was lacking were warm showers. After having discarded my clothes into a pile on the bed, I stepped under the water for all of two seconds, as long as I could endure the scalding water and then jumped out while I soaped up my body and shampooed my hair. But too tired and hungry to complain, I kept the room. I washed my face (and the entire bathroom floor in the process), changed into fresh clothes, and headed for the hotel restaurant.

Dinner turned out to be a bland meal of chicken, rice, black beans, and plantains. But it was food, and I was sitting down so I was content. Besides, I was in a foreign country yet again and had no plans—anything could happen. I was starting to get the hang of this whole spontaneity thing.

• • •

One of the nicest things about travel in Central America is that it gives you an excuse to strike up conversations with strangers, something that's nearly impossible to do in Los Angeles. Try leaning over your grilled eggplant at any trendy West Hollywood lunch spot to ask the guy at the table next to yours, "Where are you from?" or "Where are you headed?" and he will likely mistake your banter for the existential prying of a Jehovah's Witness, the only people who talk to strangers in Los Angeles.

However, in Costa Rica wherever you went—on the streets, in restaurants, on the bus—everyone went around gabbing with each other. "Be sure to be friendly to strangers," Central American mothers taught their children from birth. The effect of this was that any time you leaned over your beans and rice in a Costa Rican eatery and asked a guy seated nearby for the time, he would gladly tell you "Seven-fifteen," which segued nicely into a rundown of his whole life history, beginning with conception.

When you were in a hurry, dealing with this cultural tendency could be a bit inconvenient, but sitting in the hotel restaurant my first night in San José, I actually had a couple of hours to kill, the time it would take waiting for my floor to dry. So bravely, I gathered up my collection of Spanish verbs and nouns in my head, ordered them into a sentence, and addressed the nearest man with a watch, hoping he was the kind of guy to give me the time of day.

Sure enough, he informed me that it was quarter past seven, though I hadn't expected him to respond to my request in perfect English. He gave me a warm smile and added, "If you don't mind a piece of advice—be careful who you talk to around here. When a man sees a woman traveling alone in this part of the world, sometimes he gets the wrong idea."

"Not you?" I teased.

"Well, if anyone's going to get the wrong idea, I want it to be me."

He was about my age, with dark skin and big brown eyes, and he invited me to join him at his table. It was sure to be another one of those travelers' conversations, full of trivial stories of going and coming that would end with an exchange of addresses and a false promise to write, but this was more interesting than watching the only event going on in my room: evaporation.

"Let me guess where you're from," he said, taking a sip of his orange soda. "Well, I know it's not the United States . . ."

"Why do you say that?"

"We've been talking for nearly a minute now and not once have you used the word 'fuck.' "

Cute *and* funny, I thought. This conversation was beginning to look up.

"You know, the first time an American told me to take a flying fuck, I had no idea what he was talking about. I mean I can do it a lot of ways, but how do you do it flying? Later, I asked my friend Jeremy what that guy meant. Jeremy said, 'Don't worry about it. He was just giving you shit.' So I said to Jeremy, 'Well, what did he expect me to do with his bowel movement?' "

I had been prepared for a discussion of woven handicrafts, the wonders of coastal algae, or the burgeoning mold population, but here he was pleasantly surprising me with scatology. My first impression had been completely wrong. And not only that—I had mistakenly pegged him as a Costa Rican.

You don't expect to be running into Arabs in this part of the world. After all, they're supposed to be hanging around the Middle East, drinking thick coffee, smoking strawberry-flavored tobacco, and picking fights with non-Arab nations. But to my surprise, the man sitting across from me shook my hand, introduced himself as Michel, and informed me that he was from Kuwait.

"The Middle East is one of the oldest parts of the world. I know who my father's father was twelve times back. The biggest religions in the world, Christianity and Islam, where did they start?

Americans like to think they invented everything, but you don't hear many stories about Jesus crossing the Delaware or the Hudson."

I giggled and took a sip of lukewarm coffee, thinking that Costa Rica might turn out to be a lot more interesting than I had anticipated.

Lying in bed that night, glowing from the evening's conversation and Michel's ability to make light of serious topics, my head was still spinning with his stories, making it impossible for me to sleep. Luckily, this was the only type of insomnia that bothered me these days: I was never awakened by stress or anxiety; it was only excitement or giddy anticipation that kept me up at night. I was simply too happy to sleep.

Tossing, turning, and grinning, I realized that my irresponsibility plan was working out brilliantly. I was twenty-six years old and for the first time since leaving Peru so long ago I actually felt like a kid. Before I was even an adolescent, my mother had already been relying on me to clean the house, pick out her clothes, and discipline my younger sisters. My childhood had alternated between running the house and the terror-filled days at school, and by age sixteen, I had possessed the mature gaze of a woman of thirty. Now that I was actually just a few years away from that age, most people took me to be about nineteen.

Even my life in Los Angeles, the few months in between traveling when I did the overpaid writing jobs required to finance my next trip, had taken on a surreal quality. During the day, I would work in my robe and slippers in front of my computer, sipping steaming cups of coffee. At night, I'd finally get dressed and head out to my favorite dark bar where I'd stay up late, a glass of bourbon never far from reach. And in an ultimate act of rebellion, I had even taken up smoking.

I happily stretched out in my double bed, realizing that there was finally no one to take care of but myself. There were no commitments, not even to the clock. Bedtime was whenever I was tired. Waking up happened when I was no longer tired. And if laughter or good conversation kept me awake at night, no problem: I could sleep the next day.

Here I was in a foreign country with no plans (unless you counted the date I'd made with Michel who'd offered to show me around San José the next day). I rolled over in my bed, giggling like a six-year-old, realizing I had become the person I had always wanted to be.

The next morning, walking through one of the city's dusty, unappealing parks, Michel had the chance to tell me a little bit about his life. He explained about the scar under his chin, the one under his eye, and showed me where a grenade had torn through his leg. This was a man who had seen things I had yet to understand.

" 'Desert Storm,' you Americans called it. It was terrible. Everyone was getting killed, but my brother and I didn't have to fight. My family is wealthy and influential—my father was a cabinet minister, and he said, 'Sons, you don't have to go. The Americans will die for us.' My brother went anyway. When he died, I wanted to die too. So I joined the guerrilla movement."

"How did you do that?"

"I filled out an application form and they accepted it." He gave me a mischievous grin and we both laughed. "When I was leaving, my grandmother said, 'Don't worry. God takes care of fools and children so you should be okay by both counts.' But I was a terrible guerrilla. I am probably the only Arab you will ever meet who is a coward. And I can't shoot anything. I would fire here and here and here and miss. At the training camp, you know those silhouettes that go by? They had forty-eight go past and I had an AK-47. I didn't hit one. Not one. But my instructor was very nice. He said, 'Don't worry, you're still a very important part of this group. And when you go out on the field, it doesn't matter if you don't hit a thing. You can act as a diversion.' "

I couldn't help but snicker. He started cracking up too and we found ourselves in a contagious bout of laughter, both of us gasping for breath and hanging on to each other to keep from falling over. I gripped his shoulder for support, and as I raised my head, we found ourselves in one of those well-choreographed movie positions, my lips just inches away from his.

But the moment was quickly destroyed. "There's something I have to tell you," he said.

I was hoping he'd complete the sentence with something light-hearted, something like, "You have great hair," but of course, the only time you heard that phrase was when you paid a stylist forty bucks to say it. Besides, "You have great hair" didn't need to be prefaced with the severe "There's something I have to tell you" line. "Hey, girlfriend," "Miss Thang!" or "Well, sop me up with gravy and call me a biscuit" usually sufficed.

"What's the matter?" I wanted to know.

"Have a seat." We sat down at a nearby bench. "You know, this really isn't the best time for you to be meeting me."

Sure it was, I thought. No matter what drama he got me mixed up in, I still had a prepaid ticket out of this potential relationship in a matter of weeks.

"I really wish I could take you out to dinner and the movies, but I'm stuck in a bad situation." He took a deep sigh. "I originally came to Costa Rica to try and buy a house for my parents. When my brother died, they were devastated and I thought the best thing would be to get them away from the memories. It was also to make things up to them—right after my brother got killed, I disappeared on them. I ran off to Venezuela, to stay with a friend I had known in boarding school. Anyway, I was living in Venezuela and I called my family and mentioned the idea of them coming down. We thought Costa Rica would be the perfect place. It was a great idea. I was going to make amends with my family and we'd all be away from Kuwait for a while."

"What happened?"

"I found the perfect house. This yellow Spanish-style place with a pool, six bedrooms. It was beautiful. So my mother sent me a check for the down payment. I had to go to the town of Limón to complete the transaction and I got robbed. They took everything. The check, my wallet, my passport. They even took the suit I was wearing."

"How terrible."

"It really wasn't that bad. I figured my mother could cancel the check and all she'd have to do would be to transfer more money to me. She wired twenty-five thousand dollars to a bank here, but there was a problem: I had no way to pick it up. The robbers had taken my ID."

The same thing was always happening to me: I had money, but so many times it seemed as if there was no way to get it. Latin America was filled with fickle ATM machines that spewed out money on a whim. With thousands of dollars in my account, in Mexico I had been denied a twenty-dollar withdrawal. Another time, my balance was down to a matter of pennies when the machine in Honduras cheerily spit out fifteen twenties. "Open the pod bay door, Hal," I intoned as my mantra every time I walked up to one of these temperamental machines.

"I needed a passport," Michel continued, "but there's no Kuwaiti embassy in Costa Rica. So I had to go through the OIJ, the Costa Rican equivalent of the FBI, who would verify my identity and give me a temporary ID. But this wasn't free. They wanted to charge me 320 dollars.

"Well, I didn't know anyone in this country. I hadn't eaten for days. And I met this girl, this chubby girl who began taking care of me. She brought me sandwiches and said she'd help me. She came up with this idea of transferring the money in her name. She offered to pick it up for me and said she'd give it to me. Guess what?"

"She ran off with the money."

"Yep. I was going to offer her half, but she took it all and disappeared."

Financial problems were always wreaking havoc with my life too. Chubby girls, fickle ATM machines—it was all the same thing. I couldn't help but sympathize with his plight. "I don't have tons of cash on me, but the least I can do is buy you lunch," I offered.

"You really don't have to. You have to understand that this is really humiliating to me. But I really thought you should know."

"Don't mention it. Rice and beans is not going to bankrupt me."

Ironically enough, the thing I always missed most about the United States was Mexican food. You couldn't go more than two blocks in Los Angeles without running into a taco place—how come it was so difficult to find Mexican food in Costa Rica? I imagined warm enchiladas, cheese-laden burritos, spicy tacos, and crunchy nachos as I stared at the unappetizing meal in front of me: white rice, flavorless black beans, and a slab of meat, the same ingredients as Mexican food but without the spices. Edible, but boring.

Luckily, if you were able to say the word "*guanábana*" (pronounced wah-NAH-bah-nah) the whole meal was redeemed by the drinks. *Guanábana con leche* was a blended mixture of milk, sugar, and a rich white fruit with a thick sweet pulp. Unpeeled, *guanábana* was terrifying looking, the kind of fruit even Adam would have had no problem refusing. Sometimes reaching the size of a football, the whole thing was covered in a thick, green lizard-textured skin. But after giving me a description of the creamy drink, Michel had tempted me into trying it and now we were slurping down *guanábana* juice like old friends.

I had to admit that I was having a great time. Here I was in what was undoubtedly the most peaceful, dull, and overtouristed of all Central American nations, and I'd already found myself in the midst of an adventure—accompanied by a wealthy, well-traveled Kuwaiti who was trapped by unpleasant circumstances. I couldn't help but up the ante.

"Send the money in my name," I impulsively said.

"You don't have to do this," Michel responded.

"Look, I have to be back at my parents' in time for Christmas, but if you think your transfer will arrive by then, you can have your mother send it in my name and I'll be happy to pick it up for you."

"That's so nice of you. Wow, I don't know what to say. Yes, I do— I'll give you half of it."

"Don't be ridiculous. Just buy me lunch when your money arrives."

"I hope you like Venezuelan food. When this is all over, I'll treat you to lunch in Caracas."

It did occur to me that receiving a twenty-five-thousand-dollar transfer from a stranger in Kuwait could have serious implications. Drug money, stolen bills—who knew where the money had actually come from? But as I gave it more thought, I realized that I was blowing the situation out of proportion—unscrupulous bank transfers were just the kind of things they wrote books about. And since I was considering putting together a book about my travels, receiving a little tainted money wouldn't be such a terrible thing.

Besides, this was Costa Rica and nothing exciting ever happened in this country. At least this was what my copy of *Costa Rica: A Natural Destination* warned:

There's something different about Costa Rica. It is a country without an army in a world that counts tanks and missiles and nuclear warheads as the measure of a nation's strength. The national hero is not a general but a young, barefoot *campesino* (farmer). Schoolchildren, not soldiers, parade on Independence Day. . . . Located in a region where violence is too often the order of the day, Costa Rica lives in peace. It has one of the highest literacy rates in the Western Hemisphere and a Social Security system that offers health care to all its people. Costa Ricans like to say they gained through evolution what other countries try to attain through revolution.

Lines of literate Costa Ricans waiting for their social security benefits—it wasn't the kind of event that made for compelling material. My only hope was that Michel would actually turn out to be an internationally wanted criminal.

Besides, at the moment, I was going through another more immediate ethical dilemma which was the fact that although Michel and I were getting awfully cozy on my bed, I was having second thoughts. I was seeing someone else in Los Angeles, who had nothing to do with Michel, who I was seeing in a completely different way, being that his naked body was the one directly within my line of sight at the moment.

I had been casually seeing Chris for just over a month now, and although I had warned him that I was wary of commitment and even of monogamy, we had settled on an open relationship qualified by a fair warning clause. This meant I could see whomever I chose; I just had to tell him before I actually slept with anyone. It had sounded like a good compromise that night over Absolut Kurant, but now that I was nearly nude in a hotel room with an exotic and attractive Kuwaiti, I was beginning to realize the inconvenient aspects of this agreement.

I had my own moral code and although it did not preclude me from going to countries illegally or having more than one beau at a time, I did have a problem with lying to anyone who wasn't an American border official. I was a woman of my word and dammit, I was going to make that telephone call.

"Hi, Chris, just want to let you know, in accordance with the terms of our relationship, that I am about to have sex with another person." That was how I rehearsed it in my head—quick, efficient, and to the point. I reached over to grab the phone, when it suddenly occurred to me that I hadn't seen the phone in my room for some time, which made sense considering that there had never been one. The lobby phone was a possible option until I remembered the large sign in front of it that politely requested no overseas calls. That left the international phone center, which would require a walk of six blocks to get to, not to mention that the staff preferred to deal with customers who were fully clothed.

At this point, torn between two difficult options, I decided to leave it up to the reader, like those "choose your own adventure books" so popular when I was a child:

If you think Wendy should sleep with Michel, continue on to the next nonitalicized paragraph.

If you think Wendy should keep her promise and wait until she is able to find an international phone line before sleeping with Michel, proceed on to your nearest Mormon church and ask for the conversion application form.

It was definitely the right decision. Hours later, as the sun came up and both of us collapsed exhausted finally ready for sleep, I closed my eyes, thinking happily that this was the way traveling was supposed to be.

The next day, while Michel went to the bank to make the arrangements for the transfer, I decided to check out San José on my own and turned to my guidebooks for advice, opening the less utopian of the two, the *Berkeley Guide*. The most interesting sight sounded like the criminology museum, a monument to the most notorious crimes committed in the country, which promised formaldehyde-preserved body parts and aborted fetuses.

Just as I was preparing to leave, I felt a wave of nausea wash over me that seemed to have nothing to do with the thought of seeing amputated hands and feet. What was worse, for the past week, a red rash had been steadily getting worse on my left hand.

My guidebook had been so eloquent on the subject of grim attractions; I hoped it would be just as informative when it came to Central American diseases. Sure enough, in addition to the usual warnings against cholera, typhoid fever, hepatitis A, yellow fever, and dengue, the authors had been kind enough to go on about other less glamorous illnesses.

> *Filariasis* is contracted from mosquitoes that transfer a parasitic worm, which then inhabits the lymph nodes and tissues. It can occasionally lead to enlargement of the extremities (elephantiasis).
>
> *Leishmaniasis* is contracted through the bite of a sand fly. It causes fever, weakness, and in some cases a swollen spleen or skin sores.
>
> *Chagas' disease* is contracted from the excrement of the reduviid bug, also known as the cone nose assassin or kissing bug. You may have no symptoms or fever in the early stages of this disease, but it could lead to heart disease, an enlarged intestine, or possible paralysis. There is no vaccine available and treatment is limited.

This wasn't the kind of cheery reassurance I was looking for at the moment. Figuring a slightly more optimistic outlook couldn't hurt, I turned to the section on staying healthy in my other guide: "I used to say it was okay to drink the tap water in San José and most other cities in the Central Valley." Of course you did, I thought sarcastically. "Then in 1991, a study revealed that only 50 percent of municipal systems have water not contaminated by fecal material." I threw *Costa Rica: A Natural Destination* against the wall and vowed to never use that guidebook again as long as I lived—which, come to think of it, didn't seem like it was going to be that long.

Feeling sicker by the minute, I raced to the bathroom just in time for an unpleasant intestinal experience. Deciding to put off the criminology museum until the day when my stomach would be a bit more up to the sight of amputated body parts, I put myself into bed and fell into a deep sleep.

"Hello, I am your doctor and I will be forcibly tearing your fingernail out this morning." Any normal mother would have taken this introduction as a bad sign. I was six years old, living in Peru, and my mom had taken me to the hospital for a tetanus shot after I had stepped on a rusty nail. And since we were there, she had thought it would be a good idea to have the nice doctor take a look at her daughter's fingernail, which had slight indentations and was pale yellow. There was only one cure, he informed us. I did not understand what he was proposing—my six-year-old vocabulary did not include the word "extraction." But he wrapped me tightly from head to toe in a sheet to prevent me from struggling, shot me up with a mild local anesthetic, and began ripping my fingernail out from its roots with a scalpel and a pair of tweezers as my screams echoed throughout the halls of the hospital.

After some time, my fingernail grew back in (pale yellow and indented, I might add), but my fear of Latin American doctors remained. (The upside was that this event had created copious amounts of guilt material to be used as needed on my mother:

"Remember that time you took me to a doctor and he performed the same technique on me used to torture prisoners of war?") Now that I was in Costa Rica, concerned that I had contracted some terrible tropical disease, the last thing I wanted to do was visit a medical practitioner, who would surely advise that the best way to get rid of a rash was to amputate my hand.

But Michel had insisted. His Costa Rican friend Jessica knew of a great doctor, he informed me, and too weak to put up much of a fight, that afternoon I found myself on a bus headed toward the office of another Latin American M.D. Twenty minutes into our ride, I couldn't help but cheer up slightly as we left the dirty, loud, and congested center of San José and entered an area of rolling green hills and peaceful farmland. Besides, my visit to the doctor had turned into quite an impromptu party.

When Michel had first mentioned Jessica, I had expected her help to extend as far as a telephone number and an address, but earlier that morning, as my hotel room had gotten more and more packed with Jessica's friends, relatives, and loved ones, I began to suspect that my diarrhea had become the social event of the season. After the onlookers shook my hand and wished for my speedy recovery, the room finally dwindled down to three others and myself, the number of people who would be accompanying me to the doctor. In this part of the world, even getting over a bad case of the runs was seen as a group endeavor.

Now there were four of us on the bus. Michel was at my side, and Jessica, who had turned out to be much more beautiful than I had expected, was behind us, bubbly, radiant and with a head full of dark corkscrew curls that bounced along with the bumps in the road. Seated by her was her buddy Maritza, a slightly plump, good-natured twenty-year-old who went along with anything Jessica suggested. At the moment, that seemed to be shouting out the window of the bus, informing male bypassers on the street that they had very attractive hindquarters.

This was performed all the time in Costa Rica—shouting out a compliment at an attractive stranger was called a *piropo*—but it was never done by women. Men were stunned to hear a woman dispensing information about the shape of their buttocks, and the fact that Jessica was so charming and beautiful only unnerved them further: They didn't know whether they were being victimized or complimented. They generally turned a bright shade of crimson, their staunch machismo dissipating with every step as the four of us rolled in the aisles. By the time we arrived at the doctor's office, even I was in good spirits, considering the fate that surely awaited me.

In my own country, a physician's questions generally had something to do with the symptoms at hand, topics such as fever, achy muscles, and congestion. However, I was in a distant tropical nation where the professional queries were a little less to the point.

"Citrus fruit?" Dr. Guzmán asked after I had explained the nature of my visit.

"No, thank you. I'm not up to eating anything right now."

"No, no—I mean what has been your contact with citrus fruit?"

My contact with citrus fruit? I had always thought oranges and lemons were the right kind of fruits to be hanging out with, but he was making them sound so dubious.

"I . . . eat them?" I said, hoping it was an acceptable response.

"Yes, yes, but do you peel them first?"

Apples, pears, peaches—those were the kinds of fruit you sometimes didn't peel. But citrus fruit? Who ate oranges without peeling them first?

"I haven't eaten any citrus peel, not that I'm aware of."

"That's not my question. Have you been peeling citrus fruit?"

Of course I had—how did you eat an orange without peeling it? On second thought, come to think of it, in Costa Rica, the bags of oranges came with the fruit already peeled. Actually, I hadn't been peeling any oranges in Costa Rica.

"No lemons or grapefruit either?"

I thought back. There hadn't been any citrus fruit—unless you counted the innocuous-looking limes in Tegucigalpa whose peel I had used as a garnish for one of my mother's Christmas cakes.

Dr. Guzmán nodded accusingly and pointed to my left hand. "This is what happens when you peel citrus fruit in Central America."

Oranges, grapefruits, and lemons had always seemed so benign to me before. I could only imagine the consequences of peeling something exotic like pomegranate.

"What is going to happen to me?" I needed to know.

"The rash will clear up on its own, though it may take a month or so. As for the diarrhea, it's merely a case of tourist's disease."

A disease just for tourists? This sounded a bit xenophobic to me.

"It means you're not used to the bacteria in the food. Drink lots of water and control your food intake a little bit. You'll feel better in a few days."

That was it. I was going to be just fine. My extremities weren't going to grow to mammoth proportions, no tapeworm inhabited my intestines, no parasite was going to start sucking the life out of my heart.

I paid the doctor his fee, the full price of six dollars since I didn't have Costa Rican medical insurance, and walked out to greet my waiting entourage, all fingernails and major appendages still in place.

The next few days, as my body slowly recovered, Michel's situation steadily worsened. He had gone to the bank every day in hopes of good news, but there was simply no information. In typical Latin American fashion, no one had any idea when the transfer would arrive or what the holdup was. Worse yet, I was going to have to be leaving in a few days if I wanted to make it back to my folks' in time for Christmas, which meant that when the transfer arrived, since it was in my name, it would be impossible for Michel to claim it. Torn between letting down my new lover or my family, I settled on a compromise.

"I want you to take this money," I said to Michel, handing him a stack of twenties, the day before I was scheduled to leave.

"Oh my God, no, I can't."

"Look, I have to get to my parents'. But with this, you can pick up your ID and have your mother send the money in your own name. You'll be fine."

"Sure. Fine but without you."

I didn't know what to say. I was going to miss him too, but he didn't understand that travel was just a game to me. It was the only place where I would never be faced with tough decisions. It was another reality that I mucked about in for a while, where I got to take rash (no pun intended) and juvenile actions—and then left without ever having to face the consequences.

As if sensing my thoughts, Michel gave me a halfhearted hug good-bye and that morning went off to Limón to claim his ID. It wasn't the last time I would see him—he'd be back that afternoon and I wouldn't leave until the next day, but it still felt so final.

I spent a grim morning with Jessica and company. She and Martiza showed up unexpectedly at the hotel, and discovering that I was alone (a state they regarded with the same suspicion as heroin), they swooped me up and dragged me off to their work. Their job consisted of getting corporate sponsorship for the Costa Rican Foundation for the Blind, something they did on a contract basis out of their own office, not too shabby for two girls who hadn't yet reached the American drinking age.

The last words I'd had with Michel had left me glum and not much in the mood for talk, but my companions were occupied in other things anyway. Jessica's boyfriend Olman had shown up and the two of them were absorbed in the task of making out in the room upstairs while Martiza read through a stack of papers on her desk, lighting one cigarette after another and occasionally passing one along to me.

I stared out the window of a rainy Costa Rican day, feeling guilty and missing Michel. Why did he have to complicate the lightheartedness I had worked so long to cultivate?

Unlike in my own country, where we defined the relationships between people on something logical—on a tangible real-life person named Kevin Bacon, in Latin America, lines were drawn on the basis of relatives who had been visited by the Virgin Mary. Just as I had never met Kevin Bacon personally, no one I came across in Costa Rica had actually seen the Mother of God, but everyone's cousin or cousin's cousin or Aunt Beatriz had definitely been privy to the experience.

This wasn't too peculiar, considering that this was a land of mystery and magic, where churches offering the word of God were much more ubiquitous than cable lines offering HBO to the people. This was a place where wishes were granted as a result of faith, and when Michel arrived at the hotel later and informed me of what had happened to him that day, I suddenly began to understand why Latin Americans were so obsessed with religion. Praying to a statue of a virgin to recover a lost passport was a lot more likely to bring results than relying on government organizations.

As usual, nothing had gone right for Michel. The Costa Rican officials had taken the money, but they'd given him a hard time for being an Arab and insisted on running an additional check before they'd give him his ID. Michel had no idea how long it would take. And this was the last night I was going to be able to spend with him.

"There's always the possibility that the transfer has arrived at the bank," I wagered optimistically.

"You must be a religious woman," Michel said sarcastically. "Because what you're speaking of would be a miracle."

Nevertheless, I convinced him to at least give it a shot and both of us squeezed through the doors at the last minute just as the guard was closing up for the evening. From the lobby of the enormous Bank of Costa Rica, we ran up the escalators to the third floor, and raced through the halls in the direction of the international transfer department.

A grumpy woman anxious to go home entered the number of the transfer into the computer.

"What is the country of origin?" she requested.

"Kuwait."

"Hmmm. No, I don't see anything from Kuwait."

"Don't you have *any* information?" I pleaded.

"The computer only shows me what transfers have arrived. I can only tell you whether or not your money is here. It isn't."

"How much longer should it take? It's already been a week."

"Ten days is the usual time. Though we're closing tomorrow for the holidays. We'll reopen the day after New Year."

January 2 was more than a week away. I couldn't believe it. The bank was closing for nearly ten days.

Both of us silent on the walk back to the hotel, I was reminded of what had happened to me in Cuba, how I had nearly run out of cash with no access to any of the funds I had in the United States. If it hadn't been for Alberto and Mercedes, who knew what would have happened to me there? Alberto had found me a cheap place to stay and Mercedes had offered me cash. Of course, I didn't accept the money, but the mere idea that she suggested it had deeply touched me—it had taken her twenty years to save seventy lousy dollars, yet she had been willing to relinquish a quarter of it to an American tourist she'd known for just a week.

Here I was, on the other side of the fence, completely able to help someone out of a bad situation. If nothing else, I owed it to Mercedes.

"I'll call my parents and tell them I can't make it."

"You're kidding!"

"Merry Christmas, Michel."

•   •   •

𝓘t was a grim December 25. This was the first time in six years that I had missed Christmas at my parents', and the brief phone call I'd made to my dad in Honduras hadn't gone very well. Our short chat hadn't been long enough to explain everything; there had just been enough time for me to note the disappointment in his voice.

Frankly, I wasn't any happier about the situation. I was as devastated as a girl being deprived of something like—well, like Christmas. Granted, in Honduras, it wouldn't have been a traditional holiday with cranberries and turkeys and a tree (this year, instead of fighting with pine branches, my parents had given up and just decorated the ficus plant), but it was still the only time of year everyone in my nomadic family got together. I was going to completely miss seeing my sisters this year.

Now I was in a nearly deserted city, eating lunch in the only place open, an overpriced tourist restaurant famous for its extra-large quantities, which meant an even bigger serving of tasteless black beans and rice.

Sensing my misery, Michel came up with a suggestion. "Look, we'll head out of here tomorrow. If you're committed to sticking around for another week, we might as well have some fun. Let's get out of this city and go to the beach."

It was a wonderful idea. I hadn't yet seen anything of Costa Rica and the thought of whiling away a week on the sands of the Caribbean was a lot more appealing than hanging around the smoggy, thief-infested pandemonium of San José. Finally, I'd make it to the ocean.

𝓜anzanillo was a quaint seaside location filled with seagulls, tropical breezes, and tranquil villagers, where the most stressful moment of the day was watching the sun rise through the languid fronds of beachside palms. The afternoons were lazy, the nights loud with Afro-Caribbean music, and the food a savory blend of seafood, coconut milk, and exotic spices. It was the kind of place that we were nowhere near at the moment.

To get to Manzanillo, you first had to pass through Limón, a grimy and rambunctious Caribbean port town, where the occasional roaming sailor was the most reputable person you were likely to run into. Those native to this rundown hellhole were usually drunk and disheveled, on drugs, or simply up to no good. It was the place Michel had initially been robbed of his twenty-five-thousand-dollar check and hoping that thieves were like lightning (not in terms of speed, but rather that they wouldn't strike the same place twice), I had surreptitiously slipped Michel the bulk of my money for safe-keeping.

On the nerve-racking walk to the bus station where we planned to purchase our tickets to Manzanillo, I repressed the urge to look behind me, but I couldn't help but play out the worst in my mind: some unsavory character holding us up at gunpoint, demanding our money, and tossing us into his vehicle. Of course, this was just a fantasy. Reality was, it would take *five* men to grab Michel at gunpoint and toss him into their vehicle.

It all happened so fast that I didn't have time to comprehend what was occurring. One minute we were just steps away from the bus station and the next we were surrounded by five bulky guys who encircled Michel, told him not to make a scene, and forced him into the back of their pickup. I simply stood there dumbfounded, not understanding, until one of the men grabbed my arm and reassured me, "Don't worry. We're from the police."

This did not make me feel especially better. But before I had time to ask any questions, they were gone—and they had taken Michel along with them.

I found myself suddenly alone in Limón, a place whose name in Spanish means "lemon," and I'd already learned how much damage that particular fruit could cause. I was completely lost, far away from home, and in a treacherous town where men disappeared faster than one-night stands. What the hell was I supposed to do?

Suspecting that this sort of problem was a little beyond the scope of either of my travel guides, I entered the nearest café, ordered a papaya smoothie, and sat down for a smoke and a long think.

What were my options? First of all, I could always return to Honduras. I'd hop on a bus to San José and head back to Tegucigalpa. A good plan—but Michel had most of my money. Not only that, because he was such a damn gentleman, he'd been holding my suitcase, and the cops had taken it along with them. This was definitely the last time I was going to let a man carry my bag for me! I needed my cash and my clothes—and frankly, I needed to figure out what was going on. Unable to come up with a better alternative, I realized there was only one thing I could do: I was going to have to find him.

I walked up to the counter to pay for my drink and asked the woman at the cash register how to get to the police station. I could tell by her expression that this was not the question she was expecting.

"Is everything okay?" she asked.

I did my best to force a smile and nod. Realizing she wasn't going to get an explanation out of me, the cashier reluctantly wrote down the directions.

I wandered out of the restaurant nervous and disoriented. I wanted to take a cab, but I knew the tiny quantity of money that still remained in my pocket wouldn't stretch that far. I was going to have to walk, something that had been bad enough at Michel's side and was worse now that I was a woman facing the streets alone.

The town was like the bad parts of San José only much smaller and rowdier. I tried to avoid a passing child determined to sell me a pack of gum when a man stumbled out of a bar and bumped into me, shouting something unintelligible to me in pigeon English. I ignored the proposition or the insult—I wasn't sure which—and kept moving, guided by my crude directions. I turned the corner and the next street was nearly identical: one-room concrete buildings converted into bars, restaurants, or tiny markets.

Soon, I had picked up an unwelcome guest, a red-eyed man reeking of alcohol who kept grabbing my shoulder. I jerked myself away but the man persisted.

"You're so pretty. Pretty eyes," he slurred in Spanish.

I tried to ignore him, but he grabbed my hand. This had happened to me before and I had found that the best tactic was to stop, face the man head on, and shout at him. But I didn't have the strength. I just wanted him to go away. I wanted the whole damn town to go away. I wanted my money back and my clothes back and I wanted my faith in short-term vacation romances back.

I sped up to a run. My pursuer was out of sight within minutes but I kept up my pace anyway. I realized I was making a scene—I was the only foreigner in this part of town, not to mention that I was racing through the streets, but I needed this journey to end as soon as humanly possible.

Red-faced and panting for breath, I finally arrived at the police station, a peeling white structure surrounded by a large fence, where in place of grass, there was just a huge rectangle of mud separated by a concrete pathway. I walked up to a bored-looking guard at the entrance and tried to explain what had happened.

"I was walking down the street an hour ago . . ." I got out between gulps of air.

"Did you get robbed?"

"Kind of."

"What did they take?"

"My boyfriend."

By the look he gave me, I suspected this was not the kind of thing that went on all the time, not even in Limón.

"The people who took him," I added, "they said they were from the police."

"Who's your boyfriend?"

"Michel Omar. He's from Kuwait."

"Hang on." The guard picked up a handheld radio and asked about everyone who'd been brought in during the past hour. "No one named Michel? No one from Kuwait?"

He turned to me and shrugged his shoulders. "Well, whoever it was who took him, they didn't bring him here."

Great. Now where was I supposed to look?

"Though they might have been from the OIJ. You might want to try going there."

It was another six blocks to the federal building, which meant I would have to brave the streets of Limón again. I turned away from the guard and headed in the direction he had pointed me in, too exhausted to keep running.

Retracing my steps for three blocks, I thought how ironic it would be for something to happen to me on my walk. I was halfway between the police station and the feds' office—how fitting.

Fifteen minutes later, after having been shouted at, groped at, and stumbled into, I brushed the hair away from my face and dragged myself up the steps of my destination. I was mentally drained and out of breath, but I figured that as far as bad days went, this one could not possibly get any worse.

Figuring that your day could not possibly get any worse is the kind of thought it's safe to have in a place like, say, SeaWorld. What's the worst-case scenario? The cotton-candy machine is broken, the dolphins are out with a bad case of the sniffles, the puffer fish get deflated. Fall into the sea-lion tank, and you can safely assume that your day is about as bad as it can get.

However, find yourself stranded in a foreign country, your companion suddenly snatched out from under you by a group of plainclothed men in a pickup who claim they are on official business, and you can be assured that your day is unlikely to start looking up any time soon.

Walking up to the information window at the offices of the OIJ,

I wasn't certain what would constitute good news in this case. If Michel was actually here, it would mean that he'd been arrested. If he wasn't here, it meant he had been kidnapped. A criminal or a hostage? Which did I prefer?

At the moment, what I really preferred was a carefree day at the beach followed by a candlelit dinner and a massage, but the slender, bearded man behind the window wasn't selling tickets to Manzanillo, romantic meals, or hot oil. All he had for me was information, news I wasn't sure I wanted to hear.

"Kuwait?" he asked, slightly amused. "There's no one here from Kuwait."

"Thanks anyway." I turned to go, wondering how I was going to get home now.

"But your boyfriend is here," the official slyly informed me.

"What?"

He handed me a passport bearing a photo that was obviously Michel.

"Is this your boyfriend?"

It wasn't the time to explain the exact nature of our relationship (besides, I didn't know how to say "fling" in Spanish) so I just nodded.

"As you can see, it's not a passport from Kuwait."

I rifled through the pages filled with stamps from countries all over Latin America and turned to the cover: Trinidad and Tobago.

"Have you given him any money?"

I didn't know how to respond.

"Look, why don't you come back here, take a seat, and we'll have a little chat. I'm a detective. My name's Luís. Don't worry. You're safe now."

Luís was a kind man with sad eyes who gently offered me a seat and a steaming cup of coffee.

"Your boyfriend, Charles—"

"His name is Charles?"

"Yes. Did you give Charles any money?"

He hadn't really taken anything from me. I'd offered every time— and it was just food I'd bought him, plus the 320 dollars I'd given him to reclaim his passport. "What exactly do you mean?" I asked.

"Charles is a con man. The last woman he tried to swindle, he gave her a story about a bank transfer coming from Kuwait."

I hung my head.

"Do you want to tell me about it?"

Later that night, having recovered my suitcase and my cash in return for a strenuous day of testifying, I lay depressed and confused in the hotel room that Luís and his partner, Walter, had found me for the night. Too much had happened too fast and I hadn't had time to make sense of it all.

Staring up at the ceiling in a glum mood, I was startled to hear a knock at my door. I hesitated to answer it: I'd had enough excite-ment for one day and wasn't up for company. Of course, there was always the remote chance that this was opportunity visiting me, but then the knock came twice, eliminating this as a possibility.

"Wendy?" a voice called. "Wendy, open up."

Who possibly knew I was here?

"Wendy, don't be afraid. It's Luís."

Great. Now the Costa Rican FBI was knocking on my door. I climbed out of bed and opened the door to find myself face to face with the five men who not three hours earlier had grabbed Michel and tossed him into their truck. What did they need? More testi-mony? My passport number?

"We're going out for drinks and dancing and thought you might want to come along."

This was too confusing. First, the man I cared about turned out to be my enemy. Now the people who took the man I cared about wanted to be my friends. I was going to have to start making these people wear color-coded name tags to tell them apart.

An hour later, seated at the bar of a cheesy seventies-style dance club, I found myself surrounded by rum and Cokes, federal officials, and the reflecting lights of a disco ball. I was still depressed, but at least now I was semi-intoxicated, accompanied by others, and well illuminated.

Luís did his best to cheer me up, moving from lighthearted topics like Top 40 Bee Gees tunes to the best cocktails in Costa Rica, but even his jovial attempt at conversation was unsuccessful at pulling me out of my black mood.

I fell into a distracted silence, and as if reading my thoughts Luís leaned over and whispered to me, "Just remember, we are the good guys."

I wanted to believe he was good. He was warm and gentle—but, then again, that was how Michel had seemed. How could I possibly have been so wrong?

Good guys, bad guys. Was life as black and white as that?

In the stories I grew up with as a child, it wasn't too difficult to tell the protagonists from the people who were antagonizing them. The antagonists were the ones wearing black clothes and big pointy hats who wandered about trying to interest young maidens in large, shiny poisonous apples. Run across someone with green skin, crooked fingers, moles, and a raspy voice, and it was a pretty strong indication that you didn't want to give them your name for a twenty-five-thousand-dollar international money transfer.

But Michel had none of these traits. He had been funny and sweet and had taken me to the doctor when I was sick. How could he have betrayed me? This was the first question I planned on asking him. The previous night, I'd done a little bit of cautious detective work of my own and after some innocuous-seeming but intentional questioning at the disco, I'd gotten Michel's current whereabouts out of Luís. Impelled by a surge of angry determination, I'd fearlessly marched through Limón in the morning, where *I* became the one frightening people on the streets. I had demanded directions of anyone I encountered without as much as an explanation, a kind word, an introductory greeting, or a smile.

Now I was on a rickety bus wandering through territory I didn't recognize, wondering if I would even be allowed in to see him. But I had come this far and I wasn't going to back out now.

"This is it," the driver shouted to me.

I stood up and walked to the front of the bus.

"Good luck," he said as I stepped onto the street.

The doors shut behind me as I took stock of my location—the green countryside, the pastures with grazing horses—had the driver made a mistake? I turned around to ask him, but the bus was already in motion. It sped away, leaving me alone at the side of a remote two-lane highway.

There were only four buildings within my sight: two farmhouses, a small restaurant with two kids playing in front, and a lime-colored building surrounded by a tall chain-link fence. Was this the prison?

I walked across the street. As I neared the building, two men came into view, obviously guards. This had to be the place. Now, how was I going to convince them to let me see Michel?

"I'm here to see my boyfriend. He was brought here yesterday," I informed the closest of the two uniformed men sitting in the guardhouse.

"Visiting days are Thursdays and Sundays. Come back then."

"I have to leave the country tomorrow," I fibbed. "I'm flying back to the States. Please, isn't there anything you can do?"

The older guard in the rear approached the window and addressed his partner. "It's okay. They just brought him in. He's entitled to one special visit. They'll let her in to see him."

With a nonchalant shrug, the guard pulled open the gate, and for the first time in my life, I stepped onto the grounds of a prison.

One of the most intoxicating aspects of travel is that it gives you the ability to wander through a foreign environment without feeling like you're actually part of it. There is a dreamlike quality to moving through an unfamiliar place, a sense of false protection—the way that journalists and photographers can often believe they are somehow outside of the story—as if bombs and gunfire somehow respected a reporter's observer status, understanding that writers are merely there as witnesses.

This was how I felt walking up to the door to the main office of the prison: It was not real. Real things only happened in New York and Los Angeles (and once in a great while in Miami). This was Costa Rica, an otherworldly state that I would soon wake up from. Here it was acceptable for me to visit a jail cell (something I would never have considered in my own country). In fact, it was necessary. I had never met anyone who had been arrested before and I needed to understand. For the moment anyway, irresponsibility had taken a backseat to my quest for answers.

A female guard who had patted me down minutes earlier accompanied me to the administrative office and asked me to take a seat on a bench. I sat down in what could have been any Costa Rican business office. There was a large counter staffed by two employees, conference rooms off to the sides, and people walking around with files.

"Charles will be with you in a moment," the woman behind the counter said.

I smiled back at her and waited. What would Michel—what would Charles—what would whatever-the-hell-his-name-was have to say to me?

I watched a fly zip across the room, its buzz suddenly audible to me in Dolby 3-D stereo. An imaginary music score began playing in my head. I was simply the character in a movie. None of this was really happening.

Looking up, I saw Michel only steps away from me, which only heightened the strangeness of the situation. This was the same man I had spent the past week sleeping next to and here he was in a prison.

He sat down calmly at my side and waited for me to react. There were so many things I needed to know, so many things his betrayal had made me question.

"I just came to ask you why."

Even though I had asked, I was still determined not to believe a word Michel told me. He was a liar and a thief. I wasn't interested in what he had to say. I had come to visit him to allay a nagging worry I'd had since his arrest—I had always been such a good judge of character, able to size up a person within minutes of meeting them. I needed to figure out how I had been so wrong about Michel.

Michel was speaking to me, laying out his confession, but I wasn't really interested. In my mind, I was a little girl with her hands over her ears singing to shut out the sound of his voice. There was no reason to trust him now. There he was droning on about innocence and regret, words I had no reason to believe, except that they weren't the words he was using at all. I suddenly heard what he was saying. It was a huge confession, a horrible one. He was giving me the names and dates of all the crimes he had committed. I was stunned. I was the plaintiff, he was the defendant, and he had suddenly provided me with all the evidence I needed to destroy him.

There was a stint as a mercenary, a guerrilla, involvement with even less reputable groups. He had fled his home country after his brother was assassinated for treason. From there, he had wandered the world, surviving as best he could. The money I had given him was to go toward leaving Costa Rica to go anywhere but Trinidad and Tobago—that passport was fake. There were additional details, some of which I do not remember, some of which I choose not to write. But by the time the guard came to take him away a half hour later, I was torn by conflicting urges: the gut instinct to flee from the dangerous man in front of me and the journalist's desire to stay, to remain part of what had turned out the be the most interesting story of my life so far.

I was sitting right next to a man who had done things I couldn't begin to imagine. It was like coming face to face with the Godfather. Did you run in fear or did you stick around to hear his stories? What I really wanted was to start over with the truth, to spend days getting to know him again in an attempt to understand. I wanted to comprehend this man who had been willing to lay down his life for a political cause. I wanted to know what had drawn me to him and, stranger still, why that attraction still remained. Did I see the good inside of a bad man or had he been a good man all along, one blurred by false truths?

The world was such a complex place. Memorizing the dates and names of world events was easy, but understanding the meaning behind these conflicts, what compelled people to lay down their lives for a cause was something I would never fully comprehend. Had I been born in a warring Middle Eastern country, had I watched my family members get killed by an oppressive government, would I have made the same choices as Michel?

I watched the guard lead Michel away, wondering who he really was, this man with the boyish charm and the complicated life. I would never really know.

"You are the most dangerous person I have ever met," were the last words he said to me. It had been his idea of a compliment, his joking way of explaining his need to confide in me. He claimed I had been enough to shake his worldview.

But he was wrong. I hadn't been trying to change his mind. I had just wanted to figure him out. I had learned long ago that it was impossible to draw that moral line for anyone else. And anyone who foolishly believed they could invariably got themselves mixed up in a violent armed conflict. Lebanon versus Israel, Cuba versus the United States—had any of these attempts made progress? Was it really possible to alter anyone else's view?

Bill, George, Fidel, Ehud, Benjamin, Ariel, and Yasser—*they* were the dangerous ones. I was simply trying to understand. I was just trying to make sense of a war-torn world.

Chapter Five

Avoiding Prison and Other Noble Vacation Goals

Before visiting Costa Rica, I'd only ever met one person who had ever been there, but now it seemed that everyone I ran into had spent significant amounts of time in the country. Wherever I went in Los Angeles, somebody had a story to tell. A guy I bumped into at a bar wanted to talk about Guanacaste. A friend had photos of the Caribbean coast tacked up on her office wall. The checker at the grocery store turned out to be from Limón. It was like the experience of looking up a new word in the dictionary—you go twenty-five years without ever needing to use a term like salubrious, but the minute you learn what it means, all of a sudden the word pops up everywhere.

I had only been back in Los Angeles for a month, but while salubriously tossing items in my cart at the health food store, I began to think over all the things I had heard about Costa Rica since my return. My own experiences were nothing like the stories I had recently been told, which got me thinking—was it possible I had visited an entirely different country? Maybe Costa Rica was like Vietnam and Korea—maybe it was a nation divided; perhaps there was a communist part and a regular part and I had gone to the wrong half by mistake. How else was I supposed to reconcile my bizarre, prison-related experience with the stories I kept hearing of aqua-colored beaches and picturesque cloud forests?

At least I knew who could give me the answer. Since returning to Los Angeles, I had kept in touch with Jessica through a series of faxes and overseas phone calls. We had become friends during my last three days in Costa Rica. After Michel's arrest, she had raced over to my hotel in San José to see if I was okay—an article about Michel had come out in the paper and she had recognized my name. After hearing my side of the story, she quickly shifted her alliance from him to me, figuring I would make a better friend anyway: I was unlikely to swipe her money and, besides, it would be a lot easier getting together for coffee with someone who wasn't in prison.

As I waited until there was space available on the bus to Tegucigalpa, she had helped me pass the time. She had made me temporarily forget all that I had just been through, and hanging out with her had been surprisingly fun. She was seven years younger than me and at first I thought the age difference would mean we had nothing in common. After all, I had been on my own for the past nine years whereas she still lived with her parents. However, it was this very fact that ended up appealing to me. She reminded me what it was like to be nineteen—or what it would have been like had I not been somber and hardworking, weighed down with the anxiety of putting myself through college. Spending time with her was like getting back the teenage years I had missed. The act of smoking a cigarette or drinking half a beer was still a major event for her; to me these actions had ceased to be any big deal, but she made them fun again. Together we reveled in the depravity of it all. Just walking down the street, we'd crack each other up. A simple walk to buy ice cream was an event that would inevitably turn into an infectious gigglefest.

Although my life in Los Angeles had greatly improved over the past year, it still paled in comparison to my last few days with Jessica. I wanted to laugh like that again. I wanted to act silly. I wanted people to roll their eyes at me as I giggled too loudly in the street. Maybe I had missed out on all the fun things there were to do in Costa Rica. Maybe I should give the country one more chance.

• • •

While waiting for my bags at the San José airport, I thought to myself that this trip to Costa Rica really was going to be different. It was going to be a real vacation, just as Jessica had promised. I was going to visit nature preserves, museums, and exotic restaurants. I was going to sip tropical drinks out of ripe coconuts. I was going to throw caution to the wind and get myself a tan. And no way in hell would there be any need for me to visit the local jail.

"What are we doing tomorrow?" I asked Jessica once I had arrived at my hotel in San José and was able to use the phone.

"Actually, Wendy, I hope you don't mind, we're going to visit the local jail."

This was not a good sign.

"Jessica, I'd love to, but I have to go to a beach or a mountain. I have to get a tan."

"Wendy, remember when you said how lucky I was to have a boyfriend who wasn't in prison?"

"Yeah."

"Well I'm not so lucky anymore."

The irony of this situation was not lost on me. The last time I'd been in Costa Rica, we had turned Michel's incarceration into a joke. Every time Jessica uttered the slightest complaint about her aching feet or her growling stomach, I'd turn to her and jokingly remind her that things could always be worse: She could be in my shoes. "At least your boyfriend isn't in prison" had become my ongoing refrain.

How was I supposed to console her now? "Well, at least you know he's not sleeping with other women" didn't come out as encouraging as I had hoped. But more important, what was going on in this country? Given the number of men I had met in Costa Rica and the percentage of those men that had wound up in prison, I was beginning to suspect that getting arrested was something that went on all the time.

My phone conversation with Jessica ended before I got any real information. Her father walked into the room she was calling from, and since he was blissfully unaware of the recent events in his daughter's life, Jessica was unable to give me any details of the situation, leaving me with a lot of unanswered questions. Lying in bed in my hotel room (I'd gone back to Hotel Venecia, not because it was especially nice, but it was cheap and familiar—it was a wonderfully worldly sensation to arrive in a foreign country and get recognized by the hotel staff), I thought over what I knew about my new friend. As far as getting involved with criminals went, she didn't seem the type. She made the sign of the cross every time we walked past a Catholic church, ran her own business at age nineteen, and refused to sleep with Olman until they got married (which at the rate things were going looked like it wasn't going to happen anytime soon). The only thing in her life resembling corruption was her one-cigarette-a-day habit, which she indulged in with the same guilty glee as if her menthol Virginia Slims had been laced with crack.

I chalked up the strange turn of events to being in a foreign country with a penal tradition different from the one found in the United States. Unlike in my own country where wealthy and powerful criminals actually had to have a trial before being declared innocent and freed from prison, here they often did away with the inconveniences of scheduling hearings. Bribes were standard practice throughout Costa Rica and it was common knowledge that a checkbook was the most important legal document anyone could carry.

This sort of simplified the whole judicial process and made life a lot easier on wealthy, law-disregarding citizens, but if you were foolish enough to have been born poor and got on the wrong side of the police, your chances of seeing the outside world again were about as good as those of Siberian tigers hoping to get paroled from the San Diego Zoo.

"The police can do whatever they want to you," my father had explained to me in Honduras. "In fact, if you get robbed, think twice about going to them. They won't do anything unless you bribe them and they've even been known to plant drugs on unsuspecting Americans."

Given this information, I was just glad that my admission to the prison the next day was scheduled to take place through the visitors' entrance.

"Jail is no picnic," my mother used to warn me on the especially mischievous days of my childhood. Being just nine years old, it was hard for me to imagine what prison could possibly be like: nothing to do all day, living without my siblings, no mother or father to eat breakfast with. Of course, I was sure there must be a downside too. Jail couldn't possibly be a fun place to be.

But walking up the steps to San Sebastian prison with Jessica on my second day in Costa Rica, I began to suspect that my mother had been wrong. The scent of hot dogs was wafting through the air, men were busy grilling pork over a barbecue, and families were relaxing on blankets spread out over the ground. It seemed like—well, prison sure looked like a picnic to me. It reminded me of the huge company outings my dad felt obligated to attend and would routinely drag us to as kids, except that here everyone seemed to be having a good time—which I attributed to the fact that on prison visiting days half of the people came here willingly.

Jessica and I were in a long line filled mostly with women, all of whom carried plastic containers filled with steaming meat, gravy, rice, and potatoes. In order to be allowed into the outdoor courtyard on the other side of the chain-link fence, we had to sign in with our passports and subsequently get patted down by a female guard. Once we finally made it inside, Jessica and I seated ourselves on a bench and watched the prisoners filing out of the cellblock and into the arms of their families.

While waiting for Olman to appear Jessica had the chance to tell me the story. Three days earlier he had been arrested in a mix-up, in which he was mistakenly accused of selling drugs. The OIJ had recordings of Olman's phone calls that went something like this:

"Meet me at the gas station in fifteen minutes. I think I'm going to sell at least five thousand *colones* worth today."

"Well, I have a contact at the Pepsi plant. He has plans to help me distribute."

It would have been very incriminating if Olman had been discussing cocaine or heroin instead of the raffle tickets that he was selling for the Costa Rican Foundation for the Blind. But the OIJ had shown up at his house one morning and led him out in handcuffs, along with his uncle and brother who were with him at the time.

Olman entered the courtyard just as Jessica was nearing the end of the story. She spotted him in the distance, raced over, put her arms around his neck, and asked how he was doing. I walked over, gave him a kiss on the cheek, and asked him what it was like being a drug dealer.

I would have continued the conversation further, but I realized that Olman's tongue was tied up with other things (namely Jessica's)—which was my distressing first clue that I was going to have to find a way to kill the next four hours on my own. For a brief moment, I thought that I would just mingle, but then I remembered that the attendees at this picnic were not my dad's innocuous mining engineering colleagues—these were convicts.

And even assuming I would be brave enough to strike up a conversation with one of them, what would we possibly talk about? Of course the nagging question would be what the guy was in for but asking that was sure to be a breach of prison etiquette. "Hi, I'm Wendy. What crime did you commit?" didn't seem the best way to start a friendly chat. And even if I did manage to get the question out, what would I say to his response? "Oh, you killed your wife and three children. So, tell me, what was *that* like?"

The fact that I was visiting yet another Costa Rican prison was just beginning to sink in. Did these things happen to other people on their vacations?

I figured the best course of action would be to keep a low pro-file and take advantage of this unique sociological setting by merely observing. Sitting at an outdoor picnic table under a covered awning surrounded by Olman's family members, I timidly nibbled at the food Jessica had brought and spent the next hour as follows: for twenty minutes I watched Jessica and Olman's near-pornographic display, for twenty-five minutes I came up with possible escape plans in case I ever arrived at this jail by the back door instead of the vis-itors' entrance, and for fifteen minutes I stared dumbly at Olman's brother Jorge, wishing to God I had something to say other than, "So, what's it like being in jail?"

Luckily, Jorge finally broke the silence by piping up, "Do you want to know everyone here who's gay?"

"Okay," I said.

"Him, over there, with the red half shirt. Gay. And the one with the long hair and bad skin. That's his boyfriend."

That topic of conversation having worn thin, there followed a long uncomfortable silence. Finally, I had to ask, "So, what do you do all day?"

"Mostly just drink."

"Really?" I asked, relieved to have finally found some common ground. "I thought it wasn't allowed."

"It's not. We make it ourselves. That's why the guards won't let anyone bring in fruit, juice, or tortillas. We ferment them in a plas-tic Coke bottle and hide it under our mattresses."

"And makeup? Why couldn't I bring in makeup?"

"Some prisoners have tried dressing up as women to escape."

"Say, would you do me a favor?" Olman's uncle chimed in.

"Sure," I said, hoping he wasn't going to ask to borrow my lip-stick.

"A friend of ours couldn't come out into the courtyard because no one is here to visit him. Would you tell the guard you're here to see him?"

• • •

The first thing Francisco Sánchez did after thanking me for having called him out was plop himself down at my side and ask what a nice girl like me was doing in a place like this.

"Just visiting," I answered with a nervous laugh. "But the more important question—"

"What's a nice guy like me doing here?" He pulled out a picture of a smiling, doe-eyed little girl. "That's why I'm here."

"Pedophilia?" I wagered.

"She's my daughter. I'm in jail because I came here to see her. I'm from Colombia. But it's no big deal. It's just a mix-up. I should be out of here in a week or so. Do you want to hear the story?"

Had this been a U.S. prison, I would have shrugged him off and found a plausible way to slip away, uttering some excuse like "Sorry, but I have to go sneak someone a file," but he seemed so nonthreatening. In fact, looking around me, everyone at the prison did. Men were cuddling their babies, kids were tossing balls on the lawn, husbands were snuggling up with their wives. This was not the way prisoners were supposed to be. Where were the knife fights and swearing matches? Someone had to have a swastika tattooed on his forehead.

The man sitting next to me had to be the least threatening one of the bunch. He didn't look anything like a typical Colombian—he had pale skin, light blue eyes, and was exceptionally tall for a Latino. And he was so gentle and boyish that I quit worrying about my safety and began to wonder about his—how could a man like him have wound up here?

"Everyone here has a story," he said with a sad, knowing look.

"I'll hear yours on one condition."

"What's that?"

"No lies. My last boyfriend only told me lies."

"Is that why you broke up with him?"

"No. The OIJ took him away. He's in prison in Limón."

"Sounds like you have a story too."

"Yeah, maybe I do."

Francisco's account of his situation had something to do with his ex-wife and a car that she accused him of stealing. According to Francisco, he was completely innocent—he had bought her the car in the first place and had sold it because she had bailed on him and left the country. I highly doubted his story (based on a healthy suspicion of all men in prison), but innocent or not the whole encounter had been harmless enough and Francisco's stories about Colombia with its warring guerrillas and drug cartels had turned out to be an entertaining way to spend the afternoon. I had survived my second trip to a Central American prison.

"I guess I'd better go," I said after the prison bell rang, signaling the end of visiting hours. "I'm supposed to meet my friend Jessica outside."

"Let me walk you to the exit," Francisco said, as casual and well mannered as if we had just gotten together for an afternoon chat in the park.

We strolled to the gated door, a walk of less than a minute, but within that time the atmosphere at San Sebastian completely changed. For the first time that day, I actually felt like I was at a prison. The music stopped, the chatter ceased, and an ominous silence filled the courtyard, in spite of the fact that it was still filled with people. Earlier that morning, the hellos had been boisterous and cheery, but the good-byes were silent—by now, all the trite encouraging words had already been said.

At the exit, I couldn't help but glance at the woman next to me who clung to her husband and quietly shook with sobs. It was such a private moment but there was no privacy to be had here. My problems were so insignificant compared to hers, I thought, suddenly

feeling guilty and out of place. I was like the uninvited guest at a fu-
neral, the one who gets trapped listening to the reminiscences of the
widow, who doesn't have the guts to admit she never even knew the
deceased.

"Take care of yourself," I said to Francisco, truly meaning it. "I
hope you get your case settled."

"Thanks," he said, holding out his hand. "And if you ever want to
talk, you know where to find me."

I smiled and turned to go, acutely aware of the significance of
the next four steps I would take. I was casually strolling out of a
prison. How easy it was for me and how impossible for the blue-
eyed man left waving at me through the fence.

"Well, I'm glad that's over," I said to Jessica, once we were both
speeding away from the prison in the safety of a cab.

"What do you mean?"

"I survived visiting day at a prison. Now I can say I did it."

"Does that mean you don't plan on going again?"

"Jessica, this may seem strange to you, but I am twenty-six years
old and I have already been to two prisons more than I had counted
on by this age. What reason would I possibly have for going again?"

Looking at Jessica's distraught face, I realized that in a moment
of utter selfishness, I had completely forgotten my friend's perspective on the whole afternoon. What for me was an exceptional event,
an adventure most people would never experience, for her was a
painful reality. Her boyfriend was actually in prison.

"I was hoping you'd come with me again on Thursday," Jessica
said.

I wanted to be a supportive friend, but I had come a long way
for this vacation. I had counted on lighthearted fun with Jessica, but
now that this didn't seem possible, I hoped to at least visit volcanoes
and beaches, to have a well-deserved good time after my trouble-

some experience with Michel on my last trip. Besides, I was an American. Going to prisons wasn't a normal vacation activity where I came from. We went to Disneyland and SeaWorld and Alcatraz Island—we didn't go around visiting jail cells.

I told her I'd wait and see, guiltily knowing I had no intention of actually following through, figuring the next day I'd look into buses headed to Manzanillo.

I had an itty bitty problem with money the next day which was that I had only an itty bitty bit of money—itty bitty being defined as absolutely zero. At least, that's what the words on the ATM screen informed me.

This presented a problem for several reasons. First of all, I was fond of eating. And besides, I really liked the little blue Costa Rican bills with the picture of the toucan on the front. After all, we didn't yet have watermarks in my own country.

"Don't worry!" was Jessica's predictable response upon hearing the news. In fact, it was her standard phrase upon hearing any form of bad news. Assuming I were to tell her that I hadn't yet paid for my past few days' hotel stay, my Visa card was being mysteriously denied, the only possible friend I could borrow money from was in some unknown country in Europe, one of my new writing clients was late paying me the ten thousand dollars I was owed, my permission to remain in the country would expire shortly, and I hadn't yet gotten around to purchasing a return ticket to the States, what would she have told me? That it was really nothing to get concerned about.

"Everything will be fine," she insisted, sitting on the double bed in my hotel room. "Just relax." If her idea of relaxing was trembling my way to the store on the corner, barking for a pack of cigarettes, smoking half the box on my way back to the hotel, running to the bathroom, placing my head under a faucet of cold water, and returning to kick the wall a dozen times, then relax is exactly what I did. "I am relaxed," I said, crumbling an empty cigarette box in my hand.

"Let's examine my options," I said, thinking this sounded like a rational, composed thing to say. Unfortunately, she couldn't hear me over the sound of my foot shaking against the floor. I repeated myself.

"That's right. Let's examine your options."

"We just did, Jessica. There is nothing to examine!" I said, holding down my knee with the palm of my hand. "I have two thousand dollars in that account. And the ATM machine won't let me get to any of it."

"Don't worry," she said calmly. "There is nothing to worry about."

Luckily, all heavy blunt objects were well beyond my reach.

"It'll all turn out okay," she consoled me.

What did she know about these things? She was a nice enough girl and she'd been kind enough to show the visiting gringa around the city, but she was just a child. She was nineteen years old, she lived with her parents—she was a virgin for God's sake! Short of coming up with cash or getting me an airplane ticket, what could she possibly do?

"I'll talk to the hotel manager about your bill. In the meantime, you can stay with me," she cheerily informed me.

"What will your parents say?"

"They won't mind. It'll be great."

Jessica was offering me an easy way out of all my problems. All I had to do was stay with her for a few days until I figured out what was going on with the bank. Of course, there had to be a catch.

"And we can go to the prison together on Thursday," she added cheerfully.

That was the rub. I either got tossed out of my hotel penniless and pesoless onto the streets of San José or I crashed at Jessica's, obligating me to go with her to San Sebastian. Homeless in a foreign country wasn't a particularly appealing option. But then again, neither was hanging out at a prison. On my last visit to Costa Rica, I had vowed *never* to set foot on the grounds of a prison again.

"I'll pull a cot out of the closet and sleep on the floor," Jessica added. "You can have my bed."

Never, I repeated to myself. Unless you counted next Thursday.

Jessica lived forty-five minutes away from San José in the rural community of Santa Ana, which was like a halfway village for wannabe farmers. The town was filled with midsized homes on large plots of land, which offered enough room for most people to accommodate several trophy animals but not enough space to actually earn any money from them. When a farmer referred to his "cattle," he was speaking about his one dairy cow. When he mentioned his farm animals, he meant his dogs and roaming stray cats. And when he talked about his orchard, he was alluding to the three mango trees in the front yard. These were well-off poseur farmers, the kind that owned businesses in San José during the week and spent their weekends gathering their farm animals around, calling each by name.

Jessica's family had a horse, a dairy cow, a pack of dogs, and a family of roaming chickens. They also had a barn, several cars, and a three-bedroom home, making them comfortable by Costa Rican standards.

"Are you sure your parents won't mind that I'm here?" I asked Jessica as she flung a pack of stuffed animals off the bottom bunk in her bedroom and onto the floor.

"No, they're dying to meet you. I've told them all about you."

Sure enough, Jessica's parents were completely nonplussed when she strolled into the living room and informed them of the circumstances and her intention to have me stay for the next week. Hugs and kisses and friendly words were immediately showered upon me; however, this attention ended as abruptly as a beauty queen's plans to attend medical school.

"We're so happy to . . ." Jessica's mother's voice trailed off as she turned her attention away from me and joined her husband on the couch.

"Shhhh!" Jessica's eight-year-old sister pleaded and everyone complied, turning to face the television set in unison.

"It's *telenovela* time," Jessica explained.

Over the next week, the Arguedes family members would go out of their way to explain the plotlines of the soap opera they watched every night. During lunch, Jessica's sister would express her conviction that the relationship between Tomás and Flora definitely wasn't going to work out. Over coffee in the living room, Jessica's mother would insist that Teresa was a bad person and a liar and that you couldn't believe anything she said, especially when it had anything to do with Jorge who was actually a saint in spite of that whole unfortunate incident with the loaded gun. The only person who didn't discuss the series at length was Jessica's father. After all, he had more important things on his mind.

"*Mangas,*" he'd correct me, every time I called my favorite Costa Rican fruit a mango. "The big ones are *mangas;* the small ones are *mangos.*"

Apparently, there was some confusion on this important matter. A Costa Rican fruit vendor had explained to me that the distinction had to do with the degree of ripeness. The young green ones were *mangos;* the ripe yellowish-orange fruits were referred to as *mangas.* But Jessica's father was sure it was a size issue. He'd lay them out on the table, quizzing me, convinced that he would not let this particular American return to her own country before she had learned the difference.

"*Mango,*" I'd say, looking at the small fruit in front of me.

"That's right. It's a small one. And this one?"

"*Manga.* Because it's big."

"Good. Very good."

"How about this one?"

"*Manga.*"

"No, no, no! It's a *mango,*" he said, amazed how slow his American pupil could be.

"But it's big," I said defending myself.

"That's right. It's a big *mango.*"

"Not a small *manga?*"

"No, definitely a big *mango.*"

For the benefit of anyone who may someday visit Costa Rica, I have included the following cut-out, wallet-sized continuum:

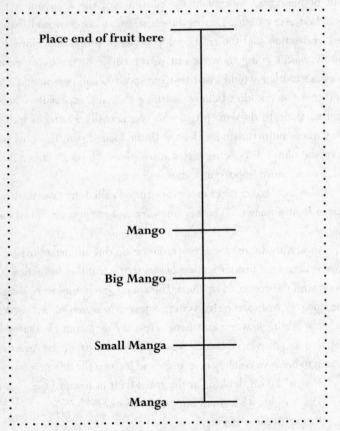

Place end of fruit here

Mango

Big Mango

Small Manga

Manga

Instructions for use: 1) Cut along dotted lines. 2) Photocopy at 150 percent. 3) Enjoy!

• • •

Unlike in the United States where only losers and serial murderers lived with their mothers past the age of twenty-four, in Latin America it was the only socially acceptable thing to do. The fact that I was twenty-six years old and already supported myself was seen as a suspicious sign of independence, and it was barely tolerated in my case because I was a foreigner. Costa Rican girls who got their own apartments before marriage were seen as rebellious tramps, whose first night on their own was sure to be filled with drunken revelry and animal sex—in other words, the same reasons we left home in my own country.*

Since Latinos rarely fled the coop (and if they did, it was usually only for a long weekend that ended with them bringing a wife back), Costa Rican homes were filled with people. What was odd at the Arguedes household was that everyone seemed perfectly content with the situation. This for me was going to require some getting used to. After all, I came from a family where successfully separating yourself from all others was seen as the highest form of bliss. As a kid, doors were shut, solitary walks were taken—anything to accomplish "alone time," as my mother so adamantly referred to it.

However, after wandering about Jessica's house for a few days, I came to the conclusion that Latin American families didn't have the same need for privacy as those from the States. They shared rooms, they shared beds, they shared clothes. As long as no one was actually standing on your toes, you had no personal space issues to complain about, they figured.

---

*This belief was so firmly entrenched that it would be two years before I encountered Lena, the only Latina woman I've ever met who had actually accomplished it. She was a bold, independent, and bright Bolivian capable of earning a living on her own who still struggled with the guilt laden upon her by her family for having left home at age twenty-five. She was also lots of fun and remains one of my favorite people to this day.

At first, I had assumed it would be a bit of an adjustment for me to get used to living with a family again—I had been on my own for nearly ten years. So I was amazed at how quickly and contentedly I adapted to life at the Arguedes'. They rapidly incorporated me into their routine and assured me that their house was simply an extension of my own. From Day 1, it was taken for granted that I would help myself to anything out of the fridge, go to bed whenever I was tired, and not stand on ceremony if there was something I felt like doing—just as it was assumed that I would help with the dishes and light household chores.

At Jessica's house, I was just one of the kids, which was strangely comforting. I got bossed around by her parents and referred to them as *señor* and *señora*. Had I been a decade younger, at that adolescent age when you insist you are a grown-up, I probably would have resented this juvenile treatment, but I had already made something of myself and I was bored with being impressive. In Los Angeles, you always had to be someone or have accomplished something for people to want to hang out with you, but the Arguedes family didn't expect anything of me. They didn't know that I was earning five-hundred dollars a day. They didn't know that I had put myself through college or that I occasionally conducted interviews with Hollywood celebrities. They just liked me, period. Their affection for me was real. And being a kid for a while was actually a nice respite.

Over the next week, I tagged along with Jessica like a sister, comfortably settling into her routine: days spent between her office and the streets of San José, an early-evening dose of television, and nighttime walks that were completely magical for me. In Los Angeles, I had always shut myself away after sunset. Darkened city streets were no place for a woman walking alone so my friends and I invariably met up at movie theaters, bars, coffeehouses—anyplace indoors. But with Jessica, I embraced the night. Fearlessly, the two of us raced each other through darkened fields, climbed trees, and picked wild fruit, the same way I had spent the best days of my childhood. There was no discussion of California wine, independent film, or nouveau Asian cuisine—just giddy laughter over scraped knees and orange-stained hands sticky with fruit juice.

On one of these nights, while Jessica and I happily frolicked through a neighbor's cornfield in an attempt to find anything edible, I suddenly realized that all of my roaming around the world had come down to this—not corn (granted, it was one of my favorite vegetables but it didn't quite seem worthy of an international quest)—but rather the ability to act like a kid, to stomp through cornfields at eleven o'clock at night and have nothing else matter. It wasn't pure irresponsibility I had been searching for, the kind that entailed running away from everything I cared about; rather, it was the desire to be taken in and taken care of, to have someone else think about bills and insurance and rent checks while I had time for the small important things, like stealing the neighbor's produce. Come to think of it, my journey around the world *had* come down to corn.

The next day, bursting with good intentions, I slipped out of Jessica's office and walked to the international phone center, where I invested what was left of my cash on a phone call to my parents in Tegucigalpa. All this time with the Arguedes clan was making me miss my own family.

"Hi, Mom, it's Wendy," I said, happy to hear the sound of a familiar Dale voice.

"Wendy, you shouldn't call international long distance. It's so expensive."

"I know. I just missed you."

"We miss you too, dear."

"I'm in San José and was thinking of popping in for a visit in a few weeks. What do you think?"

"Oh, Wendy, we'd love to see you, but it's not a good time. We're really busy."

"What are you doing? I thought you guys didn't do anything."

"Normally we don't. But this week, we're moving to Bolivia. Didn't you get the e-mail?"

In typical Dale-family fashion, they had made a spontaneous decision to leave the country. Bored with their lives in Tegucigalpa, they'd begun a massive relocation campaign, which began with reading travel guidebooks for a week and ended with plans to move to a city they had never even visited.

"Cochabamba sounds like a great city," my mother gushed. "It's called the city of the eternal spring. And the best thing is, it's really poor. So our money will stretch a long way."

As my mother droned on about the other merits of Cochabamba (though being poor was the one that seemed to get her most enthusiastic), I decided that this was really one of my parents' major character flaws—not the fact that they were making a habit of spontaneously moving to foreign countries (I was actually sort of proud of this egregious disregard for societal convention) but rather that they often failed to inform their children of their plans beforehand.

The previous time this had happened, I had been a sophomore at UCLA. One day I called them at their house in Montana and got the out-of-breath voice of my fifteen-year-old sister Heather on the other end of the line explaining that at the moment our mother was currently too busy to come to the phone, given that the family was in the middle of packing to move to Arizona. This was news to me—I had never heard of any family plans to relocate and it was the first time it ever occurred to me how easy it would be to completely lose contact with my parents.

"How are your folks?" I imagined my friends asking.

"Well, they moved and I don't have their new address. You know how it is with people you haven't talked to for years. We just fell out of touch."

That was the difference between my folks and families like

Jessica's: The Arguedes family viewed maps as innocuous wall hangings, pretty pictures that coordinated nicely with the colors in the couch. My parents saw maps as suggestions. To a Dale, Rand McNally was an international relocation guide.

I finished up my phone call with my mother and in a glum mood, I left the international phone center and headed toward Jessica's office. It was a five-block walk I was beginning to know well. There was the ice-cream parlor, the record store, the souvenir shop, the man selling coconuts. There was a money exchange place that I had entered a few times, the T-shirt shop I recognized, and the woman I had bought papaya from. And there was an ATM machine that I had never seen before in my life.

On an impulse, I decided to try the ATM. After a wait in line, I entered the gated cubicle and crossed my fingers in the hopes of good news. I pressed what I hoped were all the right keys, stood back, and gave the machine time to process my simple but international request. After what seemed an exceptionally long wait, the machine cheerfully spit out three hundred dollars.

I was so relieved at having discovered an ATM machine that could be troubled to give me access to my funds and I had been having so much fun with Jessica that I hadn't realized how fast time was going by. I had already been in Costa Rica for several days—or had it already been a week?

"What day is it?" I asked Jessica one evening at her house, realizing I had lost count.

"It's one day away."

"One day from what?"

"One day from Thursday."

"You mean it's Wednesday."

"Yeah. Isn't that what I just said?"

Unlike most people, who had a way of defining days by using names such as "Sunday," "Monday," and "Tuesday," Jessica's life revolved around prison visiting days and the amount of time it would take to get to the next one.

"Visiting day is tomorrow. And we'd better think about starting to get ready," she informed me in an uncharacteristically serious tone of voice.

"What do you plan to do? Sleep with your makeup on? How can we get ready *now* for tomorrow morning?"

"Silly, we have to cook what we're going to bring."

It had never occurred to me that a prison was the kind of place you didn't want to show up at empty-handed. "You mean like a cake with a file in it?" I inferred.

Jessica rolled her eyes. "Wendy, we're going to a prison. A prison."

"What? You'd bring a cake with a file to a *dinner party*?"

Jessica cracked a smile. "Seriously, all that Olman has there are the things we bring him."

"I'm sure they give him food and clothes."

Jessica looked down to the floor. "Wendy, they didn't even give him a mattress. I had to give him the money to buy one. I have to bring him clothes, food, soap—even toilet paper."

"You're kidding."

But from the way Jessica looked at me, I knew she wasn't. It was slowly beginning to dawn on me that the situation was a little more serious than I had first imagined. Up until now, it had kind of just been a joke for me because people I knew didn't go to jail. The most embarrassing thing they ever did was occasionally show up at really lame parties—though there was the one time that my artist/interior-decoration-obsessed friend, Lisa, smoked way too much pot and woke up in the morning to realize that she had tried to fit her apartment with a new floor. In her drug-induced state, wood hadn't seemed natural enough; she was going for something a little more rustic so she decided to cover her oak floor with something earthier—like earth. (What I wanted to know was how the hell she expected to clean a dirt floor. And how would she know when she was done mopping?)*

But having a boyfriend in prison was a reality for Jessica; it wasn't just the source of embarrassing jokes. She was in a really tough situation and I had no idea whatsoever how to help her.

"Jessica, you know I'm just kidding," I said, giving her a big hug. "I'm there for you, you know."

"Thanks," she said, recovering her usual good cheer. "Come on, I'll teach you how to make *arroz con pollo.*"

Entering San Sebastian was a lot like getting into those trendy clubs on Sunset Boulevard in West Hollywood. There was a tremendously long wait in line and a tough-looking guy checking IDs at the entrance. Besides, it really helped to know someone if you wanted to be let in. To ensure that wandering tourists didn't get it into their heads to just pop in for a quick tour, if you wanted into San Sebastian you had to know the name of an inmate. After all, this was a prison and there had to be some attempt to keep out the riffraff.

"Vázquez, Olman Mora. Cellblock A-2," Jessica said to the guard. He found Olman's name on his list and put a check by it.

"And you?" he said, turning to me. "Who are you here to visit?"

I was about to say Olman's name when I suddenly remembered the Colombian who had seemed to be the most harmless form of entertainment at the place.

"Francisco Sánchez," I said impulsively.

---

*Lisa doesn't smoke pot anymore. Now she makes art with the corpses of dead animals. However, she's thinking of moving on to another medium now that "that dead thing has gotten so trendy."

• • •

"I didn't expect to see you again," Francisco said after having spotted me in the courtyard and racing over to greet me.

"Me neither. Believe me, there are a million other places I would rather be."

"I know exactly what you mean," Francisco said with an ironic smile that made me laugh.

He looked just like I remembered him. He was wearing the same clothes and had the same sad blue eyes. He had the lanky walk of most tall and slender men—arms and legs flailing all over the place, which made it seem as if he were shuffling from side to side as he moved forward, and he hunched over slightly, what I assumed was an attempt to make closer eye contact with the people he towered over.

As we sat down at one of the outdoor tables where Jessica was dishing out bowls of steaming *arroz con pollo,* I hoped that Francisco wouldn't misinterpret my having given the guard his name. I wasn't trying to make friends here, but talking to him would protect me from unwanted advances, and he seemed genuinely nonthreatening, unlike some of the less savory characters who had tossed glances my way the last time.

"Are you hungry?" I asked.

"With the food they give us here, I'm always hungry. You'd think this was a jail or something."

I laughed but still felt a bit nervous, the way I always tended to be when talking to new people at a prison. I was curious about the man sitting next to me, whose life was like the stories I only read about in books, but I didn't know how to go about asking such personal details of a stranger.

"Does your family know you're here?" I finally managed to ask.

"No. My parents are dead."

"I'm sorry."

"Yeah. My mother died of cancer when I was fifteen. My father couldn't deal with it so he drank himself to death. He died three years later."

"Don't you have anyone else?"

"I have two sisters, but I haven't wanted to call. They limit us to eight minutes. Have you ever tried explaining how you wound up in prison in an eight-minute call?"

I shook my head and smiled, feeling a lot more at ease. Francisco seemed so open about his life that I ventured asking him the question I had wondered about ever since I had set foot in San Sebastián: "What is it *really* like being here?"

"It's about living in the future. It's about waiting. It's about time. Time is the enemy. You count every minute, hoping it will go by. And then there are moments like these when time goes by and you don't want it to. But it does anyway."

I was silenced by what he had just said, trying to take it in.

"I can't really tell you what it's like, but I can make you feel it."

Francisco slid over closer to me and put his lips close to my ear. And then in a quiet melodic voice, he began to sing:

Libre, como el sol cuando amanece yo soy libre, como el mar.
Libre, como el ave que escapó de su prisión y puede al fin volar.

It was the song of a prisoner, a man sitting in a jail cell calling to mind everything in his former life that reminded him what it was like to be free: the sun rising, the tide coming in, birds flying overhead.

Francisco had been singing only to me, but the others at the table had overheard him and conversation had stopped. Olman's uncle looked to Francisco and complimented him on his voice while I turned to Jessica to whisper, "Who *is* this man?"

"Olman's been telling me about him. It's really sad. Everyone talks about what happened to him. His ex-wife just got him tossed in here in an act of revenge. Olman says his cellblock would be completely quiet if it weren't for Francisco. His singing and his crying are the only two things Olman hears at night."

At the end of visiting hours, as Jessica hugged everyone good-bye, Francisco pulled me off to the side. "You know, I'm supposed to get out of here any day. Maybe we could go to a movie or something."

"I'm leaving in a couple of weeks. I can't really stick around."

"Well, you'll come back to visit, won't you? Say, you know what, why don't you come to the dance they're putting on tomorrow?"

"My Spanish must be really bad," I answered in my really bad Spanish. "I thought you just said the jail was putting on a dance."

"That's right. With food and live mariachi music."

I'd never heard of such a thing—a prison putting on a party?

"You're kidding, right?"

"No, I'm not."

I looked at him for a minute, trying to gauge his expression. "Funny. Very funny. I believed you for a second." I turned to Jessica. "This guy is giving the poor *gringa* a hard time. For a minute I actually believed him when he told me the prison was putting on a dance."

"You mean the one tomorrow?" she asked. "Why don't you come?"

I wavered for a minute while images of volcanoes and jungles and beaches raced through my brain one last time. A small "no" was all that was required of me at that moment. It was a tiny word really and so easy to say. But even as my lips formed the sound of the "n," I heard my voice get ahead of me and blurted out, "What the hell?"

•   •   •

"You like him, don't you?" Jessica accused me outside of the prison as we waited on the curb for a taxi.

"Don't be ridiculous."

"What's not to like? He's gorgeous, he's nice, he's a great singer—"

"He lives in a prison."

"You seem to be fixated on that fact."

"Jessica, in my country, people I hang out with don't go to prisons."

"So . . ."

"Here, everyone seems to."

"But you like him. I can tell."

"Sure, he's cute. But attraction is cheap. You can come across it just about anywhere. And sometimes you just have to walk away from it."

It was a sound sensible mantra—and what's more, I truly believed it, but I was still worried. I was completely capable of blowing off a handsome man, but a handsome man with entertaining stories, whose words bore the mark of a life well lived, this was the kind of man whose secrets I was dying to tear into. I hated the fact that Francisco was a prisoner, and what I hated even more was that I had more to talk about with him than the men I ran across in Los Angeles, guys who saved their passions for Range Rovers, the film industry, and arugula salads with radicchio.

As Jessica and I jumped into the cab she had flagged down and sped off through the streets of San José, I thought back to the last conversation I'd had back home, days before I had boarded a plane to come to Costa Rica. At a bar, a tall attractive stranger had scooted his stool up closer to mine and had tried to break the ice with mundane questions: "Where are you from?" "What do you do?" A month earlier, I might have been excited by the possibility of where the conversation could lead and would happily have responded to his queries, but my experience with Michel had changed me in a way I had not realized until that moment. As I began to answer, I suddenly felt that writing radio commercials and being born in Arizona were arbitrary details. They had nothing to do with my real life. What mattered to me was that I had just visited a Costa Rican prison. But this wasn't the kind of topic you broached with a stranger; I was having a hard enough time explaining these things to my friends.

This travel thing had started to get to me and I was losing the ability to separate my double existence. A year ago, Lebanon, Honduras, and Cuba had been like distant movie settings that I could walk out of any time and back into my reality. But now Costa Rica followed me around. Even in Los Angeles, I hadn't been able to shake it from my life.

And that was really why I had returned. I had come back to Costa Rica to try to make sense of how a lover of mine could have wound up in prison—and the irony of it was that the man capable of explaining it to me was a soulful, kind Colombian inmate. I was completely screwed.

"So where do you meet all these men?" my friends in Los Angeles would later ask me. "Coffeehouses? Movie theaters? Singles bars?"

"No, actually singles bars would be a step up."

Meeting men in prisons had its advantages. So they didn't have a phone number and sex was a bit inconvenient, but you always knew there was someone keeping an eye on them while you were away. Besides, if every man I met in Costa Rica was going to wind up in prison anyway, wouldn't it simplify the process to just start meeting them there? This was what passed through my mind as I walked through the entrance of the prison with Jessica on Friday.

"So, what's the cover?" I jokingly asked the woman at the front counter as I handed her my passport.

"There's a donation of five hundred *colones,*" she said, serious as a prison guard. Figuring I couldn't finagle my way in for free by sneaking in a back entrance, I handed her a bill as she stamped my hand.

I spotted Francisco in the courtyard twenty minutes later and nervously walked over to greet him. The day before, he had just been someone to talk to, but given that only adult women were allowed in the prison during the dance, today it felt suspiciously like a date, and one I wasn't completely prepared for. After all, first dates were awkward enough when you were in a room filled with quiet music and candlelight. They were even more unsettling when you were surrounded by rapists, murderers, and thieves.

"So, would you like to meet some of my friends?" Francisco asked after giving me a kiss on the cheek.

"These friends . . . I don't assume we're talking about doctors and accountants and engineers?"

"No, most of the people in here are politicians. Come on," he added, grabbing my hand and leading me through the courtyard.

He introduced me to Valencia, a short, thirtyish Colombian who felt the need to lecture me on injustice.

"It's unfair, unfair, unfair! The cops cook up these false drug charges because they don't like that I'm a foreigner and I own beachfront property in Puerto Viejo. So they plant cocaine in my hotel. That's the kind of thing that goes on all the time in this country. Not like in Colombia where the cops are people you can trust. Have you ever been to Colombia?"

"No, but I may get there this Christmas when I visit my parents in Cochabamba, Bolivia."

"That's a great city," he said, lost in a moment of reverie. "Some of the best cocaine in the world."

"Really?" I said, making a mental note to pass this tip on to my parents.

We walked past the mariachi band and over to a group of men who had gathered by the fence. Francisco pointed to a tall, chestnut-haired one and explained that he was an American who had been caught selling drugs. Apparently, this American hadn't made it to a beach or volcano either. (I decided not to ask him if he'd managed to avoid having a boyfriend who was in jail.)

As far as first dates go, I had to admit that it was going rather well. We weren't sitting in a four-star restaurant and there was a decent-sized possibility that someone might try to kill me, but at least I wasn't going to be faced with the tough decision of whether to ask him up to my apartment.

Besides, the man sitting next to me was beginning to get to me. Jessica was right—he was awfully good looking and he had the most striking blue eyes I had ever seen. And in spite of what had happened, he seemed to be strangely in control of his life. Granted, he lived in a prison, but this was beginning to seem more like a positive attribute than a flaw—where else was I supposed to meet a man capable of relating to my bizarre existence? Blockbuster Video? The Dairy Queen?

With other men, I had always blindsided them with any discussion of my past. I couldn't help it, but my experiences were always disastrous conversation stoppers. "So, there was this time that I lived out of a station wagon with my parents and two sisters." What could any normal person say in response to that? And the only thing lonelier than not ever sharing any personal details about myself was making a difficult disclosure only to receive a blank stare.

But somehow I sensed that I could trust Francisco with this information. Without making any effort, the stories of my life came pouring out. He didn't flinch when I talked about my recent visit to a prison in Limón or when I spoke of my trip to Beirut.

Over the next hour, the topics of conversation kept spilling out. Every story he recounted inspired two anecdotes of my own, which reminded him of four more incidents. It was a conversation of geometric proportions. I had topics lined up like ducks at a shooting gallery—I'd have to let some of them slide past—there wasn't time to get to them all.

Finally, knowing our time was growing distressingly short, I wanted him to explain again how he had wound up in prison—I hadn't really given him my full attention the first time and suddenly the topic seemed terribly important to me.

"Nice to know my stories really matter to you," he said with a wink.

"Well, back then, for some strange reason, I had somehow assumed you were, you know, a *criminal*."

He smiled and indulgently launched into the story one more time. He had visited Costa Rica on vacation, fallen in love with a woman, and stayed in San José to live with her for four years. The marriage had fallen apart and he had finally returned to Colombia, but he couldn't stop thinking about the daughter he'd left behind. He made plans to go back to Costa Rica, but there was a problem: His relationship had ended badly, in bitterness and disputes, and in a final act of vengeance, Laura, his ex, had filed charges against him, claiming that he was a mere acquaintance of hers, that they had never had a relationship, and that he had stolen her car. After all, Francisco had gone to Colombia and wasn't around to tell his side of the story, which was that he had bought her the car in the first place and had sold it when she had run off to Holland and had been incommunicado for over a year.

By calling a friend in San José, Francisco had found out about the false charges, and knowing that officials weren't too understanding about listening to both sides of the story at the border, in a rather foolish but very typical Colombian move he decided the only way to enter the country would be under an assumed name with a fake passport. He crossed the Costa Rican border successfully but ten days later he'd been unlucky enough to be asked by several police officers to show some identification and he had pulled out the false document.

So here he was. His lawyer said the case was cut-and-dried, that the car charges were a hoax, and that walking around with a fake passport wasn't such a big deal in this part of the world.

Francisco gave me his lawyer's phone number to verify his story. I took it, thinking that I would call just in case, but I really did believe what Francisco had told me. What was worse, I found myself sadly wishing that the two of us would be able to walk out of the gate together once visiting hours were over. But, of course, I knew this was impossible.

All too soon the prison bell rang. Over the loudspeaker boomed an authoritative voice. "The visit has come to an end. Please make your way to the front entrance."

"They want us to leave," Francisco said. "Guess we'd better go."

He walked me to the gate. "So, what should we do now?" I asked. "Shopping, the beach, maybe catch a movie?"

"Why don't we grab a bite to eat?"

"I'm starved."

"Me too. Wait a minute," he said, slapping himself on the head. "I just remembered, I have somewhere I have to be."

"What a shame," I said.

"What a pity," he echoed.

"Actually, I'm going to be pretty busy for the next few days. But I think I'm free on Sunday from 8 A.M. to noon."

"Where should we meet?"

"Why don't I see you here again? You seem to like this place."

"All right," I said, quickly pecking him on the lips. "Don't be late."

"Isn't it great?" Jessica said to me the next day, while milking Lorenzo, her family's cow. "Who ever thought we'd have boyfriends who were roommates!"

Apparently Cellblock A-2 was a prestigious place to be. The day before, we'd read in the paper about a high-ranking government official who had been caught trying to sell cocaine. "He's in A-2," she said excitedly. "We'll have to ask Olman and Francisco if they know him."

In addition to the advantage of being able to network with top government officials, hanging out with a man who was incarcerated began to feel strangely safe to me. During the next few visits, I shamelessly poured out the darkest secrets of my life to him in part because I knew that soon I would leave. Getting seriously involved with him was so unreal that it posed no danger; it was a fantasy that couldn't possibly be. Before, my international flings had ended with my departing flight. This one only existed from 8 A.M. to noon on Thursdays and Sundays.

In between those days, I would hang out with Jessica and occasionally with her business partner and friend, Maritza, trying out strange Costa Rican fruits and teaching my friends English swear words. But this proved to be a bit of a challenge.

"Shit," I told Jessica, when she asked me to teach her a bad word in English.

"Yeah, yeah, I already know that one."

"Fuck."

"Yeah, I know that one too."

We went through the list: bastard, dick, pussy—but she'd heard them all before. And this was a woman whose only other English expression was "Happy New Year."

"What is it you want to know how to say?"

She thought about this for a minute. "I know," she said in Spanish, "teach me how to say, 'I sucked him off and then kissed him, spitting the cum into his mouth.' "

"Jessica, I thought you were a virgin!"

"I am, but Maritza's been talking to me."

"Maritza!" I said, looking at my other Costa Rican friend in a whole new light. Apparently she'd learned more than just a few

English swear words from her boyfriend, Marco. There was just one problem with her relationship, she explained. Marco only wanted to see her one time a week.

"You should have Marco arrested," I advised her. "Then you'd get to see him two days, on Thursdays and Sundays."

"And you'd get to talk to him on the phone every day," Jessica chimed in.

This was a bit of a ritual with us. Every day, sometime between seven and eight-thirty at night, Jessica and I would sit in her kitchen, eating and chatting, waiting for the phone to ring. This arrangement presented just one small problem. Jessica's parents were often huddled around the table at this hour and she had yet to tell them about her boyfriend's change of address. What she had explained was that he was in northern Costa Rica for several months because of his job and he could only call her once a day.

This fib worked rather well until I started getting a phone call too. "Take care of yourself, Olman," she'd say, ending the call and handing the phone to me. "Wendy, Olman wants to say hello to you too." Telling Olman I was thinking of him, that I was looking forward to seeing him again may have seemed a bit overly affectionate, but fortunately, Jessica's parents never said anything.

Every time I had started up a relationship with someone in Los Angeles, it had been the norm to have sex first and ask questions about each other later. There was no "Where were you born?" "What is your family like?" "Who should I contact in the event of an emergency?" The guys I became involved with revealed more information to their employment applications than they ever did to me.

However, the man I was currently seeing didn't live in Hollywood or Santa Monica or Pasadena, which meant that sex was definitely out of the question—he wasn't free to come over to my place, and although I went to see him at his place twice a week, staying the night was not a possibility. After all, Francisco had 230 other roommates.

With our situation the way it was, there was nothing left to do but fall back on spending quality time together. Over the next few weeks, we continued to delve into the inexhaustible well of subjects we had to talk about. I discussed California and Arizona and he went on about Cauca and el Valle; I mentioned American Coke and he explained about the Colombian kind.

On the few occasions when the strain of translating my stories into Spanish became too exhausting for me, we would sit on a blanket spread on the ground, my head resting comfortably on his lap while he sang to me. Slowly I was beginning to distinguish the *baladas* from the *boleros,* the *cumbias* from the *vallenatos.* Sometimes he would write down the lyrics to his favorite songs and hand them to me as visiting hour drew to a close, timidly turning them over like secret love notes.

I was even growing accustomed to the amount of effort required to see Francisco. I was getting used to the early mornings, the long prison lines, the women patiently waiting outside with their shopping bags filled with food. There was a camaraderie there. Everywhere else in Costa Rica, I was a *gringa,* an outsider. But at the prison, I was a woman whose man was locked away. This mutual circumstance was bigger than issues of culture or race. They treated me as one of them.

How easy it was to arrive in a new country, how simple to brush up on a foreign language, to taste new foods, learn new customs. How difficult it was to leave.

Several days before my flight was scheduled to depart from San José, as I sat alone in a café writing in my notebook over a strong cup of Costa Rican coffee (while Jessica took care of some errands for work), I thought back on all that had happened to me in this country so far—meeting Michel, Jessica, then Francisco. How had I managed to get so involved with the place?

A month earlier, I had planned to lounge on the sands of white beaches, drink pineapple drinks laced with rum, dance late into the night, and plunge myself into the warm waters of the Caribbean. I had done none of those things. So why was I struggling with the idea that soon I would have to leave?

As I scribbled my thoughts down, fittingly enough, a group of noisy and enthusiastic American backpackers filed in to the café and settled in at the table next to mine. By now, I knew their type well. These travelers sauntered their way through Latin America, weighed down by nothing but their backpacks, their specially designed gear offering ideal weight distribution, lightweight aluminum frames, and a wide assortment of pockets that were perfect for quick storage of Swiss Army knives, portable alarm clocks, and collapsible silverware. I knew—I too had read the catalogs.

On my previous trip to Costa Rica before Jessica had shown up, my loneliness had made me want to be part of them. Walking past them in the streets of San José, having given up Christmas and then Michel, I had longed for one of them to start up a conversation with me. I had wanted to discuss the inane details of traveling, notes about where to go and how to get there, details as insignificant as the brand of jeans it had seemed so essential to be wearing in high school. But now I realized that it was too late. What these people had to say about traveling seemed as worthless to me now as the prom queen's advice on what type of lip gloss to be using. They were so far removed from my notion of Costa Rica that I really had nothing to say to them.

Just like the popular kids at high school with their homecoming parties, proms, and football keggers, these travelers had their own obligatory events, a list of required sightseeing that in order to be one of them, you had to necessarily attend. But I didn't have the right brand of extra-durable, element-resistant traveling jacket and never would. Hell, I didn't even own a backpack.

"So what have you been doing the whole time you've been in Costa Rica?" It was such a simple question for them, something they responded to with a long list of place names. But for me the answer required a degree of self-revelation that I reserved for those able to understand.

My real friends were the ones who knew the details of my life. In spite of all my whining about Jessica's dragging me to a prison, I had to admit that I had a deep respect for her. She was a tough but emotional nineteen-year-old who refused to follow in anyone's footsteps. And as much as the thought frightened me, I knew that Francisco too had become my friend. We both possessed the melancholy souls of those with unconventional lives, those who are poorly understood—who in each other's presence finally lose their loneliness.

I forgave Francisco for not being able to say good-bye to me at the airport. Apparently, there was something he just couldn't get out of. But Jessica and Maritza were there.

"When will we see you again?" Jessica wanted to know as we stood in line at the "migration counter," where travelers waited to get exit visas stamped in their passports.

"It may be a while."

"When? A month? Two months?" Maritza asked.

"It will take me a while to arrange things. I have to do one more freelance job, go to the consulate, get a visa."

"But you don't need a visa to visit Costa Rica," Jessica said.

"No," I smiled. "I just need one if I want to live here."

My two friends looked at me and then each other. "You're joking," Maritza said.

I thought over what it was I had in Los Angeles. I had a successful freelance writing business, a lovely apartment with wood floors that I'd spent years decorating with antiques. I had a car, a budding screenwriting career, and connections with the most important bartenders in town. And what did I have in Costa Rica? A guy in jail, a Costa Rican family, and two friends, one of whom had just spent the past week sleeping on her floor.

"See you in July," I said.

I hugged my friends one last time and started toward my gate, passing the point through which nontravelers were not allowed to pass.

"You have to come back, Wendy," Jessica called after me.

"Don't worry, Jessica," I yelled back, trying out the phrase she had taught me. "Don't worry."

Of course, I'd be back. After all, there were beaches to swim and volcanoes to climb. And besides, there was still one prison I hadn't yet visited.

Chapter Six

The Exit Strategy

At some point during our temporary separation (Francisco remained in prison; I was back in Los Angeles), the unexpected happened: I made a commitment to Francisco. Other couples did this all the time, moving gradually toward a life together, eased in slowly through late-night champagnes and shared morning coffees. With Francisco, it was all or nothing. It meant giving up Los Angeles, giving up my hard won freedom, giving up other men.

It had not been an act of faith. I had not made any conscious attempt to give relationships one more chance, nor did I think to aim one more time in the direction of responsibility. It was not something I even thought over. I had survived war-torn Beirut, communist Cuba, illegal entry into some of the world's most threatening places, yet here I was, powerless in the face of one man.

I wanted to understand what was happening to me, to categorize it the way my father had taught me, to explain it. But my analysis always came up short. There were a hundred reasons to commit to a man and a thousand reasons not to commit to this particular one, but I did it anyway, not because I should or shouldn't, because it was good or bad, the right thing or the wrong thing—but because it was the only thing that occurred to me.

My existence became divided up into moments spent speaking to Francisco and moments spent waiting to speak to Francisco. My life in Los Angeles ceased to exist—it was just time spent waiting—waiting for the phone to ring, waiting to hear his voice. And each call was an unbearably short eight minutes, counted off second by second by a guard with a stopwatch—enough time to say, "I miss you, I'm thinking of you, I'll be back for you," but not enough time to tell him about my day or the funny article I'd read in the paper or about what happened the other morning in line at the drugstore. And it was certainly not enough time to tell him about the pit in my stomach, the gut instinct when things began to feel not quite right—not with him or with us, but with his situation.

The pieces of news foretelling what was to come had begun falling into place one by one, lined up like dominoes ready to topple at the slightest pressure. At first, the lawyer had assured us that Francisco would see the light of day before the month had passed. Once thirty days had gone by, the lawyer simply shrugged his shoulders, offered no explanation, and prescribed patience as the best remedy at this point. And after two months had gone by and the attorney no longer visited Francisco or accepted his calls, I resorted to a number of expensive but necessary phone calls to the lawyer myself. Each time, upon hearing Francisco's name, he abruptly hung up on me.

I was concerned, but from a distance of twenty-seven-hundred miles, my options were limited. I sent Francisco five hundred dollars to find another attorney and did my best to stay focused on the task at hand: getting out of Los Angeles. Once I was in Costa Rica, I would be able to take control of the situation and help him out. Until then, there were so many personal errands I needed to check off my list in order to make it back to him—subletting my apartment, selling my car, sorting out my essential (i.e., portable) belongings, getting certifications and identifications, visiting government agencies, and canceling every membership in my name, which turned out to be so problematic that I began to suspect I was the only American who had ever moved out of the country.

"Is there a reason you are canceling your subscription to *The New*

Yorker? Have you been dissatisfied with your service?" the female voice at the other end of the line had asked during a phone call earlier that week.

"No, no problems at all. It's that I'm leaving the United States," I had politely explained.

"I see. But don't you want to continue receiving the magazine? That way you can read the past issues when you get back."

"No, you see, I don't know when I'm coming back."

Given the woman's uncomfortable "uh-huh," I figured that saying that I belonged to a tribe of cannibals would probably have been less shocking. Sure, Americans left the country all the time. Unlike me, however, they all planned on coming back.

After a week of repeating this news and having grown used to the astonished silence at the other end of the line, I finally realized the positive side of my unique situation: I had the strongest ammunition ever invented against obnoxious telemarketers, a crafty, overzealous bunch of people who normally had a response to just about anything. "You don't have any money right now? Pay later." "You are a busy person and don't have time for this? This timesaving device will save you hours." "You just got your arm amputated and aren't interested in a free tennis racket? Not to worry. Your trial membership also includes a free prosthetic limb."

Telemarketers had rebuttals for any conceivable situation, every situation, that is, but one—they had neglected to sufficiently prepare for the news that their intended customer had imminent plans to move to the Third World. I could actually hear the shocked look on their faces, feel the uncomfortable pause as they rifled through their papers, hoping to come across the scripted answer that their supervisor had promised would work in any situation, and, finally, the anxious clearing of the throat and the ultimate defeated words, "Well then, have a nice day."

In addition to the never-ending quantity of small details I was working out in order to leave the country, there was also the slightly larger issue of how I would support myself. Counting the checks that had yet to come in, I was going to have about sixteen-thousand dollars to tide me over, a decent chunk of money that would magically stretch five times further when converted into *colones* and spent in Costa Rica. Plus, there was the chance that I would be able to telecommute, doing some boring but well-paying business writings for Hughes Aircraft from Costa Rica.

Of course, the final obstacle to overcome was breaking the news to my folks. Happily, my parents' move had already been precedent-setting, so my disclosure didn't phase them in the least. They saw it as their eldest daughter simply following in their footsteps. Besides, now that they were safely settled in their home in Bolivia, having me in Costa Rica would mean I was that much closer.

Granted, I hadn't quite let them in on the whole Francisco situation, but this was what our familial fondness was founded on: lack of information. I had also never spoken at length about any of the other men who had passed through my life—and it didn't seem to be the ideal moment to begin the process of self-revelation, now that my current boyfriend lived in a prison.

My friends in Los Angeles as well as my sisters actually did have all the details, but they still remained characteristically supportive. Heather was all for it, Catherine gave it the thumbs up, my buddy Michael offered his blessing, and Lisa sat me down and said, "You know, most people taking this kind of step, leaving the country and all—I'd say they were running from something. But with you, it's different. I think that you're actually running *to* something."

She was right. But not even she could have predicted the situation I was about to get myself into.

Four days before I was due to leave, something odd happened—Francisco failed to make his scheduled Wednesday morning call. I checked to make sure the ringer was on, that the cord was plugged in to the wall, that there wasn't a message on my voicemail. But there was nothing.

I spent the entire day fidgety and anxious, hoping that it would hurry up and get dark so that sleep would rid me of the pit in my stomach. I even went to bed with the phone by my side in the hopes of a call in the morning, even though I knew it was unlikely. Prisoners followed a regular schedule—if one of them failed to make his Wednesday phone call, there were no make-ups the following day.

At seven A.M., however, the phone actually did ring. At the other end of the line, I heard a tiny depressed voice that I barely recognized as Francisco's.

Delivering bad news within eight minutes does not allow for subtlety or procrastination. "I've been arrested," he said.

I didn't understand how they could arrest a man already imprisoned, but Francisco continued, "There was a breakout. They claim I was the mastermind behind it. I had nothing to do with it. And they've transferred me to La Reforma, a high-security prison."

There was silence while I tried to take this new information in. Francisco must have suspected what I was thinking so he added, "Please, tell me you're still coming."

The thought of another false charge against Francisco was terrifying, but it wouldn't deter me. In my life, I had always gone after whatever I desired with a single-minded determination—the bleakness of the situation wasn't enough to scare me off.

What had made me pause was the tiny worry that the new charge against Francisco might turn out to be true. I didn't seriously believe Francisco was capable of lying to me, but I had been lied to before and I needed to be sure.

I had just four minutes to make up my mind. There was no way to call him back, no possibility of deciding another day.

My mind reeled. Three months had gone by. There had been long letters, reassuring calls. Three months of longing, waiting to see him again. It felt so real to me. But emotion didn't count. Feelings could deceive. To answer, I needed logic, cold hard rational thought.

There were just three minutes to go. I had to make up my mind, decide my fate.

Then it hit me. Francisco was supposed to be released any day. Every official had told us as much. Even the prison guards believed it. He was as good as a free man, no reason to treat him like a criminal. Francisco had never lost hope. And that was it, the reason I needed. A man who believes he is going to be freed doesn't gamble everything on a risky escape attempt. It wouldn't make sense.

"I'll see you in three days," I said.

There was just a minute left to go and there was so much left to say, but it didn't matter. I would see him in three days.

I arrived at my new Costa Rican home with a suitcase, a carry-on, and a tremendous hangover. Not knowing when they were going to see me again, my friends had planned a small going away party the night before and managed to ensure that I left the country drunk, happy, and quickly—before there was any time to even consider backing out.

But just like airplanes, all drunks eventually come down, and the next morning I found myself in San José, burdened with fully functioning reasoning capabilities, the disadvantage of which was that I had to think about what I was doing with my life. The thing was, getting on an airplane had always been as easy as drinking piña coladas, because tucked away in my pocket I had always had a nice safe return ticket, and tucked away in my mind was the knowledge that I could always come home.

But this was no round-trip. This was one way, all the way. My belongings were now packed into two pieces of luggage and a cardboard box, which caused me some dismay when I realized that the cabdriver picking me up would have no difficulties whatsoever fitting everything I currently owned into his small Toyota Tercel.

Of course, there was a bigger problem facing me, and that was the fact that although my things fit very nicely in that cab, they could not remain there indefinitely. At some point I would have to take them out and I wasn't sure exactly where this was going to be. Luckily, Jessica was home.

"Don't worry, I found you a place to live," her bubbly voice informed me over the phone. "It's a one-room guest house owned by a family in Santa Ana and they're expecting you. It's next to the butcher shop, the white house with the white fence."

"Great. What's the address?"

"I just gave it to you."

This was one of the anomalies of the city of San José. There were rarely street names and the buildings were never numbered. So a Costa Rican address read something like this: "From the Park Morazón, go one hundred meters to the south, fifty meters west, and where you see the Beer Cheap sign (sometimes covered up by the line of people in front of it), enter the alley. We're located right across from the fat man who usually sits at the corner."

The whole thing got further complicated any time an address included a bank, because every financial institution in the city had nearly the same name. There was the Bank of Costa Rica, not to be confused with the National Bank of Costa Rica, which was completely different from the Popular Bank of Costa Rica.

My own address was pretty solid by Costa Rican standards. "Next to the butcher shop, the white house with the white gate" actually fit on a standard-sized envelope, the only inconvenience being that I would have to send out change-of-address cards every time the family I would be staying with decided to paint the house.

"You're skinny. I'm going to make you fat." These first words I heard after hauling my things from the cab and knocking at my new abode were uttered by a pudgy woman in her forties who kissed me on the cheek, introduced herself as Cloti, and took me around to the backyard to show me my new place: the tiny detached room without a kitchen or a phone that I would be calling home.

"You must be Wendy. And your husband?"

"My husband?"

"When will he be arriving?"

"My husband will be arriving . . ." About never, I thought, marriage being one of the few bad habits I had managed to avoid. "You must mean Francisco," I said, wondering what stories Jessica had primed my new landlady with.

"Francisco, yes, that's right. And where is he now?"

"That is a very good question."

It *was* a good question; however, it seemed that Jessica was the one with all the answers when it came to queries about my life. Luckily, Cloti changed the subject, there being something more pressing that she needed to know.

"Your husband, tell me, is he very attractive?"

It was not a typical Latin American query. "What does he do for a living?" "How many brothers and sisters does he have?" "Is he a drug trafficker?"—these were the questions I usually got when people found out I was dating a Colombian. But Doña Cloti wanted to know about Francisco's physical features.

"Actually, he looks a lot like me. Blue eyes—"

"Blue?" she asked, moving in closer. "Is he tall?"

"One hundred ninety centimeters," I said, hoping that this was the correct conversion for six-foot-two and not sixteen-foot-two as I feared it might be.

"Oooooh. That's tall."

"Fat or thin?"

"Thin, but a nice chest. Strong arms."

She gripped me about the arm and in a hushed tone asked, "Wendy?"

"Yes?"

"Does he treat you well?"

I had been a bit puzzled by this first conversation, but I would soon find out what it meant. Two days later, over a breakfast of bread thick with butter and topped with sweetened condensed milk (her desire to make me fat was nearly succeeding, kept at bay only by the forty-five-minute run I put myself through every other day), Cloti asked me, "Wendy, how long has it been since you've seen Francisco?"

"Three months now."

"Don't you think it's strange that he's not with you?"

Knowing that the obstacles keeping us apart included a large fence, forty-five armed guards, and several locked and barred exits, I didn't think being separated was all that peculiar. After all, I'd dated men whose psychological walls had kept us far more distant.

However, Doña Cloti knew none of this. What she thought (thanks to the story that Jessica had fed her) was the following:

- Wendy was a nice American, who like most of the nice Americans who had lived in her house before, had moved to Costa Rica to enjoy the beaches, volcanoes, and tropical beverages.
- Wendy was married to a nice Colombian, who unlike most nice Colombians, had nothing to do with cops, prisons, or breakouts.
- The nice Colombian to whom Wendy was married was currently in the country of his birth, starting up an import-export company, after which time he would make it to Costa Rica to begin living with his nice American wife who had never visited a prison.

These facts were necessary, according to Jessica, because no one from Costa Rica ever went to jail. (Other than her boyfriend and the fifty-two hundred Costa Ricans who made up the prison population.) Besides, Santa Ana was a small community and everyone there seemed to be far more interested in what was growing in their neighbor's garden than what they were harvesting in their own backyard.

Adding more sweetened condensed milk to her bread, Doña Cloti continued, "Don't you think it's strange to be married to a man who is living in another country?"

After dating a man in jail, being involved with someone living on another continent was starting to sound pretty run of the mill.

"You don't really know what he's doing when he's that far away," she continued.

"No, I guess not."

"Does he have another woman there?"

"No," I laughed, picturing Francisco living with nearly two thousand men.

"How do you know?" she asked bitterly. "My husband has another woman and a family up north that he has been visiting and supporting for over twenty years."

Infidelity, it seemed, was the national pastime in Costa Rica (probably because they realized their soccer team wasn't going anywhere). Any time I sat down in San José's central park for more than two minutes, I was sure to be approached by a married man older than my father who would invite me to have drinks, dinner, or sex with him. Luckily, I'd amassed a lot of experience dealing with unwanted advances (being one of the few women I knew who had been felt up on four *continents*) and I knew how to deal with these sorts of things. The best tactic was having them arrested by a dozen armed police officers, a helicopter spotlighting them from overhead.

I had learned this little trick when I was nineteen years old, working alone in a retail clothing store in Los Angeles, when a man had entered, taken off his pants, and begun masturbating in front of me. Not sure exactly what to do (the path to the door being blocked by a large penis), I suddenly remembered the panic button. Two minutes later, a very surprised naked man was arrested (literally with his pants down) by an armed group of police officers, a helicopter flying overhead while my distressed manager explained to me, "Wendy, it's not a panic button. It's an armed-robbery button."

However, my last time in Costa Rica I had realized that this tactic was not going to work very well in this part of the world because the cops at the jail were propositioning me as often as the prisoners. Having discovered that being married was often the only way to get rid of a Latin advance, I had told one particularly persistent guard that I was at the jail because I was visiting my husband. Not one to be deterred, he had responded, "Well, if he's in prison, how's he going to stop you from going out with me?"

They say that patience is an acquired skill, but I have yet to learn where exactly one goes to acquire it. Personally, I think that the ability to sit calm and contented for long periods of time is located next to the gene that controls the gallbladder, which is very unfortunate for the many members of my family, including myself, who as a result of surgery, happen to be living without that particular organ. Luckily, neither gallbladders nor patience is required to sustain human life as long as one avoids greasy foods and prison visits. However, as fate would have it, my first week in Costa Rica, these two vices formed the basis of my existence.

Since I didn't have a kitchen, Cloti insisted that I take my meals with her family, which made her suddenly responsible for the bulk of my dietary intake. She'd pile up the outdoor patio table with chunks of fatty meat, oil-drenched rice, and butter-soaked bread as I sat down to an al fresco lunch with the entire clan: her, her husband, Yuliana (her eleven-year-old daughter), her younger brother, and her mother-in-law.

Besides putting up with the heavy food that was wreaking havoc with my fragile digestive system, my bigger worry was Francisco. Upon arriving in the country, I had had to wait three days for my scheduled "special visit" with him, which I had acquired as a result of being a foreigner, under the pretense that my stay in Costa Rica was limited. After what felt like an interminably long period of time, the days had finally gone by and on the scheduled morning, I was able to slip out of the house without Doña Cloti's knowledge, sparing me the usual barrage of questions that followed any time I left or returned. A bus dropped me off in the center of Santa Ana, where I flagged down a cab to take me to the prison.

"Where to?" the driver asked, reaching over to open the door.

"La Reforma," I said, suddenly remembering Jessica's warning to not give out too much information to anyone. In her paranoia, she'd even come up with a list of explanations in case the cabdriver began asking any questions.

"Tell him you're a foreign exchange student and your project is to study the prisoners in Costa Rica."

"Jessica, that's not exactly the type of project the Rotary Club endorses."

"Oh. Well then, tell him, tell him—"

"What?"

"Tell him that you're a missionary and you're bringing food to feed the prisoners."

"Carrying just one bag of groceries? What do I say—that I'm going to multiply the bread and the fishes?"

"Okay, okay, let me think."

"Jessica, I don't see why—"

"I've got it! Plants!"

"Plants?"

"Yes, tell him that you like plants. See, there's a nursery not too far away. Have him drop you off there and then you just have to walk four kilometers to the prison."

"Four kilometers?"

"Yeah, it's not far. What is it? Two, three miles?"

Luckily, the cabdriver was not that curious about what I was doing visiting La Reforma; he was far more interested in what I was doing visiting Costa Rica.

"Have you seen a lot of beaches and volcanoes?" he asked enthusiastically.

Fortunately, I had finally learned the appropriate response to this question. "The Caribbean—it's always been one of my favorite seas."

La Reforma was located outside of San José, in a valley surrounded by lush green mountains, with air so fresh it hurt my smog-accustomed LA lungs. Not even the prison officials had the power to remove the hills and trees, and I imagined that being an inmate there couldn't possibly be so bad.

Of course, Francisco didn't have access to this view. Being the supposed leader of the now famous breakout, he had been transferred to top security, where he was kept locked indoors all day in a cell the size of my dining room, which he shared with seventeen other inmates.

To visit him, I had to go through a body search and two inspections of the bag of groceries I was carrying. The prison guard smashed my bread, ripped open my carton of orange juice, and confiscated my keys (rather, the one key I now owned). Then I was invited to take a seat and wait.

This seemed to be the ritual at La Reforma, what I would come to refer to as "invisible lines." It didn't make a difference what time I arrived, if there were people ahead of me or not, no matter what, I was going to have to wait. My visit had been scheduled for nine o'clock that morning but at ten-fifteen, I was still there, sitting on a bench, waiting.

"I realize Francisco's very busy and has a ton of things to do," I said to the bored guard sitting in front of me, "but do you think he'll have time to see me today?"

"I'll see what I can do," he said, picking up the phone. "Hey Ramírez, about Sánchez—is he coming up or not?"

Ten minutes later, I heard footsteps making their way up the ramp. And finally, three months, ninety days, 2,160 hours, thirteen bottles of rum spent waiting for him, there he was, walking toward me.

It is a strange sight seeing the man you are in love with wearing handcuffs. It's even stranger when you were not the one who put them on him. Accompanied by a guard, he made his way up the path to where I was standing. Thin when I had left him three months ago, he was gaunt and pale now, walking too slowly, his head down, steps that were far too small for his six-foot-two-inch frame.

Later I would learn what he had been through: a day in solitary confinement in a cell four feet wide, the stench of urine making sleep impossible, where the only attention he received was to have half of the cell doused in a continual stream of water. Then the transfer to a new prison, where the "hole" had been even worse, even smaller, this time full of cockroaches and mosquitoes that had slept on the concrete with him. Finally, the move to top security, where he had been robbed of everything except the clothes he was wearing and where he was still sleeping on the concrete floor (not having the twenty dollars necessary to buy himself one of the prison mattresses).

I embraced him silently, not encountering the words to tell him how sorry I was. Instead, I was reminded of someone else's words, a line from a Billy Bragg song I had heard long ago: "This isn't a court of *justice*, son, this is a court of *law*." This is what the legal system is doing to an innocent man, I thought. This is what the justice system is doing to my life.

This was a special foreigner's visit, but because it was in addition to the regular Thursday and Sunday visits that went on all morning, it was just an hour long. I was being eased in slowly. The next visit would be in *mediana cerrada,* top security at the prison, where we'd sit on the cold, damp concrete floor of a windowless room inhaling the stench of raw sewage, surrounded by the menacing looks of murderers and rapists.

We were ushered into a small room filled with rows of desks

that reminded me of my junior high school classrooms. God only knew what went on here. Reeducation, I imagined. We both squeezed into desks made for people half our size, and Francisco reached for my hand silently. There was so much to say that neither one of us knew where to begin.

We had a full hour, the first time in three months that we had been allowed to speak for so long, but the additional time made finding the right thing to say all the more difficult. We hadn't expected anything of an eight-minute phone call, but sixty minutes was enough time to share something meaningful. There were so many things to reveal, so much that had happened to us both during our months apart, but there was a guard outside counting off every second, ensuring that we didn't get away with even a minute more than we had been rationed. With so much pressure to cram everything in, my mind raced to sort out the most important facts.

At a loss and in an attempt to inject a little levity into a moment that was in desperate need of some cheer, I finally asked, half joking, "So, what have you been up to while I was gone?"

Francisco laughed. "Well, for one thing, I moved, as you can see. What do you think of the place?"

"Well, it seems pretty safe. Bars on all the windows."

"Not a single thief could get in here."

"I bet. Say, Francisco . . ."

"What?"

"How the hell am I going to get you out of here?"

The situation did not look good. Francisco had made front-page news in two of San José's papers: "Leader of Prison Breakout Faints During Escape." "Colombian Leads Escape of Seven Prisoners from San Sebastian." They'd even publicized his name on the television news. But what had been lacking was Francisco's version of the story.

He explained it this way: Seven inmates had attempted an escape and were all caught outside of the prison, half of them while

making their way down the wall, the others after they had successfully cleared the building and were fleeing down the street.

"And you?" I asked Francisco. "Where did they catch you?"

"The night it happened, everyone knew about the breakout, but I
never even left my cell. The next morning while I was on the phone
with my daughter, an announcement came telling me to present myself at the director's office. I showed up and that's where they told me.
They informed me that I had been the one to mastermind the escape."

I knew Francisco was a smart guy and could probably plan a
breakout in his sleep, but to actually carry out the escape while he
was sleeping, now that was a different matter entirely.

"What kind of proof do they have?"

"One member of the escapees says I did it—he has always hated
me and has found a way to get back at me. But there are thirty prisoners in my section who've signed a document testifying that I never
left my bed."

Before we knew it, a guard came to give us a warning that time
was nearly up. It seemed unfair to me. I had paid for this hour with
three months of waiting and now it had been eaten away, minute by
minute, just like that.

"I can't believe I already have to go."

"Wendy, I can't believe you actually came."

He was right. At least we were in the same country now. At least
he wasn't going through this alone.

"I'm going to do everything I can to get you out of here." I meant
it, even though I had no idea what I could possibly do. "In the meantime, do you need anything else?"

"Do you think I could borrow your lipstick?" he said with a grin.

"When a man loves a woman very very much—and they're
married—well, the man puts his penis in the woman's vagina and

that's where babies come from." That was the extent of my mother's advice on relationships and that useful bit of information I received (and subsequently imparted to the rest of the neighborhood children) when I was just four years old. I searched my brain for anything more recent. Of course, there was my mother's description of what sex was like ("it's like a tickle that you don't want to stop"), but other than that Mom had been pretty brief on the topic of relationships and had neglected to mention any helpful tidbits on getting my boyfriend out of a Costa Rican prison.

I was clueless how to begin, but at least I knew who would sympathize with my situation. Jessica could certainly relate and maybe she'd even offer some helpful advice—"Ten tips for freeing the man you love" or something like that.

"What about bail?" she suggested as we strolled from the ice-cream shop to her office, raisin-rum purchases in hand. "That's what my lawyer's trying to do. I want to get Olman out, see what his chances are and if it looks like they're going to convict him at his trial, we'll leave the country before the court date ever comes up."

"That's your plan?"

She nodded.

"You'd leave the country just like that?"

She shrugged her shoulders.

"What about clearing Olman's name? What about your family?"

"Wendy, where do you think you are? If you think you're going to find justice here, forget it. If I have to choose between having Olman in a foreign country and not having him at all, I'll leave here in a second."

Was my chance of seeing justice in this country as slim as all that? What about due process, what about a fair trial, what about all those rights with Latin names that we had in my country—habeas corpus, e pluribus unum, carpe diem. Maybe Jessica was just uninformed. Surely, Francisco's attorney would take a more proactive view.

The next day, seated in a café in downtown San José, I expressed my concerns to the slightly chubby, mustached man across the table from me. "What about habeas corpus? What about gluteus maximus? Isn't there anything we can do?"

"There is nothing you can do but wait," Francisco's attorney casually informed me, apparently unaware that he was speaking to a woman without a gallbladder.

"Easy for you to say," I said, watching him digest his greasy food with ease. "Exactly how long am I going to have to wait?"

"Trials around here take a while. It shouldn't be more than, say, three or four more months."

"They're going to keep an innocent man in prison for a total of ten months?"

"Probably longer. There are three charges and we're going to have to wait for three different trials."

"Well, what about bail? How come bail hasn't been set in his case?"

"He's already had three different lawyers. Among them, they've requested bail a total of five times. It's always been denied."

"Why?"

"It's tough to get bail on behalf of a foreigner. As a Colombian, there is nothing tying Francisco to Costa Rica. The court assumes that the minute he's set free, he'll flee the country."

"So there's nothing we can do?"

He shook his head. "Just be patient and wait."

In eleventh grade, while my classmates were off doing typical Montana things like preparing for snow, preparing for the rodeo, or preparing to overthrow the U.S. government, I would shut myself away in the library, away from big trucks, big cows, and big guns and lose myself in a world of literature. It was on one of these cold winter days that I was first introduced to Latin American culture viewed through the lens of linguistic determinism. According to the author (whose name I never did pay any attention to—who spent time remembering things like writers' names?), Latin Americans' *Weltanschauung* was reflected in the way their language was constructed, and a simple analysis of the sentence "*El plato se me cayó de las manos*" ("The plate fell from my hands") was enough to illustrate the Latin American view of life, the universe, and gravity. Unlike most Americans who lived in a world of cause and effect and believed themselves to be primarily in control of the events that happened to them (reflected in the American way of expressing this same sentiment: "I dropped the plate"), the author claimed that Latin Americans viewed life as something that just happened. "I didn't drop the plate. The plate simply fell from my hands." For Latinos, life was lived in the passive tense.

Ten years had passed since I first encountered this text (what I had come to refer to as the "nonflying saucer theory"), and now the evidence supporting this idea was all around me. In Costa Rica, disaster was seen as something that simply occurred. Who were you to try and avoid it?

"Sorry, I'm late for work. I got drunk last night."

"Oh, I was almost angry—but if you got drunk—well, what are you supposed to do?"

Of the Costa Ricans I had met, none of them wore seat belts, and given the number of cabs that had left me stranded halfway to my destination, few taxi drivers could even be bothered to remember to put gas in their tanks. The electricity went out constantly, but no one complained. Buses broke down all the time, but passengers were rarely refunded the cost of their tickets. And open manholes were to be found along nearly every city sidewalk, but no one sued. After all, nothing could be done to avoid such calamities—if it was God's will that you should fall through an opening in the street, land in a pile of hepatitis-infected crap, and break a leg, so be it. The Lord worked in mysterious ways.

This Costa Rican laissez-faire may have worked well for Jessica and Francisco's attorney, Jorge, but I was a woman of action and I needed a more American way of dealing with my problems. I needed to *do* something, not lounge around slurping papaya juice while things just happened. I needed the advice of people who saw the world as I did—so I figured I would try and plead my case at the U.S. embassy.

Walking up the steps of the imposing grandiose building, I knew I had come to the right place. The American flag waved proudly in the wind, marines guarded the entrance, and you could practically smell the apple pie wafting through the air. They would help me out here, I figured. I was one of them. I was a citizen of the most powerful country in the world.

At the entrance, I smiled patriotically at the guard, envisioning myself as a brunette Elisabeth Shue seeking solace at the embassy in the movie *The Saint*:

> Chased by a Russian mafioso, Elisabeth Shue's life in peril, it's only fifty steps to the U.S. embassy. Then thirty, twenty, ten. She's finally three slow-motion steps away. The Mafia guy reaches out to grab her shirt and at the embassy gate she screams, "I'm an American!" These are the magic words. The gates are flung open as Ms. Shue runs through them in slow motion and embraces the marine who so kindly opened the gate.

Granted, my entrance wouldn't be quite as dramatic.

"I'm an American," I said, smiling patriotically at the guard and walking past him.

"Whoa! Hang on a sec," the guard said, blocking my path. "You think you can just stroll on in?"

Gee, they hadn't asked Elisabeth Shue for ID. I pulled my passport out and handed it to the guard.

"Now I need to check your backpack."

After performing a thorough search, I figured I was free to go.

"Where you going there, sweetheart?" the guard asked me.

Damn, how many Russian mafiosos did a girl have to be chased by to be let onto American soil? "What now?" I inquired, hoping this marine knew he had ruined all chances of getting a hug from me. He pointed to the metal detector and I walked through.

Inside the embassy, after deciding that American Citizens' Services was the office that would probably deal with my particular problem, I entered a room that looked more like a DMV than my romantic notions of a U.S. embassy. A group of bored-looking people filled the waiting room, whiling away the time until it was their turn to plead with a U.S. official.

"Number 56," a woman's voice called out in a dull monotone over a speaker. "Number 56," she repeated.

A tall, blond man stood up and walked up to the counter as I took a number and sat down to wait.

After half an hour of reading pamphlets on topics such as staying healthy overseas and registering at the embassy during travel abroad (I noted with some concern that there was nothing on freeing your loved ones from a Central American prison), my number was finally called.

"Seventy-eight," the monotone voice announced.

I stepped up to the counter and addressed the woman behind the bulletproof glass, hesitating to announce my problem out loud to the room of waiting people. "It's kind of personal. Isn't there any place I can discuss this matter in private?"

"I'm sorry. It's not allowed for security reasons."

"Well, I have a legal problem," I said, hesitating before speaking the words out loud into the microphone in front of me. "My boyfriend is in prison here. They've accused him of several crimes and they are holding him without proof, without bail, and without having set a trial date. He's been there for seven months now. I was hoping you could offer me some help."

"I have a list of attorneys," the woman informed me, as formal as if I had just asked her to withdraw three hundred dollars from my account. "However, I'm required to inform you that their appearance on this list does not constitute endorsement by the U.S. embassy. These are simply the names of attorneys compiled by Americans who in the past have claimed to have positive dealings with them."

"I already have an attorney."

"I'm sorry. That's all I can do."

I was completely appalled. I wanted a new U.S. embassy, one that actually helped its citizens, offering safety, comfort, and hugs at the entrance. I needed help, not a scripted answer, carefully worded to avoid any potential legal ramifications.

My look of distressed agony must have been pathetic enough to make its way through even the bulletproof glass, because the expression on her face softened and exactly as I had imagined in my fantasy, she reached out to me with all the comprehension in the world and gently asked, "Listen, are you okay?"

I wanted to tell her that of course I wasn't okay, that I had left everything behind in the United States—my friends, my apartment, my clothes, my furniture, my car—and now I was stuck in a foreign country in love with a man who I couldn't even go to the movies with. I lived in a tiny room without a kitchen or a phone and had to pretend that everything was fine every time I sat down to lunch with the people who were not my family. My boyfriend was in prison for crimes he didn't commit and no one in this country gave a damn, least of all his attorney. And my own country, with all its rhetoric about justice and the pursuit of happiness, didn't intend to lift a finger to help me. How could I possibly be okay?

This is what I wanted to say, but there was a plate of bulletproof glass between us and these weren't the kind of things you said over a microphone. So I shrugged my shoulders and uttered, "Sure," as I walked out of the embassy and onto the rainy streets of San José.

• • •

Ironically enough, I had come to Costa Rica with the fantasy of finding my perfect life. I had imagined an idyllic existence, shaded by palm trees and warmed by ocean breezes—Jessica, Francisco, and I in our reclining beach chairs lined up side by side. In the land between two oceans, I planned to live out my second childhood, away from the meaningless monotony of life controlled by the clock, of always having somewhere important to be. I had never counted on a prison breakout to interfere with my fantasy. It wasn't the kind of thing I generally needed to figure into my plans.

Now I had all the time in the world in a country bordered by two breathtaking coastlines yet my potential beach buddies both had other commitments. These days, when Jessica wasn't visiting Olman, she was preparing to visit Olman, and now that Francisco had been transferred to La Reforma, her path rarely crossed mine. Even more distressing was the situation with Francisco—the possibility that he would one day join me at the beach was beginning to look more and more remote.

On my last visit to Costa Rica our visits at San Sebastian had been casual, friendly, even fun. In fact, it was one of the things that had so impressed me about Francisco—he had remained amazingly upbeat in spite of such trying circumstances. San Sebastian had been filled with lesser offenders (lots of the men were there for simply failing to pay their debts), but La Reforma was a completely different place, a prison that averaged ten murders a year. And Francisco was in top security, living with the country's worst offenders. A week after I arrived in the country, a knife fight had broken out in the next cellblock that had left Francisco nervous and depressed. "The guards just stood back and watched," he explained to me, trembling. "They bet on who would win."

Two days later, a group of prisoners had crept up on Francisco while he was sleeping, surrounded his bed with newspaper, and lit it on fire. Luckily, only Francisco's legs had gone up in flames and he was spared his life, but I couldn't look at the blisters on his skin without wondering how much more time he'd be able to hold out there.

If there was ever a time for me to flee responsibility, this had to be it. Other men had required less of me and I still had fled the burden of their problems. Yet the very gravity of the situation was what compelled me to stay. My boyfriends in the past may have lost a few nights sleep over me; I knew that Francisco would be in serious jeopardy of losing his life.

Although Francisco was mild mannered and gentle and had little chance of holding his own in a fight, he had an advantage over the other inmates: my money. Twenty, thirty, forty dollars a week was a small price to keep Francisco alive, and with it he was able to make friends, offering cigarettes, food, and a bill now and then to the other prisoners who knew better than to bite off the hand that fed them.

This was what it had taken for me to commit to the long haul with a man—the threat of my boyfriend's impending death if I didn't. It was the universe's big joke on me: "You can't deal with another person's neuroses, annoying personal habits, and bad morning breath? How about this: Fall in love with a man who loves freedom as much as you do and now, let's see here, we'll have him locked away in a prison." Good God, even destiny had a sense of irony.

Reaching out and touching someone was relatively simple if you had to dial a mere seven numbers plus an area code, but making contact with my family was getting increasingly complicated. It wasn't just the elaborate international prefixes, the problem of being heard over crackling Third World phone lines, the prohibitive cost of a ten-minute call; the reason I didn't pick up the phone to have a detailed heart-to-heart about what was currently happening to me (i.e., the whole boyfriend/prison/breakout inconvenience) was because of the fact that it was completely impossible to have a serious conversation with my parents. Sure, they were a blast to hang out with when everything was fine, but when it came down to the worst tragedies of my life, my parents had always proven themselves useless in a crisis.

Recently I had traced the path from birth to this point in my life and all the places where things had gone wrong, guess who was to blame. That's right: Mother & Company, headed by none other than Cathie Dale herself. (My father was like a low-ranking receptionist at Make Wendy's Life Miserable, Inc., sharing a small portion of my resentment but only loosely affiliated with this baneful institution.)

I submit the following examples as proof:

Difficult life circumstance endured by Wendy Dale	*Circumstance due to error on behalf of Mother & Company?*	*Circumstance a result of other factors?*
1. Painful childhood	Yes	No
2. Genetic predisposition toward intestinal problems	Yes	No
3. Living in a car (first occurrence)	Yes	No
4. Putting self through college with no outside financial help	Yes	No
5. Living in car (second occurrence)	Yes	No
6. Getting boyfriend in prison	Mostly	A negligible amount

Conclusions

Wendy Dale's unhappiness quotient is due in large part to the actions taken on behalf of Mother & Company, with blame laid at 98.4 percent and 1.6 percent for Mother & Company and other factors, respectively.

ℐf you will bear with me for a minute, let's examine the chart in detail. Items 1 and 2 are relatively apparent: Cathie Dale was obviously a witness and at times a participant in issues ranging from childhood through doctor visits. Item 3 has been discussed previously in this book (see page 25); however, Items 4 and 5 may require some additional explanatory materials (see Addenda 1 and 2 below):

Addendum 1

PUTTING SELF THROUGH COLLEGE WITH NO OUTSIDE HELP

A scene by Wendy Dale
(Based on a true story)

Wendy, age nineteen, a student working for five dollars an hour struggling to put herself through college recently wound up in the emergency room, where she was diagnosed with a stomach ulcer. She is currently at her sparsely furnished apartment in Los Angeles going through her mail. She opens up a letter and stares at it.

WENDY: *(takes a deep sigh)* Woe is me. Oh dear! Whatever shall I do? Five hundred dollars for my recent stay in the hospital where I was diagnosed with a very painful stomach ulcer as a result of the extreme stress I am under working three jobs where they pay me five dollars an hour while I try to put myself through school. Oh well, I guess I'll just have to pay for it with my tuition money that I worked so hard to save.

Two weeks later Wendy is making a phone call from her sparsely furnished bedroom in Los Angeles. (She does not have a cordless phone. She could not afford one.)

WENDY: *(takes a deep sigh)* Mom, would you please loan me five hundred dollars for my tuition at UCLA?

CATHIE: *(in a very mean voice with no compassion whatsoever)* Wendy, you know how expensive our trip to Morocco, England, and Spain was. Plus we just bought a new car.

Addendum 2

LIVING OUT OF A CAR

(A sequel to "Putting Self Through College with No Outside Help")

Another scene by Wendy Dale
(Based on a true story)

Wendy, age twenty, a college student who has paid her own tuition for two years now has wound up with no place to live due to a psycho roommate who changed the locks on their shared apartment. (Note: This psycho roommate also took most of Wendy's things.)

Wendy is at a pay phone with her car full of clothes in a very bad neighborhood that any normal mom would not want her daughter to be in.

WENDY: Hi, Mom, it's Wendy.

Wendy's mom is in a very nice house eating very expensive chocolate imported from Germany. It's obvious that Wendy's mom does not have any serious problems whatsoever.

WENDY: Mom, my roommate just kicked me out. I'm homeless. I don't have anywhere to live.

CATHIE: *(takes a bite of chocolate)* That's must be very hard for you, Wendy.

An hour later, Wendy snuggles up in her car, rubbing her hands together trying to get warm.

WENDY: It sure is hard being homeless. I guess it's going to be a long night.

Granted, this was a somewhat one-sided version of events as they occurred but it was the way the scenes played out in my head. And it was relatively close to the truth: My mother did refuse to loan me tuition money after I'd wound up in the hospital. She claimed that they just couldn't afford it right now since they'd just returned from Europe and purchased a new car. And I really did live out of my car for two months, to which my mother's only response was that my situation was undoubtedly very difficult.

These were the reasons I never told her any of the significant details of my life. These were the things I held against her—against *her,* not my dad.

Granted, my father had played his part in my life problems, but my mother was the one I blamed, mostly because my contact with him had always been so limited. He was continually working long hours to support the family, in part because my mother rejected the notion that she should get a job. He was never home when I called so any information to be imparted to him had to go through her first. I never got to plead my case with him directly, so I absolved him of any blame. Besides, we all knew that my father didn't care for material comforts. How could we accuse him of depriving us of something that he didn't value himself?

Now that I was alone in a foreign country facing what was undoubtedly the most difficult obstacle of my life, I had a very good reason not to call. I desperately needed someone to be there for me, but I already knew what my mother's response would be: "Oh, that must be very difficult for you."

I had survived tough circumstances before. Even homeless, I hadn't gone running to my parents'. I would do it again. Costa Rica wasn't going to get the best of me without a fight.

The embassy offered no help, Francisco's lawyer was discouraging, and my own formal legal training was nil, but I figured that I had years of experience in its twin discipline: ad copywriting. I reasoned that if I could sell shampoo to bald men and fireplaces to residents of Malibu, it shouldn't be that much of a stretch to sell justice to Costa Rican officials.

"The first step," I said to Francisco excitedly at our next visit, suddenly knowing what I had to do, "is get you out on bail. They've already denied you this five times because they say you're a foreigner with no ties to Costa Rica and that you'll flee if they release you."

"So what do we do?"

"What we do," I said, uttering the triumphal phrase that had gained me prestige and hefty paychecks in corporate offices across Los Angeles, "is construct a public-friendly image of you."

Francisco let out an appreciative "ohhhhh."

"The way I see it, they view you as this foreigner who came to Costa Rica with every intention of stealing your ex-wife's car. We're going to create a different image. You are a father, a responsible citizen, a man with a Costa Rican daughter who considers this country his home. What is missing from your files is the other side of the story: that you lived and worked here for four years, that you have a daughter here, that you have good credit, anything that will show you're a respectable human being."

"Respectable human being?" Francisco let out a dejected "ohhhh."

"Yes, I realize. I have my work cut out for me."

Knowing that Francisco had worked at a travel agency for three years in Costa Rica, I figured I could get a good reference from his employer.

"Where do you think your old boss is now?"

"That seems to be the million-dollar question, doesn't it?"

I wasn't the only one looking for this man; half of Costa Rica was after him. The travel agency where Francisco worked had turned out to be a front for laundering Yugoslavian money, which meant that even if I could get in touch with him, his reference probably wasn't going to do Francisco a lot of good.

"But the travel agency manager will help me out," Francisco said.

"Great. Where do I find him?"

"Well . . ."

Francisco wasn't exactly sure where his old manager was (it had been more than three years since Francisco had left Costa Rica the last time), but he had a friend named Rafael Quiroga who worked at another travel agency and could help me get in touch with him.

The next day in search of Mr. Quiroga, I entered the largest, most bustling travel agency I had ever seen. After stumbling into three offices and failing to find reception, I finally found the right room and asked a busy secretary wearing a headset where I could find Rafael Quiroga.

"Rafael Quiroga? Rafael Quiroga? Carlos, is there anybody here named Rafael Quiroga?"

"I don't know any Rafael," the man said, gliding past the receptionist.

A woman carrying a stack of files rushed by. "Do you know anyone here named Rafael?" the receptionist asked her.

"Ask Jaime," the woman responded, sliding out of the room.

The receptionist made a phone call. "Jaime . . . yes . . . yes . . . anyone here by the name of Rafael Quiroga? Great, thanks."

"There's a Rafael Quiroga in Accounting," the receptionist informed me. "Down the hall, third office on the left."

Sure enough, there was a Rafael Quiroga in Accounting. He just wasn't the Rafael Quiroga I was looking for.

"You must mean the Rafael Quiroga who works for us on a contract basis," the wrong Rafael Quiroga informed me.

"Where do I find *him?*" I asked.

"Talk to Rolando in Administration, down the hall, exit the building, go around the corner, and it's the first door on the right."

"Rafael Quiroga, of course I know Rafael Quiroga," Rolando in Administration said, reclining in his chair. "I have his number here in my Rolodex. Let's give him a call."

He dialed seven numbers and waited.

"Rafael Quiroga, please—what? What number have I called? And there's no Rafael Quiroga there? Sure? Well, thanks."

"Wrong number," he said to me with a shrug, replacing the useless card back into his Rolodex. "But he has to come in here tomorrow. Would you like to leave him a note?"

"Sure," I said, frustrated. "Could you loan me a pen?"

"Hey, anyone around here have a pen?" Rolando shouted out.

I left a note and returned the next day.

"Any sign of Rafael Quiroga?" I asked Rolando.

"Yeah, he came by and it turns out he's not the Rafael Quiroga you're looking for. But he's a private investigator and he said he'd help you find the guy if you'd like."

"Do you have his phone number?"

"Sure, it's right here in my Rolodex."

I had once discovered that the only cure for depression was to do the thing I least wanted to. What I least wanted was to get out of bed, to face my circumstances, but in doing it every morning, in forcing myself out of the house, my depression subsided into a constant nervous anxiety. And focusing on Francisco's case kept my mind occupied, preventing my thoughts from convincing me how impossible the whole situation was. Because if I were to face the facts, there really were no grounds for hope. The Costa Rican legal system was based on the Napoleonic Code, which meant that a man was guilty until proven innocent. But try proving that someone *didn't* do something. And add to it the fact that his only alibis were criminals.

Nevertheless, I was determined to get Francisco out on bail. His ex-wife, Laura, had made him out to be some stranger who had stolen her car, but I wanted to show that they lived together for two years, that Francisco was a responsible, well-off family man who had no need to go around stealing automobiles.

Francisco did not make the job easier. I would pry him for information at every visit and he would give me vague leads, often remembering someone's first name or the neighborhood where the person lived, but he couldn't recall last names or addresses.

At least he could recall his previous address—I figured his former neighbors would provide good references. Better yet, I learned that one of them had notarized the bill of sale when Francisco originally purchased the car. Her testimony alone would be an incredible plus. She was an attorney, she had firsthand knowledge of the fact that Francisco and Laura were not mere acquaintances (as a neighbor, she watched them walk out of the same apartment building every morning), and she would remember that Francisco, not Laura, had been the one to purchase the car in the first place. There was just one problem—for the life of him, Francisco could not remember her name. But he gave me the address: "From the gas station in Rohrmoser, take a right, go three blocks, make another right, and it's the last building at the end of the street, a white gated complex with a guard standing outside."

With the help of several friendly strangers and two cooperative bus drivers, I finally found the gas station. Wandering through the streets of what had once been Francisco's neighborhood, I couldn't help but get some sense of the frustration he must be feeling at all that he had lost. He had had a job, a nice apartment in a good part of town. Eventually he had even owned his own business transporting tourists to the beach. They'd had two cars, a daughter, a life together. Four years later, this was what it had degenerated into: his ex pressing charges against him. Out of bitterness, vengeance, or greed, she claimed they had never had any relationship—"an acquaintance" was the way she referred to him. "I am not married to him or anything of that nature." And her declaration had landed Francisco into prison. This was what love had turned into, I thought, suddenly getting cheered up tremendously—after all, up until that point I thought *I* had ended my past relationships badly.

I found the building where Francisco used to live and did my best to explain to the guard the purpose of my visit: I was there to see a guest whose name I did not know. No, I did not have the number of her apartment, but I was sure she lived in one of the eighteen units.

This was good enough for him. His advice was to go door to door until I found the person I needed, which seemed like a reasonable enough plan.

As I entered the complex, I thought it was pretty ironic that all of the units were numbered. After all, the building didn't have an address and the street didn't have a name. I imagined the complications of living there, trying to write out your address on any official form: "From the gas station in Rohrmoser, it's five blocks, a white gated complex with a guard standing outside." And then you'd add: "Apartment 5."

The apartments were pretty much identical. I walked through the gate and knocked on the first door.

"Hi, is your mom home?" I asked the little girl who opened the door.

"No, she's working today. Do you want to talk to Jimena?"

"Jimena? I don't know. Is Jimena a lawyer?"

"No."

"Is your mom a lawyer?"

"No. She's a seamstress."

Okay, so it wasn't the most complex detective work, but at least kids could always be counted on to tell you the truth. I thanked the little girl and kept up my search.

At the next three apartments, there wasn't much to do—no one seemed to be home. Finally, at Door Number 5, a woman in curlers greeted me.

"I'm trying to find a lawyer . . ." I began.

"I'm a lawyer."

"Oh, do you know a man named Francisco? He lived here with his wife, Laura. They had a little girl."

"I've only been here for a year and a half."

The only other person in the unit to open the door was an elderly man in his seventies who had no information.

"Come back after six," the guard helpfully advised me as I glumly walked through the gate. "Everyone should be home by then."

Living with the territorial rules that governed prison life, conveniently enough Francisco and I had become friends with an alpha male. Daniel was a Cali cartel drug smuggler who had taken to us, and he and his wife always insisted we share their seating area and their lunch. Not ones to refuse the hospitality of anyone in regular contact with drug kingpins and hit men, Francisco and I would gingerly take their food, feeling much like the insecure kids in high school intimidated into inhaling as the bong got passed around.

"Come on, everyone is taking some," the large Colombian would insist, brandishing a huge piece of chicken. "Just try it. You'll like it."

Sure enough, we did. But chicken was just the beginning. Nancy Reagan was right (or was it Frito-Lay?): You couldn't take just one. Next came the thighs and legs and drumsticks. Then it was on to potatoes, rice, and cake. Nibbling on a cookie, I suddenly understood what parents needed to do to get their scrawny kids to eat—forget telling them about poor starving African children. Tell them about the poor Americans forced to eat under the pressure of the Cali drug cartel. ("There are people in Central American prisons who don't get to choose what to eat. They have to eat whatever the drug kingpins offer them—or else! Now be a good girl and just take a few more bites.")

In spite of this new strain on my gallbladder-deprived gastrointestinal channels, this new friendship ensured us a spot by the wall, the most coveted area on prison visiting days. Daniel and his wife would always call out to us, "Over here, guys! Come on, take a seat," and Francisco and I would obediently march over and squeeze onto the twin mattress they had laid down on the concrete floor.

Because Colombians were both feared and hated, their tight-knit group sheltered Francisco as a result of his nationality. And the fact that I was an American protected him as well.

We had become a celebrity couple of sorts at La Reforma. It was a mystery to everyone how a tall, blue-eyed *gringa* with the world at her feet who lived at Disneyland in a golden house ten miles away from the Statue of Liberty (this was how most Latinos I came across viewed Americans) would choose to spend her time in a prison, in love with a poor Latino. After all, these were Colombians—the only Americans they'd ever met in the flesh had been DEA agents.

At every visit, at least one starstruck prisoner would gingerly trek over to us to find out if I really was from the United States, and with great ceremony he'd extend his hand for me to shake. My role had grown bigger than me—I was like a young Evita Perón suddenly forced out unprepared onto the balcony.

"Uniting the north with the south," Francisco would dramatically add, as if our lust were doing two whole continents a favor. "She is from the United States. I am from Colombia. As nations, we are politically at odds with each other. As individuals, we are in love."

We were friendly with everyone but the Costa Rican *basuqueros,* the drug addicts who smoked an unrefined version of cocaine, supposedly worse for you than crack.

"Stay away from him," Daniel cautioned me one day, pointing to a scruffy-looking guy with long hair and a beard who stumbled erratically across the room. Daniel paused for emphasis, making sure I understood the gravity of what he was about to say. "He does drugs!"

I couldn't help but note the irony of the situation. "Francisco," I whispered, "isn't Daniel the one who got caught with five hundred kilos of cocaine?"

"Yeah."

"So, why is he warning me against guys who do drugs?"

"Wendy, Daniel *sells* drugs. He doesn't *take* them."

Francisco didn't find this at all odd and apparently neither did any of the other Colombians. Selling drugs to them was no big deal, just an astute business investment. But taking drugs—you might as well admit to stealing small babies and chopping them up in a blender.

In between prison visits, nothing was going right. As part of my ongoing private detective campaign, I'd made two more trips to Francisco's old apartment building and had finally tracked down the attorney I'd been seeking, but she had been cold and irritated, explaining that she just didn't have time to get involved.

I'd also had a considerable number of meetings with a lawyer at the Colombian embassy who was constantly friendly and willing to see me, but who'd merely look at me with a considerable amount of amusement, as if I were going to tell him at any minute that I was just kidding. "Gotcha! I'm not really going out with a man at a prison." He also didn't offer much help—he expected me to update him on the progress of Francisco's case, not the other way around.

Another strategy I was pursuing was trying to get my journalist's credentials, figuring I could always use the press to sway Francisco's cause. I had been undergoing a significant amount of paperwork at the Colegio de Periodistas, but each time I went in to check on the progress of my file, the staff members requested one more new document, and it didn't seem like they'd ever get around to issuing me a press pass.

Even worse was the deterioration of my friendship with Jessica.

Months earlier back in Los Angeles, Francisco had needed five hundred dollars to switch attorneys, so I had sent a money order to Jessica, figuring she would make the necessary arrangements. After all, sending funds directly to prison wasn't the wisest or most practical idea. (I could just imagine the DSL guy arriving at the prison gate: "Delivery for Mr. Sánchez. I'll need a signature please.")

What I had recently learned from Francisco's lawyer was that Jessica had given him only half of the money and kept $250 for herself.

When I questioned her about it, she had a reasonable explanation: "You can't give the lawyer his fee all at once. If you do, he won't do anything." I couldn't imagine our attorney doing anything less, but I heard her out anyway. "You give him the other half at the end when the case is over."

This made sense. "Well, would you mind giving me the rest of the money? Now that I'm here, I might as well keep the funds in my own account."

She stalled for a minute. "Sure, I'll get it to you on Friday."

Friday came and Jessica provided some excuse. Then next Friday came and then the next. Three weeks later, furious and frustrated, I finally marched up to her office and confronted her. "You spent it, didn't you?"

She didn't answer—but she didn't have to. I was so full of rage by this point that I no longer even knew who was to blame. I was sick of lawyers. I was sick of the legal system. I was sick of bullshit. I was sick of lies. But most of all, I was sick of this country that was so full of crap.

"Fuck Costa Rica!" I said and gave her door one final slam behind me.

Chapter Seven

Love in the
Time of Papalomoyo

L uck chooses strange moments. It can strike quite innocently one day when you're sitting on the couch eating a
Zero bar while watching a rerun of *Charlie's Angels*. It can happen
walking through the forest, skipping down the street, or even on
those days when you're stuck at home amusing yourself by staring at
the wall (a good thing for us writers who put great stock in wall
watching). Luck's arrival is unpredictable, arbitrary—just because
good fortune decides to show up one time is no guarantee that it will
choose that same set of circumstances again—which is a good thing.
Because luck decided to step in one day while my boyfriend was imprisoned in top security, accused of a crime he didn't commit, and I
really had no desire to repeat that particular experience.

Had I known where I was going to run into good fortune when
I woke up that morning, I'm not sure I would have bothered. I had
an address, but it was, after all, a Costa Rican address.

This time, based on Heather's information (my sister was spending her summer as an intern at the Organization of American
States), I was led to CODEHUCA, a human rights organization in
San José. The guard outside opened the gate and I made my way to
reception, where I was informed by a polite secretary that I had arrived at the *institute* for human rights and not the *commission*. Where
was the commission located? From the restaurant Spoon, one hundred meters west, then twenty-five meters east. I asked why not go

190

just seventy-five meters west, but she just shrugged her shoulders and told me that was the address she had.

I managed to arrive with the help of a taxi, a compass, and a lot of luck. I got out of the cab and stared at the human rights organization in front of me and realized with some dismay that I was staring at the *court,* not the *commission.*

A guard instructed me to "go up the hill, make a right, go straight fifty meters, and it's the third door on the right."

By the time I arrived, I had forgotten all about my boyfriend in jail and pleaded with the receptionist to do something about all the suffering brought about in trying to find obscure addresses in Costa Rica.

Luckily, she had a sense of humor, and after explaining my rather sticky problem to her, she informed me that the attorney I needed to speak to was in Nicaragua at a conference but if it would make me feel better, I could talk to the legal assistant. I told her what would really make me feel better would be two Valiums and a shot of whiskey, but as it appeared she was freshly out of both, I would settle for whatever it was she was offering.

The legal assistant, Saúl, was not what I expected—which is to say, I was not expecting Saúl. This was not some Costa Rican lawyer who would look me up and down, meet my gaze with a cold grimace, and tell me there was nothing he could do—this was Saúl, someone I had gone to UCLA with.

I was nearly three-thousand miles from home in a small Central American country where I had walked into an obscure office—yet the door I knocked on happened to be opened by a person I knew. The coincidence was mind-blowing.

"What the hell are you doing in Costa Rica?" I asked, still reeling at my good fortune.

After a lot of oh-my-Gods and I-can't-believe-its, he caught me up on what I had missed of his life in the past six years. While I had been busy collecting boyfriends from prisons in Costa Rica, Saúl had been busy collecting degrees, the latest from UCLA's School of Law. Not really that into collecting paychecks, Saúl was now working virtually free for CODEHUCA, trying to do something to change the plight of unfortunates in Third World Central American countries.

We reminisced for a while about old times, gossiping about the friends we had in common, who was sleeping with whom (and who wasn't getting anything whatsoever), and then we got down to business.

"Drinks tonight?"

"You bet. I'll meet you here at five."

Bonded by liquor, nationality, and a mutual desire to see Francisco get out of prison, Saúl and I quickly became good friends. We had known each other only briefly in college but our bouts of drinking were having the effect of bringing us close fast.

As I ran between embassies, lawyers' offices, and government buildings, I'd look forward to our Fridays out, when we'd go to the university village, huddle together around a small table in one of the student bars, share secrets, and make each other laugh. He was the bright point in my otherwise lonely existence. Now that I was no longer on speaking terms with Jessica, it was such a relief to hang out with someone who knew the whole story of what I was going through, though ironically enough we didn't discuss Francisco all that much. For me, these nights were a time to escape—for a few hours over beer and Costa Rican appetizers, I was just a normal twenty-six year old again.

Our sober hours were spent together at the outdoor produce market eating El Salvadorian *pupusas* and browsing around as I explained to him the names of the strange Costa Rican fruits. This particular habit confused the Costa Ricans terribly because with Saúl being Latino, they figured he was *from* Costa Rica and they wondered why a *gringa* was telling a Costa Rican the names of foods he'd been eating all his life.

However, my platonic affection for Saúl was showing and was making Francisco a bit jealous. After learning that Saúl and I had a standing date for drinks every Friday night, Francisco complained, "Wendy, a man doesn't ask a woman out for drinks because he wants good conversation."

"Francisco," I explained patiently, patting him on the hand, "I was the one who asked *him* out for drinks."

Seeing that Francisco wasn't particularly pleased with this response I added, "Besides, he's not just my drinking buddy; he's your human rights representative."

There were two possible ways to have sex with someone who was at La Reforma. The first was to pay two dollars to a prisoner to stand on the lookout for any guards while you and your companion went to a secret enclosed area and did the deed hidden behind a sheet. Not wanting to shell out the cash, Francisco and I chose the second option.

To get conjugal visit rights, Francisco had to submit himself to a host of HIV and STD tests while I had to undergo an interrogation by the social worker.

"Name?" the dour-faced woman behind the desk asked me.

"Wendy Dale."

"Nationality?"

"American."

"Occupation?"

"Writer. Journalist."

The woman looked up at me for the first time.

"Journalist?"

"Uh-huh," I said with a smile, conveniently neglecting to mention that I had been a *celebrity* journalist and that the weightiest news

I had ever tackled was an interview for a gay magazine with (straight) actor John Lithgow.

"Do you know why your companion is in prison?" the woman asked me, no emotion registering on her face.

"He was transferred to top security for a prison escape for which there is no proof."

"I see. And why is it that you are requesting your conjugal visit privileges?"

To have sex, you dummy, I wanted to say. "I would like to be a support to my companion in this difficult time," I managed to get out with a straight face.

Apparently pleased with my answers, the social worker scheduled our conjugal visit for the following week. There was just one small, insect-sized problem. Its name was *papalomoyo*. As of my first visit to Central America, I had lived in dread of this parasite, which has the nasty habit of imbedding itself in the skin of its host and living there contentedly for an indefinite period of time. It wouldn't have been so bad if the insect had chosen my leg, my arm, or my foot as its new abode, but one week before my scheduled conjugal visit, I began to fear that every time I took a seat, my butt wasn't the only thing I was sitting on. There was a dime-sized swelling on my left cheek that had begun to make sitting and sleeping nearly impossible.

"Looks like *papalomoyo* to me," Doña Cloti said to me after I had immodestly removed my underwear and allowed her to take a look.

"Lucky insect," her husband declared, after learning where it had chosen to make its new home.

Not thrilled with the idea of sharing my hindquarters with any creature not of my own species, I decided to take matters into my own hands: I was going to scratch.

"Well, whatever was there isn't there anymore," the doctor said to me several days later, looking at the quarter-sized hole that remained in my left cheek. "But you have a terrible infection."

He brought out a mirror and showed me the purple circle I had on my rear, the source of the incredible pain I was feeling. "Give it a couple of weeks. The antibiotics should clear it up by then."

But I didn't have a couple of weeks. I only had two days to have an insect-free, infection-free bottom.

As it turned out, it was nothing like your typical Hollywood movie love scene. There was no champagne or soft lighting. No orchestra played in the background. The scene was a musty-smelling room containing a stained twin-sized mattress, cockroaches scampering about on the floor. The main characters were one limping American writer and one imprisoned Colombian. The script read: "They embrace." But in the end, not even a Hollywood film director could have imagined it any better.

Minutes passed. Days passed. Months passed. Francisco had spent eight months in prison, nearly two of them in top security. I had been part of his life for five of those months.

I had used my time to study his case, to learn the legal code, to gather evidence if and when he was going to have a trial. The lawyer had used the time to steadily increase his fee and to constantly remind me that we hadn't any proof.

I spent my Sundays with Francisco, arriving at the prison at six in the morning, waiting in the interminable line of women for the eight o'clock bell that would signal the beginning of entering the gates: prison guards requesting passports, checking lists, inspecting groceries, and performing body searches.

Francisco spent his time reading about famous criminals who had successfully escaped from some of the world's harshest prisons.

And finally, the letter came. Francisco showed it to me at our next Sunday visit.

"They know you're here," Francisco said to me.

"What do you mean?"

"They know that my girlfriend is an American journalist."

"And?"

"And so they cleared me of the prison escape charges."

The letter explained that there was "no irrefutable proof" implicating Francisco in the breakout and that he was to be transferred to minimum security immediately. Francisco was to be given more liberty, including library privileges and an hour outdoors each day.

We celebrated with Coke and potato chips, realizing the long way we had come to end up exactly where we had started from. Francisco was now in the same position as when we had first met: two cases facing him, two trial dates that had yet to be set.

By now, I had gotten used to the bustling scene outside the prison gates. Twice a week, on visiting days, enterprising housewives converted the whole area into an open-air market, hawking tamales, fruit drinks, and sundries such as toilet paper, vegetables, bread, cigarettes, and soda that shoppers could pick up at the last minute to take in to their incarcerated loved ones. However, the heart of all activity had nothing to do with the business transactions going on all around. Rather, it was the lines, the four roped-off rows filled with visitors (nearly always women) that set the stage for what occurred here.

I had learned the hierarchy early on. It wasn't based on power or beauty—it was a happiness hierarchy. Those in the first line, *indiciados,* were there to see men whose fate was still up for grabs, men who hadn't yet been given trials, who still had hope of being declared innocent and set free. Women in this line laughed, complimented each other's clothes, chatted away about their children and their homes, even spread out blankets and had picnics on the dirt.

The next two lines were quieter, filled with women whose husbands had been convicted, lesser offenders in either low or moderate security who were biding their time, waiting day by day for their debt to society to be paid. But the last line, *mediana cerrada,* was unmistakable. No one put on the finishing touches to her makeup or dished out cookies to her friends. This was the smoking line, the line of silent exchanged glances of commiseration, where the only question to be overheard was "How long does he have left?"

It had been my line for the past two months, the place I had waited hours at a time, counting the minutes until I would be allowed in. But today, as I climbed out of my cab and walked toward the handful of women who had already gathered at the roped off area near the entrance, it suddenly hit me how much Francisco's situation had improved. I had gone straight from the misery line to the line of hope.

After my two-hour wait had passed and the women began slowly filing into the prison, I realized that entering La Reforma from now on was going to be significantly less painful. Before, I'd had to go through a passport check, a body frisking, and then a detailed inspection of the bags filled with food I was carrying in with me. After this, I'd cross the prison courtyard, attempting to fend off the inmates who would tail me begging for money, and I'd head over to maximum security to begin the search process again. There they'd keep my passport, take away my keys, and rip apart all of the food I was carrying—squeezing my bread, opening my milk, and invariably confiscating one or two forbidden items such as fruit that fermented too easily or bug spray that was too flammable.

But today as I walked out of the first examination area into the courtyard, Francisco was there waiting for me. I wasn't going to have to go through a second intensive inspection, nor would we spend the next few hours in the dark fetid area of maximum security. We got to roam about outside in an area bigger than a football field, sit in the sunshine, and have a picnic on the grass. What a difference a prison escape charge makes!

Two days later, I learned that conjugal visit protocol for *indiciados* was going to be significantly improved as well. In the past, as much as I had enjoyed the "quality time" these visits afforded (not to mention the sex), I had always hated how unspontaneous they were. The joke about blocking off time on your calendar actually applied to me. Every two weeks, "have sex with Francisco" appeared on my list of things to do.

The planned nature of my love life made these conjugal visits feel just the slightest bit sleazy. Someone else was dictating when and where I was to have sex. Since this translated into four precious hours twice a month, Francisco and I tried to cram in as much as possible during our allotted time, and the unfortunate result was that quality took a backseat to quantity (backseat being a somewhat appropriate metaphor here). The first hour was great, but every subsequent hour was controlled by nervous glances at the clock, constant reminders of how little time remained.

What I hated even more was the dreaded knock on the door signaling the end of my visit and my subsequent exit to face a bunch of horny guards who always smirked, reminding me that they knew what I'd been up to for the past few hours.

However, now that Francisco was living in *mínima,* conjugal visits here were all night long. For the first time, we were actually going to be able to sleep together—and unlike other rendezvous in my past, there was no need to worry about him leaving when the sex was over—having a group of armed guards outside the door just a hundred yards away was enough incentive to cuddle for even the most commitment-wary man.

On the day of my scheduled conjugal visit, I arrived at the prison showered and perfumed, wearing my best lingerie, a bit frazzled as usual. The line was always short for conjugal visits, but if you arrived even five minutes late or forgot your conjugal visit ID card, you wouldn't be allowed in so I always showed up a bit nerve-racked, having checked and rechecked the contents of my bag a half-dozen times on the harried cab ride over.

After the usual inspection (frisking my body, rifling through my bags, inspecting my change of underwear, my bra, my condoms—God, how I resented this invasion of privacy), I waited by the entrance, until my assigned guard showed up to take me to the conjugal visit area in *mínima.* We sauntered across the prison court-yard, my escort moving at an unbearably slow pace, a man obviously getting paid by the hour. I was supposed to stay at his side until we arrived at our destination, but when I spotted Francisco in the distance, I gave the guard my best pathetic pleading look, and apparently an old softie when it came to young couples in love, he shrugged his shoulders and let me race on ahead.

Thirty seconds later, I was in Francisco's arms, hearts pounding, our lips all over each other's faces.

"I'm making you dinner," Francisco whispered in my ear once our lips had run out of respectable places to wander. He proudly held up a bag of groceries that I hadn't noticed before.

"Where did you get that?"

"There's a store here in *mínima.* I can get a pass to walk across the prison grounds and buy stuff there once a day."

At the prison minimart (I couldn't help but wonder how many times a day that place got held up), Francisco had picked up pota-toes, yucca, plantains, chicken, and rice. It was a nice gesture, but I had no idea what good the raw ingredients would do us.

"There's a stove, too," Francisco explained, grabbing my hand and leading me in. "Come on, I'll show you our room."

We wandered into a covered patio area equipped with a small outdoor kitchen. There was a sink, a double-burner stove, and an outdoor picnic bench. Next to the patio was a courtyard that was encircled by numbered rooms, a rudimentary Motel 6 in need of a good coat of paint—or at least a different color choice, something a little more romantic than florescent lime green.

"Isn't it great?" Francisco beamed.

I had to admit that it was. Twelve hours was an incredible length of time for us to get to spend together and we had the freedom to wander back and forth between our private room and the communal open-air area half the size of a basketball court.

We raced to Room 12, set down our bags, and suppressed the urge to fling ourselves on the bed until we had fitted it with the clean sheets that I had brought along for the occasion.

"It's a double," Francisco announced proudly, distractedly tucking in the sheets. On other visits, we had always shared a twin bed that we had struggled not to roll out of. "And we even get our own bathroom!" he added, pointing to the room off to the left. "Come on, let's take a shower!"

He left the bed half tended and nearly shoved me into the tiny room. Within seconds, we were both naked and standing in the cement-walled cubicle under the showerhead.

"Water!" Francisco announced, turning the knob. And it sure was—a gushing stream of cold water. I screamed in agony.

"Make it warm!" I insisted. But I noticed that there was only one knob.

"There is no warm. You'll get used to it."

Francisco joyously splashed me with handfuls of freezing water until I pleaded with him to stop. Suddenly serious, he began running his hand over the goose bumps on my arms, my waist, my hips, and then he embraced me, distracting my mind from the cold.

So making love in a prison shower wasn't the warmest or most romantic of places, but when it came to playing the game, "Where is the strangest place you've ever done it?" I was now guaranteed to win every time, hands down.

After we had dried off and gotten dressed (the bed still remained unmade), Francisco and I headed out to the patio area where we succumbed to the fantasy that we were just a normal couple out on a regular date. It was a childish thing to do—I felt too old to be playing make-believe—but it was a pattern we inevitably slipped into.

We were just two people sitting outside on a patio watching the rain. The illusion worked for a while. As long as I focused on Francisco's face or the courtyard, I could successfully avert my gaze from the bars that encircled our fantasy motel.

How simple my needs had become. Once I had dreamed of strolling along the Champs-Elysées, traveling by Italian gondola, munching on creamy Swiss pastries. I had even gone to Honduras thinking of heading to the Estée Lauder counter. How foolish these desires seemed to me now. They were the wishes of some other person, a woman who had little to do with my life.

Now I was content with the diluted fantasy that the man in front of me was my boyfriend (sometimes he became my husband) cooking me dinner in our home.

"It smells wonderful, honey. Are you sure you don't need any help?"

"No, dear. Just keep reading your *Harper's.* I'll call you in when it's ready."

Later we'd go for a walk, perhaps run into our friends on the street, watch a movie on cable before curling up together to sleep.

My fantasy was made all the more realistic by the very real dinner preparations going on in front of me. Francisco had refused my offer to help, and now that I saw the way he prepared the meal, I realized I probably wouldn't have been of much assistance to him anyway. Granted, I knew how to chop up vegetables, but I came from a wimpy country where we generally accomplished this activity with the aid of a knife.

"They don't allow knives at the prison," Francisco explained, noticing my astonished stare as I watched him dissect tomatoes, yucca, and parsley, using nothing more than the sharpened end of an aluminum can.

The stove was also a mystery to me. It looked like a hot plate, but instead of plugging the two burners in, Francisco expertly hooked the entire apparatus up to a hose connected to a metal canister filled with natural gas. And with one swift stroke of a match, the flame sprang to life. I tried not to look amazed, the way I was always impressed by men capable of shaking a few wires under the hood of my car and making a previously useless vehicle sputter and hum again, but I felt very much like Jane dropped suddenly into the unfamiliar jungle, forced to rely on Tarzan for the simple necessities of life.

I pretended to read my magazine but watched Francisco every time he wasn't looking as he added ingredients to the pan, lovingly stirred the soup, tested the broth for salt. I was thinking about him, but it was different than what I usually felt in the presence of men involved in my life. It wasn't desire or the wish to enflame his desire. In fact, it had nothing to do with sex. What I felt was safe.

It was a really stupid thing to feel. Any woman in her right mind would have known that prisons were not appropriate places to start engaging in *Good Housekeeping* fantasies. But some primal genetic urge surged up in me, stronger than logic, stronger than rational thought, stronger even than a lifetime based on uncertainty. And damn it all to hell, I felt safe.

Of course, it was a double-edged sword. Moments like this were part of the punishment too. In prison, you didn't get a minute of happiness without paying for it doubly, and I knew that the next day, walking back onto the streets of San José would be twice as hard, twice as lonely, the contrast twice as apparent. My hearth-and-home fantasy would be revealed in all its flaws. And I would be back to where I had started from, alone and frustrated, fighting a battle, only half aware of the rules.

"The pen is mightier than the sword." It was a nice enough quote, but you couldn't help but notice its inherent bias. After all, people who came up with poignant phrases like that were obviously writers and no self-interested pen wielder was going to come up with a maxim like, "You can hack any writer to bits with a saber"—not to mention a Colt Magnum or a Smith & Wesson. However, none of these arms were (nor ever have been) in my possession. The only weapon available to me was a metal-gray Macintosh laptop with binary capabilities, fully loaded with state-of-the-art software, powered by a rechargeable battery, and connected to a Hewlett-Packard printer.

As far as writers went, I was about as armed and dangerous as they got, ready to type out pithy phrases at an impressive seventy words per minute. All I had to do was ensure that the letter I had carefully loaded into my computer would strike its intended mark. Typed in twelve-point Palatino was a request for bail on behalf of Francisco.

Francisco had been denied bail at least five times, but I wasn't willing to give up hope. The lawyer's previous whiny request had basically amounted to "Please let Francisco out. He's been in jail for a long time." But this time, I had evidence. In the past two and a half months, I had come up with a declaration of good credit from the bank Francisco had repaid a loan to, his daughter's Costa Rican birth certificate, a letter from a friend stating that Francisco had a place to stay in the event of his release, the official registration of the travel business Francisco had owned in Costa Rica, and Saúl's letter from CODEHUCA stating it was a violation of human rights to keep a man imprisoned for eight months without benefit of a trial, a document that bore a great deal of weight. Even the lawyer recognized the logo at the top of the page and asked astonished how I had managed to come up with it.

I wanted to give him a snide answer, something like, "There are people who sit around waiting for things to happen and people who get out and go drinking with human rights representatives," but I just glared at him and said mysteriously, "I have contacts."

I handed him the letter that I had typed up in Spanish, commanded him to remove any grammatical errors, sign it, and deliver it to the court.

"What are we going to do if you get out?" I asked Francisco the next Sunday, after explaining the recent turn of events.

"I'd like to eat a steak, drink several beers, and make love to a beautiful woman."

"And then what?"

"Eat another steak, drink some more, and wake up in the morning with the same woman."

"Listen, I can probably get a job with AFP here as a journalist. I have a contact here and they look highly upon John Lithgow interviews and—"

"Wendy, I don't want to stay in Costa Rica."

"Francisco, I've just spent months gathering evidence to prove that you won't flee the country if they let you out on bail."

"Wendy, what do I have here? They've even taken my daughter away from me. After the articles that came out in the papers, my ex-wife hangs up any time I call."

I looked around us at the bars, the barbed wire, and the armed guards and asked myself the same question.

Three working days later, I trembled my way up to the fourth floor of the courthouse and requested a copy of the judge's decision. A very effeminate Costa Rican man sashayed his way to the counter and opened up the file. I picked up the paper and began to read slowly, picking apart the dense and complicated legal language. I went over the paragraph once, getting the gist of its content. Then I read it again, trying not to get too excited until I was certain of its meaning. However, after digesting the document a third time, I was positive of what it had to say: After having been denied bail five times, this time it had been set in the amount of a mere $250.

I stared at the words in front of me, not quite believing them. I had waited for this day for nearly six months—three of them spent helpless and distant in Los Angeles and just as long spent battling a second-rate legal system in Costa Rica—and, finally, it had arrived. We had done it. I had stuck it out. He really was going to come home to me.

I ran to the nearest bank and deposited the money into the prison's account as I had been instructed, and raced back to the court with my receipt. The same Costa Rican who had attended to me earlier informed me that Francisco should arrive at the house later that afternoon. "Hurry on home so that he'll have someone to greet him there. And tell him to behave himself," he added with a flamboyant wave of his hand.

"I will," I said, and rushed out of the building into a bright beautiful Costa Rican afternoon.

Not long after I arrived home, Doña Cloti came around to knock on my door, informing me that I had a phone call. I thanked her and raced into her living room, eager to give Francisco the good news. Unfortunately, Doña Cloti followed me in, hoping to overhear my end of the conversation, her attempt at vicariously living out the romances of young couples in love.

Since I hadn't yet found time to unravel the yards of stories that Jessica had spun for me (Doña Cloti still thought that Francisco was in Colombia starting up an import-export business), her presence posed a bit of a problem. I was going to have to relay the news to Francisco with a bit of skill.

"How are you?" Francisco asked me, in a low depressed voice.

"I'm fine and you're feeling better than you've felt in eight and a half months," I gushed, unable to contain my enthusiasm.

"What?" he asked, not picking up on my code.

"So where do you want to have dinner tonight?"

"In Paris, under the Eiffel Tower, with a bottle of red wine."

"I don't mean in your fantasies. I'm going to have dinner with you tonight and I want to know where you want to go."

"Wendy, what are you talking about—you don't mean . . ." Finally he was catching on. "They granted me bail?"

"Yes."

"When do I get out?"

"Sometime this afternoon."

After our phone call, I figured it was probably a good time to begin deceiving Francisco that I was actually a neat, organized person. The childhood industriousness induced upon me by my mother had been replaced with an adult laissez-faire attitude toward cleanliness and my room had been left basically unattended to for the past three months. Now seemed as good a time as any to begin the arduous task of trying to straighten it up.

The first problem I encountered was that I had nothing to clean it with. Doña Cloti, never one to let me go anywhere alone, suggested that her daughter accompany me to the store. Yuliana, a shy lovely eleven year old, ended up not only helping me haul the stuff home, but she also explained what all the cleaning paraphernalia was used for.

It wasn't that I was a completely novice housekeeper; it was that the brands that were familiar to me were nowhere to be found. Comet had yet to fly into Costa Rica and Joy in this country was non-existent. Dishwashing liquid wasn't even used by housewives here; instead, there was what I called "freeze-dried Comet": a green, gritty hockey-puck-sized mound of green stuff that came in a plastic container that had to be mixed with water to wash the dishes.

After overcoming this small hurdle, I was faced with another challenge: I needed something for the floor. Luckily, mops were plentiful in Costa Rica—it was the detergent that had me stumped. Noting the puzzled expression on my face, Yuliana came to my rescue again: "You have to choose the same color as your floor." Realizing I was still at a loss, Yuliana added, "It's red." Bypassing the blue, yellow, and green plastic bags filled with liquid the consistency of runny glycerin soap, I added a container of red floor cleaner to my shopping basket.

An hour later, Yuliana and I hauled our bags into the house where Doña Cloti was there to greet us. "You're going to clean your room!" she exclaimed, happier than I had seen her in months. It was a nice contrast to her failed bonding attempt upon my arrival when she had tried to exchange housekeeping tips with me which had been met by my blank stare.

Not knowing when Francisco was due to arrive, my game plan was to do the chores in order of importance. The first hour passed. I straightened up my bed and the bathroom. Then another hour went by. I cleaned the tub and toilet and mopped the floor. Another hour passed. I started cleaning the corners of the room with a tooth-brush.

It grew dark. Francisco still had not arrived. I decided not to worry and lay down in bed trying to comfort myself with a book. Nine o'clock came and went, then ten o'clock. At midnight I turned off the lights, wondering what could have gone wrong, finally giving in to the subtle premonition that had warned me all along that it was simply too good to be true.

At eight o'clock the next morning, I left my newly cleaned room (the odor of fungus having been replaced by a refreshing lemon scent) and arrived at the lawyer's office. Jorge was not in, but the receptionist who apparently had been well trained in her employer's favorite phrase told me that I was welcome to wait.

Two and a half hours later, Jorge strolled into the office and languidly put his briefcase down on the table. "What's new?" he asked.

"They let Francisco out on bail."

"That's great."

"But he didn't arrive at my house last night."

He seemed to realize that he was supposed to react to this as if it were bad news. "Hmmm, well, I'll have to check into it."

That was it. No explanation, no apology, just a wimpy excuse to get me out of the office and deal with the other frustrations of his day. I gave Jorge my worst glare and silently stormed out his door without as much as a good-bye.

Outside the building, I took a few deep breaths in an attempt to calm down, convincing myself that anger wouldn't do me any good. What I really needed was information and the best person to provide it would be Francisco.

In theory, Francisco had a phone number, but actually getting in touch with him was nearly impossible. In the past, I had tried calling him from a pay phone half a dozen times, which had only resulted in a busy signal. On several different occasions, I had even invested an especially frustrating hour repeatedly dialing the number, hanging up and dialing over and over again in the hopes that eventually the call would go through. But it hadn't worked yet. So why hold out any extra hope today?

If this had been a movie and not real life, my attempt to use the phone definitely would have proven successful. After all, I had logged a total of four hours of failed attempts. Any scriptwriter would have realized that the heroine had suffered enough. Time to give her a break. But this wasn't the way things worked in real life. I knew. I'd been playing the "having been through enough card" for several months now.

"Okay, whoever's in charge up there, I think this has been just about the right amount of suffering," I had silently repeated so many times during the past six months. "Time to make things go right for me for a change."

Apparently, this argument had not been terribly convincing. But what the hell—one more time wouldn't hurt. As I walked up to the pay phone, I decided to put in one final silent request. "Pleeeeaaase. Not for me. Do it for Francisco."

Stupefyingly enough, my phone call went through on the first ring.

"Hello?" I said in response to the guard's mumbled greeting, not believing my luck.

"Can I help you?" he repeated.

"Um, yes, Francisco Sánchez, please—could I speak to him?"

There was a wait of several minutes while the guard went to get Francisco. Finally, I heard his voice at the other end of the line. "I haven't been granted bail," he informed me.

"What do you mean? I paid it myself."

"In the passport case. But there are the other charges. The lawyer lied to us—I was never granted bail in the car case."

"What are we going to do?" I asked, for once completely at a loss.

"We're going to court. They've finally set the trial date. Twelve days from today."

The concept of privacy in Latin America is very different from the idea we have of it in the States. According to Costa Ricans, your right to it has generally been fulfilled if you manage to find a bathroom that has a door on it. Luckily, this cultural anomaly made it very easy for me to get the names and addresses of potential witnesses, those who had the unlucky fate to either sell or purchase the car that Francisco's ex-wife, Laura, accused him of stealing. I simply walked up to the fourth floor of the courthouse and asked the clerk for Francisco's file.

"What is your relationship to the inmate?" the clerk asked me suspiciously.

"I'm his girlfriend."

"Oh, okay then."

And simple as that, he turned over the three-inch-high file to me, explaining that I had to return it in an hour but that I could make a copy across the street.

That afternoon, I tracked down the first witness. Forty-year-old Clara had initially sold the car to Francisco and Laura. Standing outside her door, I asked her the all-important question: "Do you remember who paid for the car? At least, would you recognize the man?"

"Yeah. He didn't look like a Latino. Tall with blue eyes."

Another important aspect of the case was that Francisco hadn't wanted to make a profit; he had been forced into relinquishing the car.

Francisco had driven Laura's vehicle after she had abandoned him and their daughter. His huge van used to transport tourists to the beach wasn't very practical for short trips within the city. But Francisco got into a wreck. He had no idea where Laura was or when she was coming back and he didn't have the money to repair the vehicle. He could either store the useless car or sell it for a fraction of what he had paid for it. Eventually, the car was purchased by a sixty-year-old man named José.

"It was in terrible shape," José informed me, after he had invited me into his home and his wife had brought me a warm cup of hot chocolate. "That's why I got it so cheap."

"Great. That's all I need you to say on the stand."

Finally, based on an intuitive hunch, I went to the Costa Rican equivalent of the Department of Motor Vehicles, where I made quite an impression on the employees. Never before had they imagined that a microfiche copy of a car registration could make a girl cry. But the strongest evidence of the case was right in front of me, lit by the blue screen: Laura had done exactly what she was accusing Francisco of—she had sold their other car, the one that had been registered in Francisco's name. Once Laura finally returned to Costa Rica, Francisco had already fled. And when Laura discovered that Francisco had left his van with a mutual friend, she picked it up and sold it, pocketing a nice twelve-thousand-dollar profit.

Of course, none of this proof impressed Jorge: "That doesn't change the fact that he sold a car that wasn't registered in his name," the man who was supposed to be defending him smugly informed me.

I couldn't believe it. I had thought Jorge's character defect was limited to laziness and that I would get around this by doing all the work for him. I had spent months getting to know all of the aspects of Francisco's case. I had outlined the salient points complete with supporting evidence. All Jorge had to do was stick with the script I had provided for him. But now I realized that he wasn't just incompetent—he actually didn't care.

This was Francisco's last chance. We had five days to go and we could lose everything on account of a terrible lawyer.

At my disposal, I had a large network of people in regular contact with criminal attorneys (it was one of the advantages of going to a prison twice a week). However, for months I had been asking every inmate I came into contact with for a referral and not one of them had had anything positive to say about his lawyer. Now it was down to the wire, and the probability of locating a competent attorney before the trial was like finding a needle in a haystack, an aphid on an apple tree, a tiny sliver of glass on a sparkling white floor.

That was a good simile. Hell, I had spent months trying to do this very thing, trying to pick up the final shards of the glass that had smashed to my floor in a clumsy episode of toothbrushing. It was nearly impossible to find them all, but four days before Francisco's trial, as if to remind me that nothing was completely hopeless, I actually did find the last remaining sliver. Walking barefoot across the floor, I suddenly felt a tremendous surge of pain and lifted up my bleeding foot to realize happily that it was a sign—yes, all things were truly possible.

That very day something amazing happened.

Francisco was walking through the prison courtyard when his friend and cell mate Carlos spotted an attractive, well-dressed woman.

"Get a look at that ass!"

"Wait a minute—I know that ass," Francisco responded in amazement.

The hindquarters belonged to Fabiola Valerio, a woman who had been Francisco's neighbor, car-pool partner, and confidante several years earlier.

"Fabiola!" Francisco shouted, racing toward her. "What are you doing here?"

"Remember all those years you drove me to law school? I finally graduated. I'm a lawyer now. How about you? Who did you come to visit?"

Francisco explained that he wasn't there to visit anyone, he was visiting the prison, something he'd been doing for the past eight and a half months. She was shocked, gave him her number, and told him she would do whatever she could to help him out.

That afternoon, I showed up at her office, begging her to take on the case.

"Four days!" she said aghast. "Francisco didn't tell me his trial was in four days. I really would like to help him out, but there is no way I can gather up proof by Thursday."

"Actually Tuesday. I was counting the weekend."

"Wendy, I'm sorry."

I pulled out a thick, well-worn stack of papers from my bag. "I already have all the evidence."

"The lawyer gave you a copy?"

"No, the lawyer didn't want to see it. I gathered this evidence myself."

She put on her glasses, scooted her chair closer to her desk, and perused the papers for several moments while I sat in suspense. When she had finally made her way through the last one, she looked up at me and asked, "What is it you do for a living?"

"Journalist," I said.

She grinned at me. "We're going to win, you know."

For the first time I actually believed it was true.

October 14, 1997. Laura Madrigal Vásquez versus Francisco Sánchez. Court of Hatillo. Fabiola Valerio acting as defense.

Laura Madrigal Vásquez, 32, a petite brunette, Costa Rican, takes the stand. Information comes to light that she denied having a relationship with Francisco Sánchez when in fact they have a four-year-old daughter. Her response: "I had wanted to forget that part of my life." *Point 1 for the defense.*

The first witness is sworn in, female, Costa Rican. "You originally sold the car to Francisco Sánchez and Laura Madrigal?" the defense asks. The witness responds in the affirmative. "Who paid for the vehicle?" The witness points to the accused. "Francisco Sánchez," she responds. *Defense: 2, Prosecution: 0.*

Exhibit 1: vehicle registration. Original owner of auto: Francisco Sánchez. Exhibit 2: Receipt of sale. Signature on receipt: Laura Madrigal Vásquez. *Defense retains the lead.*

Closing arguments on the part of the prosecution: a complete summary of the trial, a rehashing of all witnesses' salient points. Finally, in a very strange twist on judicial norms, it is the prosecution, not the defense, that pleads for absolution.

There is nothing left for the defense to add. The accused takes a seat, an expression of tranquillity on his face that had been missing for eight months, twenty-five days.

The next morning, I stood outside the familiar prison gate as I had so many times before. But this time, there were no inspections, no body searches, just a chorus of prisoners chanting Francisco's last name: "Sánchez! Sánchez! Sánchez!"

I saw him in the distance walking toward me and when he spotted me, he began to run. Closer, closer until we were finally touching, his fingers grabbing mine through the fence. He handed the guard his papers, and with everything in order there was nothing left to do but open the gate. And suddenly, he was walking out of the prison, as simple as strolling out of the park.

I had imagined this moment so many times over the past months. I had pictured it so many different ways. I thought I would scream or dance or shout, but I did none of those things. I clung to Francisco, not sure this was real, and I began to cry. At first it was just a few tears. And then I started to sob. I shook in his arms, shedding all the tears that had not come before on the nights I had spent alone, on the mornings I had woken up hopeless, and during every day that we had lost.

And then I realized that there was a whole world out there and Francisco was at my side, and I began to laugh. And then Francisco was laughing too. And, of course, the prisoners staring at us through the fence all got the joke and began to clap and chuckle as well.

I grabbed Francisco's hand. "So, you want to hang out here all day or you wanna get the hell out of here?"

I looked around for the cab driver supposed to be waiting for us, but he had disappeared. We would have to make our way on foot to the bus stop two miles away.

After walking a few hundred yards, Francisco turned to look behind him. We stood in silence for a moment gazing at the place we'd managed to escape.

"Thank you," he said.

Then he grabbed my hand and we began to run.

Chapter Eight

What's a Fugitive To Do?

Watching the couples that passed us on the streets of San José, I couldn't help but compare my relationship. I had met, dated, and made love to Francisco in a Costa Rican prison. Other men and women went home to fight over who left the top off the shampoo; we went home marveling at what it was like to ride together on the same bus.

I tried to imagine us alongside the couples that competed on *The Newlywed Game*. Seated between Donna and Skip, Harrison and Danielle, there would be Wendy and Francisco.

"Wendy, for one hundred points, what is Francisco's favorite time of day?"

"Bob, I would have to say . . . the hour they let him spend outside in the courtyard."

"And the first time you made whoopee, what was the line Francisco used to get you into bed?"

"That would have to be 'Conjugal visits start at 3 P.M.' "

There was so much we had yet to learn about each other. We knew the important things—how to survive separation, how to make it through the bad times, how to chop up potatoes using an aluminum can—but we were missing the details. What did Francisco drink in the morning? What kind of socks did he wear? What flavor of ice cream did he like? How did he feel about the possibility of turning into a fugitive?

This last question had been our shared worry during the previous week. Although Francisco had been absolved of the prison breakout and the car situation, there was still the matter of the false passport. In this case, they had only released him on bail.

It was relatively likely that the next trial would be a simple process. Francisco was five days short of having spent nine months in prison, and since he had been cleared of the other charges, this would count as time served toward the fake passport charges. Even better was the fact that if he was granted a sentence of two years or less, since he had no criminal priors, he would be released immediately on bail. A sentence of more than two years and nine months for a fake passport was unheard of.

Nevertheless, the thought of yet another trial weighed down on us. It wasn't just a questionably irrational fear that Francisco would be imprisoned again; it was our frustration with the legal system that by now extended to the country as a whole. It could be another six months before his trial, maybe longer. What were we supposed to do in the meantime? Squeeze into Doña Cloti's one-room apartment and wait for the months to pass? We were already bitter against the place and the people and had yet to figure out a healthy way of dealing with our resentment. (Self-help titles such as *So, You've Just Spent the Past Nine Months in Prison* simply didn't exist.) We'd been biding our time for so long now. The thought of yet another wait seemed an unreasonable request to make of us.

"If only there was some way to sneak you across the border," Fabiola said to us in her office, several days after Francisco's release. "It would be the easy way out."

We gave her counsel serious thought. In a country where justice seemed to be meted out practically at random, even our lawyer was advising breaking the law as a means to guaranteeing Francisco's freedom. This was the way things were done in Costa Rica—the system rarely worked so people stepped outside of it all the time.

After a week of contemplating our options, we had decided on a plan. We would inform Doña Cloti that we had found a bigger place to live. This way, if anyone came asking our whereabouts, she would tell them that we had moved, which would buy us time if someone decided to trail us. Then we would pack all of our belongings (which were very limited in both of our cases) and take a bus to the border of Panama.

The morning of our scheduled departure, as we fit the last of our things into the trunk of a cab, Doña Cloti chatted away excitedly, wanting to know all of the details.

"The apartment. How many bedrooms?"

"Two," I fibbed.

I could see her imagining the place in her mind. "Is it big?"

"Big enough."

She wanted more information: Did it have a washing machine? What neighborhood was it in? What color was it?

I didn't have the heart to destroy her fantasy. I knew that in her mind Francisco and I had the perfect life, proven by the fact that he and I always went out together, unlike her husband who ran off with his buddies to chase women and get drunk at night. So I gave her the specifics of the nonexistent place: a two-bedroom, second-story apartment in Rohrmoser that we'd equip with a washer and dryer, maybe even a dog.

Sharing in our joy, she embraced us both. "I'm so happy for you. But we'll sure miss you. Please come back to visit."

And it was just one more lie to say we would, even though I knew we'd never see her again.

Nervous about taking the heavily transited route, we had the cab driver let us off at a randomly chosen stop outside of the center of town. From there, we took a series of slow moving but anonymous local buses, moving successively from one town to another with the locals instead of joining the tourists on the plush, quick-moving Tica buses.

The day went by in a blur. We passed through so many towns and changed buses so many times that I never was sure where we stopped to spend the night. Was this San Isidro, San Vito, or Salitre? It didn't matter. It was a hotel on the way to Panama and nervously we checked in, reluctant to hand over our passports to the matronly woman at reception, but knowing there wasn't any other way—it was standard practice for guests to have their passport numbers recorded in the hotel ledger.

We spent a restless night, awakened by every little sound. After all, we were inexperienced fugitives who didn't have any idea what to expect. Were there officials tailing us? It was unlikely. Francisco didn't seem significant enough to merit continuous vigil of Doña Cloti's house. But at any point we could be required to show our passports and Francisco's name would surely appear on the list of those not allowed to leave the country. And then there was crossing the border, which we knew would be the toughest part.

Costa Rica is bounded by two other nations. The northern border, which it shares with Nicaragua, is characterized by gross inefficiency, immensely long waits, and a ridiculous quantity of unnecessary paperwork. In fact, Nicaragua is the only country I have ever visited that closes its border for lunch.

At the southern end of Costa Rica, the Panamanian border is a bit more orderly. It's characterized by slightly long waits, a reasonable quantity of unnecessary paperwork, and a moderate amount of inefficiency—all of which was going to fit right in with our plan. Yes, just like any self-respecting fugitives, we had a plan.

"Francisco, what's the plan?" I asked, dragging a suitcase off the bus at the Panamanian border.

"First, you get the exit stamp for Costa Rica."

"Right."

"Then you go over to the Panamanian offices and pay to be able to enter the country."

"Right."

"Meanwhile . . ."

"Yes?"

"Meanwhile, I sit in that restaurant over there drinking a couple of beers."

There was something slightly off about this plan.

"Excuse me a moment. This plan involves drinking and I'm not the one who gets to do it?"

"Sorry, darling."

"So let me get this straight: You lounge about guzzling beers while I have to face immigration officials, slow-moving lines, and paperwork?"

"Right."

"And why is that?"

"Because you were foolish enough to enter the country with a real passport, silly."

He had a point. At Central American borders, travelers had to "check in" and "check out" of every country they visited. However, Francisco's Costa Rican entry stamp was in a passport he no longer carried (the fake passport that had been confiscated), meaning that there was no need for him to get an exit stamp. According to the real passport that Francisco now carried, he had never left Panama.

I was going to do the paperwork to check out of Costa Rica and then into Panama, meet Francisco back at the restaurant, and after I'd matched the number of beers he had drunk in my absence, we'd walk across the border together, both of us completely legal in Panama. At least that was the plan.

What I hadn't counted on at the border was one of the most frustrating of Central American laws: the obligatory proof of onward passage. This requirement existed so that those of us who were in the habit of just showing up in a country would have a way to get back home, but this rule did not fit in well with my style of traveling. For instance, just to purchase a round-trip ticket required a great deal of pretrip plan making. Not only did I have to choose a date, an airline, and a seating assignment, I also had to choose a return destination—which meant I would have to know in advance where I was going to end up once I left a country.

Superfluous for most travelers, the requirement to produce a return ticket became even more ludicrous when applied to fugitives because it was nearly a given that they wouldn't be sticking around long. That was certainly the case with Francisco and me: We hadn't chosen Panama because it sounded especially appealing; its most desirable attribute at this point was that it wasn't Costa Rica.

But that was what was holding me up at the Panamanian immigration offices—I didn't have onward passage. I had nonchalantly passed through Central American borders so many times before, yet the only time I desperately needed to get into a country, officials were turning me away because I didn't have the requisite return ticket.

"Sorry, with no onward passage, I can't let you in," the official informed me, handing me my passport through the opening in the window.

I took my documents back, stunned. Francisco, a fugitive, who had entered Costa Rica with a fake passport, simply had to walk across the border. And me, the legal one, the American one, the one whose passport was the envy of all other nations for the ease with which it allowed its citizens to slip in and out of countries—*I* was the one holding up our escape from Costa Rica.

"You must have a return ticket," the official repeated, and in an attempt to soften the blow of the bad news, he added, "But we could get a drink together later if you'd like."

"How can I have drinks with you if you won't let me in the country?" I asked, amazed at his gall.

"There's a restaurant right here at the border. You don't need a visa to get in."

Yeah, I knew the one. In fact, my boyfriend was sitting there at that very moment being a fugitive.

I sized up the official, wondering what it would take to convince him. This was the most important border crossing in my life. I had to think up something. I hadn't come this far to be defeated by a minor international player like Panama.

"Look, I have a round-trip ticket from San José to Los Angeles. I just forgot it in Costa Rica. I'm a journalist. I'm just passing through Panama to do a story in Colombia. Then I'll return to Costa Rica, and if it'll make you happy, I'll use my onward passage to go back to the States."

He thought about this for a while, had a small private conference with his dour-faced colleagues seated behind him, and came back to me with a question: "Do you have any proof you're a writer?"

"Funny you should ask. I just happen to have a letter from my editor saying that I am indeed qualified to string subject-verb phrases together." This is what I wanted to say, but as far as I knew letters like this just weren't given out. Now that I thought of it, how did anyone prove they were actually a writer?

"Go ahead. Ask me anything. Gerunds, subjunctive verb tenses, onomatopoeias—I know it all." This didn't seem likely to get me very far. When official-looking people asked for proof, they always needed some kind of signed and stamped document. In my wallet, I did carry around an expired Writer's Guild of America membership card. I produced it hopefully.

After a short consultation with his superiors, the official returned to the window unimpressed. "Do you have any other cards?"

"You mean like Author's Guild or PEN—something like that?"

"No, like Visa."

With a weak smile, I timidly pulled out my maxed-out credit card and held it up in the air, hoping they weren't going to run it through the machine and discover that the twelve cents I had left on it wasn't going to buy me a return ticket anywhere.

• • •

As far as I was concerned, my credit card had already done right by me. It had substantially contributed to my UCLA education, paying for canned ravioli, coffee, and even several quarters of tuition when I had been short on cash. Having served me faithfully for years, now that it had nearly reached that magic limit and wasn't even worth the price of the plastic it was made of, here it was coming through for me again. The immigration officials looked over the credit card carefully and concluded, ironically enough, that anyone who possessed a card that let them spend money they didn't have must be financially stable and that I wasn't in danger of becoming an illegal in Panama.

Although my Visa was pretty much worthless at the moment, I really did have money on me—well, at least Francisco's underwear was loaded. After paying for lawyers and other expenses in Costa Rica, I still had six thousand dollars left, which was a lot of cash to be carrying around, so Francisco had stuffed it down his pants, which he claimed was the best hiding place (but I suspected that he actually liked the conspicuously large bulge that it formed).

The night before as Francisco and I had rolled about on the hotel bed, teasing each other while fully clothed, Francisco had stopped for a moment and said, "You realize the only thing stopping us from having sex right now?"

I shook my head.

"Six thousand dollars."

After getting my entrance stamp, crossing the border turned out to be no problem. There wasn't even anyone checking passports at the border. From the government's point of view, it didn't really matter—any traveler who hadn't gotten the required Costa Rican exit stamp followed by the Panamanian entrance stamp would pay dearly for it in fines and aggravation when trying to leave Panama.

Francisco and I easily strolled past the nearly vacant border and simply hailed the first cab that came by. We were as happy as two fugitives who've successfully snuck across an international boundary—a jubilation that lasted about five minutes. What we hadn't counted on was a checkpoint several miles later.

We were driving along a rural tree-lined road in the middle of nowhere (far away from everything except Costa Rica) when the cab came to a stop and a man in a military uniform pushed his face through the open back window, gruffly requesting to see our visas (the passport kind, not the kind I had that was worth twelve cents). Mine was fine—it was obvious that I had just entered the country— but by the look on his face when he flipped through the pages of Francisco's passport, we knew there was a problem—and we were it.

Since Francisco hadn't left Panama officially, according to the stamps in his passport it looked like he had been there for ten months, which meant he had seriously overstayed his 30-day visa.

Immigration officials are not generally characterized by their compassion and understanding, and although it may be polite in these situations to apologize profusely, it doesn't do much to get you out of trouble. (I could just imagine trying this tactic with American border officials: "Whoops, just came back from Cuba. Sorry, it was just a mistake. I promise I'll never do it again.") It was obvious there was going to be a price to pay—I was just hoping Visa would cover it.

We were immediately asked to step out of the cab while the official made a phone call to his superior about the proper way to handle the situation. After a few minutes of tense waiting, I realized we were in luck because his boss did not advocate handcuffing us to a post and beating us silly. Instead, the official kept Francisco's passport as collateral and told us that we would be dealt with the next day at the immigration office in the neighboring town of David.

In the past, authority figures had mentored me, helped me, counseled me. Now I had become the kind of person who was "dealt with."

• • • •

The room we spent the night in was modern, antiseptic white, and decorated with mirrors in place of wall art. I figured it was as good a place as any to panic in.

As Francisco and I climbed in between the sheets of our clean but spartan bed, I couldn't help but fear that this would be our last night together. We'd barely tasted freedom—I'd only had him for a week. It didn't seem fair that he could be ripped from my side so quickly.

But I had to face the truth—there was a strong possibility that the next morning Francisco would be sent back to Costa Rica. After all, any Panamanian border official could simply walk a hundred yards from the guard post over to the Costa Rican station and ask to take a look at the list of people not supposed to leave the country.

But fleeing now was not an option. Without a passport, we'd be trapped in Panama. Francisco wouldn't be allowed to buy a plane ticket or even pay for cross-country bus fare. Random identification checks were standard practice throughout Latin America, and at some point we'd surely be stopped and asked to produce our documents. Simply leaving the house without your ID card was illegal, enough to get you hauled into the police station.

What had we gotten ourselves into? I looked over at Francisco lying next to me, reminded of what had drawn me to him in the first place. The man with the stunning eyes and the interesting stories, I had thought. How right I had been. There were no signs that his life was going to get mundane any time soon, and even with the uncertain fate that awaited us, his eyes showed the same cool blue sereneness.

"Are you okay?" he asked, noticing I was staring.

"Sure," I said. "Let's try and get some sleep."

He wrapped his arms around me and we closed our eyes to the long night ahead of us.

• • •

*A*s if the night hadn't been difficult enough, the wait we endured at the immigration offices the next morning was nearly unbearable. We sat without speaking, not wanting to put our fears into words. If they sent Francisco back to Costa Rica, he would head straight to prison for having fled bail. Getting an innocent man out of prison had taxed the limits of my ingenuity. Getting a guilty one out—we wouldn't stand a chance.

"Francisco Sánchez," the irritated woman at the counter finally called out.

Walking down the hall in the direction the woman had pointed, I couldn't help but fear that this was the end of the line for us. It was the journey across the River Styx. I fully expected to encounter Hades waiting for us, growling Cerberus at his side. But as we stepped timidly into the office where our fate was to be decided, it was not the god of the underworld sitting behind the desk—just a balding man with a mustache who looked us up and down and smiled mischievously, as if we were sharing a naughty secret. He placed his feet on his desk and leaned back in his chair, pausing to light a cigarette.

"Let me get this straight. Francisco, you've been taking a course in tourism in Panama for nine months and didn't get around to re-newing your visa," he said, making the story we had fed to the guard the previous day actually sound plausible. "And you found out your American friend was coming to visit you."

Nodding seemed appropriate at this point so we moved our heads up and down in agreement.

"You just called her up and said, 'Hey, I'm here in Panama ille-gally. Why don't you come join me?' "

We both stifled a laugh. "Something like that," Francisco said.

He directed his attention toward me. "And you came to visit and he went to pick you up at the border?"

"Right," I said.

He smiled up at the ceiling, concentrating intently on a mosquito that had landed there, keeping us in suspense.

"I tell you what I'm going to do," he finally said, removing his feet from the desk and placing them firmly on the ground. "I'm going to do you a favor."

I did not like the sound of this. Any time a uniformed man holding my passport had addressed me in Spanish, the "good news" usually had come at the cost of quite a few pesos. Worse yet, here in Panama, the local currency was dollars. But at this point, I was prepared for practically anything—except for what it was he had to say.

He turned out to be the one thing I hadn't counted on—the man was—well, he was actually *nice*. He wasn't going to fine us, he wasn't going to punish us, he wasn't even going to give us a long lecture—he was going to give Francisco a way to change his illegal status at no cost to us.

"I'm going to let you out of the country for free even though Francisco should have to pay a twelve-hundred-dollar fine. All you have to do is go to Costa Rica, stay there for three days, and on your way back I'll give you a visa to stay in Panama at no charge."

It was an example of unprecedented kindness of the part of an immigration official and I would have jumped at the offer, except for one small problem: Being fugitives and all, Costa Rica was pretty much off limits.

There was only one way to respond: "Thanks for the offer, but instead of getting off for free we'd really rather just pay the twelve hundred dollars."

He was dumbfounded. He watched us for several seconds, waiting for us to tell him we were just kidding. When that didn't happen, he took a deep sigh and wrote down what we would have to do to pay the fine in Panama City. Then with one final look of great disappointment, staring at us like an Orthodox Jewish mother just come to find out that her children were taking advantage of the pepperoni special at Domino's, he shook our hands and sent us on our way.

To me there seemed to be some flaw in the immigration logic of "You can't stay in Panama for more than a month, but if you do, you can't leave until you pay." This was not the way things worked in the United States. I could just imagine the INS picking up a group of illegal Mexicans and saying, "If you can't pay, well, you're just going to have to stick around until you can." We took a slightly different view of aliens in my country and at least we were kind enough to give them a free trip back home. And considering the hefty fine Francisco and I faced in Panama, deportation was starting to sound like a pretty attractive option.

Our simple attempt to pay the fine thrust us into a Latin American bureaucratic nightmare, much like one of those dreams in which you have somewhere important to be, but your forward motion is impeded, your feet stuck in a vat of thick lime Jell-O. At the first building, we stood in an incredibly long line, only to learn that the services we requested were handled by a different office. We began the process all over again in what we only hoped was the appropriate place, and after hours of waiting, just as we were about to near the window, a loudspeaker informed us that the office would be closing for lunch and we would be required the vacate the premises until 2 P.M.

Two days later, we had finally arrived at the correct office at the right window at the right time with the right paperwork, the required passport-sized photo, and an official stamp. All that the woman behind the counter needed was twelve hundred dollars—unless we wanted to petition for a reduction in fine.

A reduction in fine? No one had ever mentioned the possibility of a decrease before. From the sixteen thousand dollars I had left the United States with six months ago, my funds had been depleted by more than ten thousand dollars. Our hotel in Panama City was eating away another two hundred dollars a week, plus there'd be the price of transportation out of the country. The idea of saving a grand or so sounded pretty damn attractive. Besides, it was unlikely that any Costa Rican official would have followed us across the border. In Panama City, we were relatively safe from arrest. Of course, it would entail beginning the process over from scratch again.

Now it was on to another building with new lines, new passport photos, new forms. Finally, after every document had been filled out, approved, signed, and stamped, we took our papers to the window and victoriously handed them to the man behind the counter.

"Now all you have to do is wait for the approval of your decrease," he said, unable to find any missing stamp, faulty signature, or problem with the paperwork. "It'll be five days. We'll let you know."

Since Francisco and I had nearly a week before his exit visa was due to come through, we had time to leisurely ponder what came next.

If there was an ideal place for major life decisions, it had to be the country where we found ourselves. It was where two continents were joined, where two great oceans connected, not so much a place in itself but more of a crossroads, the primary intersection of the Americas. Anything could occur from here, depending on what path we chose.

As Francisco and I strolled cheerfully about the Panama Canal, feeling for once like real tourists (a pleasure we figured we were entitled to now that his exit visa was nearly in our hands), it hit me that this was the zero point of the world. To my right was the Pacific Ocean, to my left the Atlantic. I had practically reached the end of the continent where I was born, straight ahead lay South America. Any direction was possible from this spot.

Francisco grabbed my hand as we watched an impressive freighter patiently wait for the canal walls to rise and fall. How easy it must be to be a ship's captain, I thought to myself. Everything was laid out for you. You not only knew where your journey began and where it ended, with a few algebraic calculations, you could even figure out when you were going to get there. But what was the fun in that?

I looked over at Francisco who had lapsed into his own reflective mood. What did we do now? I wondered out loud. We had the whole world to choose from.

I liked the idea of going to Italy, but that was just because I was fond of olives and wine and not because I had any realistic idea of what I would spend my time doing there. Francisco thought heading to Vegas would be fun, but this was just because he liked bright lights and Elvis impersonators, which I warned him would probably be too much of a shock in his fragile postprison state. Mexico was the trendy spot for fleeing fugitives, but it was in the wrong direction.

"There's an ocean to our right and another one to our left. Any suggestions?"

"I think I want to go home," Francisco confided to me.

"Me too, Francisco." I smiled at him and squeezed my fingers around his hand. "Will I know when I've found it?"

Five days later, we were flying—if you accept the loose definition of the word, the one about traveling through the air in a forward motion and not the one about stewardesses, movies, and free peanuts. It was, after all, a plane.

"Looks more like a cab with wings," Francisco said, grabbing my arm.

The tiny four-passenger plane shaking its way through the sky held us, another couple, plus the two men driving (or rather, flying) the machine. There were no stewardesses, no preflight emergency safety talk, no refreshments, or overhead lighting. There was also no PA system but this was no problem—if the pilot wanted to get our attention, all he had to do was turn around and tap us.

We were headed to the border between Panama and Colombia, a trip that had finally become possible after getting Francisco's fine reduced down to two hundred dollars, though originally I hadn't counted on going by plane—I had assumed we would make the trip by land.

"Yes, but you're forgetting one small thing," Francisco had responded to my suggestion that we go by bus.

"And that would be?"

"The Darien Jungle."

Ah, yes, the Darien Jungle, how could I have forgotten that? According to Francisco, not only was the route completely impassable by automobile, but those insane enough to make the journey on foot still had to fight off crocodiles, wildcats, and guerrillas.

So we had chosen the safer way and supposedly this was it. The pilot turned around, tapped us, and asked if we could inform both of the other passengers that we were now approaching our final destination when suddenly the plane began approaching land at a terrifying speed. For a minute I wondered if our journey was going to come crashing to an abrupt end, but at the last moment, with our seat belts securely knotted around us, the nose of the plane tipped upward, the wheels made contact with the ground, and the brakes managed to hold out for one more flight.

We got off the plane and stepped into a place where only *National Geographic* filmmakers dare to tread. After a quick look around, I realized to my relief that it was not the end of the world, but I was pretty sure that it was the closest exit ramp. It was primitive and hot and deserted, and I noted that there wasn't any graffiti—because John and Sarah and Pepe had *not* been here. I could imagine Henry Thoreau being happy in the place had he been a little more international and into poisonous snakes. His backyard would have been the jungle; his front yard, the Caribbean Sea.

This was all good and fine for hermits who wanted a little peace and quiet on the beach, but it was a bit inconvenient for Francisco and me now that our main goal was to get out of the place. As I looked at the tiny crowd of locals who had gathered around the plane to witness the arrival of the newcomers, the only event of note that ever happened here, I began to have the sneaking suspicion that we weren't going to find a major bus terminal or train station anywhere nearby.

"Which way is Colombia?" I asked, addressing the man in the village who wasn't wielding a machete.

He gave me a toothless smile and held his finger up in the air.

"Francisco, what is he pointing at?"

"I think he means the Caribbean."

As I sat in the hollowed-out log called a *panga* (which made even a canoe look high-tech), I gripped my PowerBook for dear life, hoping that the waves that were soaking me through to the skin wouldn't penetrate its supposedly water-resistant carrying case.

"This is an incredibly dangerous ride," Francisco said. "Only those who learn from childhood are able to navigate these waters."

As if on cue, our *panga* came upon a tremendous swell that I feared would topple us and for an instant my mind flashed back to the near-drowning incidents of my childhood. This time, however, the sinewy, serious, dark-skinned man navigating our tiny craft skillfully adjusted the angle of the boat, causing us to sail over the crest of the wave instead of being rolled over by it.

Sensing we were in good hands, my nerves began to settle. I remained slightly timid of the waves, but I was mostly just bright-eyed and amazed, a denizen of the city suddenly dropped helpless in a remote and wild place. There was the spray of salty seawater on my face, the heat of the sun pressing down on my shoulders, the sound of seagulls flying overhead. It was one of those rare travel moments that came when I least expected, and it was perfect, all that I required right then. I had forgotten that we were supposed to be getting somewhere and was content to simply drift. Bouncing on top of the green waves of the Caribbean had turned into enough of a reason-for-being for me.

Twenty minutes later, we spotted the shore in the distance and I realized, giddy with excitement, that the sand I was staring at was part of the wild and unruly land of Colombia. Freedom was just feet away from us, glistening in the hot tropical sun.

The *panga* bumped against land with a jolt and Francisco stepped out the boat, getting his shoes wet and stuck with sand and not caring. This was it—we had made it. We were finally safe.

We had arrived in the small Colombian border village of Sapzurro and it was an event. People raced out to the boat as if they'd been expecting us, and a mix of black and brown hands grabbed for our bags and helped me onto land. I adored each and every one of them, partly because they were friendly and full of smiles, but mostly because I was already infatuated with the whole country and they were part of it.

It had taken two Costa Rican cabs, six Costa Rican buses, a Panamanian cab, a plane ride, a *panga* trip, and a long walk to get to Sapzurro, but looking around me, I realized it had been worth it. Palms were swaying in the wind. Papayas as big as footballs were growing on trees. The air was warm and humid and carried the scent of the sea. We had arrived in a tropical paradise.

After an al fresco meal of rice, tomato salad, plantain chips, and fish sprinkled with salt and lemon juice, Francisco and I dragged our bags along a dirt path, brushing aside the birds of paradise and banana leaves that competed for space along the way. We were on our way to the home of the mayor, a man named Sombrero (which means "hat" in Spanish, but saying "We were headed to Hat's house" doesn't have

quite the same ring to it). Francisco had met him on a previous journey and assured me that it would be fine to drop in on him.

Sombrero received us with a warm smile and invited us into his
modest home that was just yards away from the beach. I looked him
up and down and came to the conclusion that he was awfully young
to be the city's governing official (then again, I reminded myself that
customs must be a bit different in a place where mothers name their
children Hat).

He offered us a seat while his wife brought out lemonade for
everyone. Francisco gave him the condensed version of what had occurred in Costa Rica and when that topic had been exhausted,
Francisco informed me that Mayor Sombrero was one of the best
storytellers he had ever met.

"Imagine the people who have passed through this small border
town between Colombia and Panama where there isn't even immigration control. Sombrero has met drug traffickers, bill forgers, hit
men, leaders of the Cali cartel. I bet he could give you great stories
for your book."

"You're writing a book?" the young mayor wanted to know.

"Yeah, but it's kind of self-centered. I mostly write about myself."

The mayor graciously invited us to stay with his family for a few
days while he told me about some of his experiences. The thought
was tempting. After all, I was in a Caribbean Eden surrounded by
water and palms and warm, humid air, where people sat on their
porches telling stories late into the night, drinking piña coladas, and
munching on fried plantains. Besides, I had a free place to stay. How
could I possibly refuse?

"I'm sorry," I said to the mayor, truly meaning it. "I would love
to—it's just time we set up new lives for ourselves in Cali."

I hated to leave, but the daily practical worries of existence had
invaded my thoughts yet again. Our money was slowly trickling
away. If we got to civilization soon, there was a chance I'd be able to

do some telecommuting work for Hughes Aircraft. But we needed to get there quickly——I hadn't e-mailed my potential clients since leaving Costa Rica and I worried they'd grow frustrated and hand the job over to someone else.

If we missed the next boat out, it would be days before there was another departure. And although I had fallen in love with Sapzurro and there was a side of me that deeply longed to stay, there was a part of me that wouldn't be able to enjoy it. It would be like going on vacation, knowing I'd left the iron on. Besides, there were still too many unknowns. We weren't sure what we were going to do with the rest of our lives, and Sapzurro didn't provide any answers, just procrastination.

We had to be heading back to civilization——though it would take a while to get there. After a five-hour motorboat ride and a brief stay in the small guerrilla-ridden town of Turbo, a day later we finally made it to Medellín, where I was never so happy to see a bus station in my life. Exhausted, we dragged our bags to the counter and bought one-way tickets to Cali.

We waited at a restaurant inside the terminal until it was time to hop aboard our bus. While trying out my first Colombian *buñuelo,* a cakelike pastry that was perfectly round and the size of a tennis ball, an older American couple seated at the table next to us tried to strike up a conversation. They were missionaries headed to Bogotá, they informed us. They were going to be in Cali in the next few weeks. It was so rare to run into an American in this part of the world. Wouldn't it be great if we could meet up in the future?

"How will we find you?" the woman asked.

With a private investigator, I thought. Why, not even the Costa Rican FBI can find us.

I shrugged my shoulders and put my arm around Francisco's waist. And together we walked out of the restaurant and into the free world.

Chapter Nine

Lessons in Laundering

There was something special about coming home. This was what I thought as Francisco and I sped through the streets of Cali, Colombia. Just as I always experienced a tinge of emotion at the sight of the Welcome to Los Angeles sign at the Bradley terminal of the airport, I wondered if Francisco was getting nostalgic at the thought of returning to guerrilla war and drug traffickers. He was home. They would take him in here—and if we were lucky, they wouldn't do it in the hopes of receiving a ransom.

"Is this your first time in Cali?" the cabdriver asked, glancing at us in his rearview mirror.

"Francisco is *from* Cali," I said with a tinge of vicarious pride.

"We're both from Cali," Francisco added. "I'm from *Cali,* she's from *Cali*-fornia."

The cabdriver looked at Francisco's blue eyes and light complexion suspiciously. "You're from Cali?" he asked, incredulous.

Francisco nodded.

"But where were you born?" the driver persisted.

"Cali."

"But your parents . . ."

"From Cali."

Francisco had come home, yet no one believed he was from the place. In fact, his biggest problem was struggling to answer all the people who kept addressing him in English. The day before at the bus terminal in Medellín, the man behind the counter had taken one look at Francisco's light skin and blue eyes and immediately addressed him in *my* native language: "Can I help you?"

Francisco had stuttered a little bit, tried to find any words resembling "purchase" or "ticket" and realizing that he was incapable of carrying on the conversation in English, he went over and grabbed me.

"Come with me. I need some help talking."

I figured that he had run into some tourists and wanted to offer them directions and hotel advice, but when we arrived at the counter, I was shocked to realize the source of Francisco's communication problem.

"Francisco, darling . . ."

"Yes?"

"Why do you need my help?"

"Because he's speaking to me in English."

"Yes and what country are we in?"

"Colombia."

"And what country are *you* from?"

"Colombia."

"Francisco, dear . . ."

"Yes?"

"Speak to him in Spanish, for God's sake!"

Francisco gave me a timid smile and reverted to his mother tongue.

Though as it turned out, it didn't matter what language Francisco spoke—there was just no way of convincing people that he wasn't an American. I would get complimented on my good Spanish and then they would turn to Francisco and add, "And you— why, you hardly have *any* accent at all."

As the cabdriver let us out and wished us a pleasant stay in the city, I looked at Francisco and laughed. "So this is home, huh?"

Francisco nodded. "Yep. The place where I belong."

•　　•　　•

Francisco and I had decided on Cali because it seemed like the most logical place to set up new lives for ourselves. Francisco couldn't enter the United States legally (getting a tourist visa as a Colombian was nearly impossible) and I had no qualms about living in South America—I spoke the language and was familiar with the culture. We didn't have a specific plan, but we had time and a little bit of money. We'd exist on what was left of my savings until the details worked themselves out.

Francisco's sister Melba had offered to let us stay with her for a while until we got on our feet. At first, I had worried that we'd be imposing, but as we shared Cokes in her small, stark living room and I watched a never-ending stream of people pour into the house, I relaxed and realized we wouldn't be a burden: There were so many people living here already, they wouldn't even notice us. We'd blend into the crowd, as inconspicuous as bare breasts at Mardi Gras.

After nearly an hour of animated chatter, Melba apologetically left the house to run some errands with her nieces, which gave me the chance to ask Francisco about our sleeping arrangements.

"We're sharing a room, right?" I asked him as we marched up the stairs to look at the rest of the place.

"Yeah, if that's okay with you."

"Silly, of course I want to sleep with you!" I said slapping him playfully on the butt.

He gave me a look that I wasn't quite sure how to interpret. As we walked into what was obviously a child's bedroom, Francisco set me down on the bottom bunk and placed my hand in his lap. "Wendy, you don't understand," he said with a sigh, giving me that look of incredible patience possessed only by ex-convicts. "When I said that we'd be sharing a room, I didn't mean with each other."

"No, it's all right, we can share a room. Really, I don't mind," I said in a magnanimous gesture of goodwill.

"You don't understand, Wendy. We *are* going to share a room. You, me, Stephanie, and Jenny."

"You mean—"

"Yes. *All* of us."

This was terrifying news. It was going to be enough of an adjustment to get used to the cold and barren two-story townhouse whose sole adornments were a few pieces of plastic furniture and some tasteless knickknacks, not to mention the fact that we were going to be living with six other people: Melba, her son, her two nieces, her nephew, and her brother-in-law. Now we were going to have to share a room with two noisy little girls who played dolls, left candy strewn about the floor, and considered Styrofoam cutouts of Disney characters to be legitimate tools of interior design.

"Do you like Princess Ariel?" Stephanie asked me later that afternoon, pointing to a bigger-than-life-sized head painted on her, um, *our* bedroom wall.

Under normal circumstances, her pageboy haircut and squeaky child's voice would have struck me as endearingly cute, but this wasn't some adorable eleven-year-old girl to me anymore. I realized that I was looking at my new roommate.

"You mean that fish woman?" I growled.

"She's a mermaid!" Stephanie said, correcting me.

"Oh yeah, right." And then straining to reach the diplomatic bone in my body, I added, "She's very pretty." And she was for a woman who was halfway covered with scales.

This forced effort apparently paid off because Stephanie beamed at me and then generously allowed me my choice in sleeping accommodations: Did Francisco and I want the upper or lower bunk?

I chose the bottom one, thinking it was an appropriate metaphor for how far down I'd sunk.

"You've made your bed. Now you have to sleep in it."

It was a nice enough saying; it had just never applied to my adult life—not because I didn't believe in taking the consequences of my actions, but because I never had acquired the habit of making my bed—or dusting my shelves or mopping my floors or putting away my clothes for that matter, at least not on a regular basis. In my own country, it had never been much of a problem. After all, America was the Land of People Phoning Before Stopping By and the hour in between hanging up the phone and answering the door was plenty of time to deceive my guests that I lived at a perfectly acceptable level of cleanliness.

This cultural norm probably would have been the same in Colombia if we had been talking about a place where everyone had a phone. But getting connected to Madre Bell was a long, complicated, expensive process, and even if you managed to get a line (an investment of more than five hundred dollars just for the hookup), you were charged for every single call, even local ones. So in Cali, people often stopped by without calling first, which I didn't really mind—I just hated the side effect: The house had to be clean at all times, which meant it had to be performed on a daily basis.

I figured it would be a good idea to follow the traditions of my host country and pretend that I was a neat and organized person, but I was sorely out of practice, having abandoned domestic industriousness when I left my parents' at age seventeen. What was worse, I knew I was being closely scrutinized by Melba. In spite of the fact that she was a year younger than I was and didn't look or dress much like a wife and mother (her hair was long and fashionable; her clothes were hip), like most Latin American women, she had taken to housecleaning like a religion. In Colombia, a dirty floor meant you didn't care about your children. Not cooking dinner meant the love had gone out of a marriage. In her eyes, my entire worth as a woman was defined by the skill with which I took over the neatness of the place. Never mind that I'd just gotten her brother out of prison; never mind that I spoke three languages and had seen four continents; never mind that I had achieved the all-time high score on Centipede in my neighborhood. Melba wanted an impressive display of my housecleaning skills. And since I wanted to fit in with the family (and, after all, she was letting us stay at her house for free), I figured, what the hell? I would start with a low-key but skillful performance of my clothes-washing ability.

I had done laundry for years in the States and I pretty much had the process down: It involved sticking five coins and a cup of detergent into a Whirlpool. But in Cali, quarters didn't exist—worse yet, the country had yet to see very many washing machines. So when I walked up to Melba and announced in a conspicuously loud voice that I intended to "Wash Some Things," she led me to the tiny courtyard patio that served as the laundry room and handed me a brush and a bar of soap.

I had figured that washing clothes by hand would mostly be just common sense, a notion that was quickly dispelled when I looked at the bizarre contraption in front of me. It was the strangest sink I had ever seen. The entire device was made of concrete and it was so long, it took up an entire six-foot wall. In the center were two basins that could be filled with water from a faucet. One end consisted of a counterlike space one and one-half feet square that appeared to accommodate some sort of washing activity. At the other end was an area the exact same size, only instead of being flat it consisted of inch-high ridges molded into the cement, which I concluded was either used for washing or the torture of small children. I had no idea how to begin.

The easiest thing would be to ask, but I knew that Melba would see this lack of experience as a character flaw. I needed some privacy to figure out the apparatus on my own. So I gave her a confident smile and remarked, "Melba, didn't I see a cobweb in the living room?"

A look of dread crossed her face and she raced out quickly to remedy the situation.

Francisco and I had already had an extensive discussion about housework and who was going to do it (him) and who wasn't (me), so when I yelled out to him to bring me his dirty clothes, he walked into the room empty-handed and looked at me suspiciously.

"What in God's name are you up to?"

"Remember when we made that deal that if I got you out of prison for a crime you didn't commit and if we succeeded in crossing the border to Panama and if one day we happened to make it safely to Colombia that you'd do my laundry for me for the rest of my life?"

"Uh-huh . . ."

"Yeah, well, I'm going to hold you to it as soon as we get out of your sister's house. In the meantime, will you please show me how to use this thing?"

Within five minutes, I had convinced Francisco that I was in fact serious about this project and that I was completely determined to learn how to wash clothes by hand. Francisco picked up a pair of jeans, and animated by the prospect that his girlfriend would know how to do housework in the event of an emergency, he patiently began showing me how to scrape the fabric against the ridged edge of the sink to get the dirt out. I watched attentively, making careful note of his technique.

"Francisco, I think I hear footsteps."

"You sure?"

"Yeah. Quick, hand me the jeans fast."

I was up to my arms in soapy water by the time I realized that it was just Jenny and Stephanie entering the room. With a sigh of relief, I handed the pants back to Francisco.

"It's only the girls. Go ahead, show me how to rinse."

Francisco dunked the pants into the soapy water, which was enough to create quite a scene. The sight of a man showing a woman how to wash clothes was such an anomaly for these two Colombian girls (I think they would have been less shocked had he shown me the proper way to wear pearls) that they immediately began buckling over in laughter. Even Francisco and I began to crack up. Of course, Melba would have to come in to see what all the commotion was about.

"I have never in my life seen a woman who didn't know how to wash clothes," she said, truly shocked.

As much as I wanted to blend in to my new home, it seemed that housework was where I was going to have to draw the line. So I sat down and explained the situation to my new Colombian family: I came from a different world, a land of dirty dishes and crumb-laden floors. Since we were going to be living together for a while, would it be too much for them to try and extend a little tolerance to those from other countries whose cultural values did not include domestic tidiness and order?

Within two weeks at Melba's house, I had failed as a housewife but I had succeeded in becoming the major source of family entertainment. The morning show began around 8 A.M. at which time the girls would gather outside the bathroom, glue their ears to the door, and wait for the screams to begin.

I had no choice but to accept the fact that most houses in Colombia had no hot water; what seemed unreasonably cruel was the fact that the shower nevertheless had two knobs: the "C"* knob which stood for cold and the "H" knob that I assumed stood for "ha ha" because it did absolutely nothing.

Bathing in ice-cold water gave whole new meaning to the phrase "refreshing shower"—because if you weren't awake after a Colombian shower, it was because you had just consumed two codeines and a bottle of rum, in which case you were guaranteed to enjoy the experience immensely.

With time, I figured I would get used to my daily dousing of cold water, but I doubted I would ever grow accustomed to the electri-

---

*In the event that you are reading this book sober, the thought may have occurred to you that most people in Colombia speak Spanish and therefore the cold knob should have an "F" for *frio*. But, of course, that would be logical and I remind you that this is South America.

cal shocks in the kitchen—the other source of physical anguish in my new household had become the stove. A typical hour of cooking would go like this: I would be happily watching my pot, waiting for it to boil—which in itself was a painfree experience (other than the fact that I wasn't much enjoying my new role as Person Who Cooks)—when I would attempt to stir the chicken soup that Francisco had taught me how to make. This did not seem like an irrational thing to do—after all there were many recipes in the United States that went so far as to advocate stirring constantly. However, in Colombia, whenever I reached into the pot with a metal spoon, currents of electricity would race through my arm. The first time, the shock was so unexpected that I quickly flung the utensil into the air and ran screaming into the other room.

I complained to Francisco that the stove wasn't working properly, that it was out to get me, and at that very moment was planning my death. Francisco sat me down and calmly explained that all stoves in Colombia were this way. It wasn't the appliance's fault. I was the one to blame: After all, how could I possibly think of cooking on an electric stove without wearing rubber-soled shoes? I told him that in the past I really hadn't ever thought of cooking; how could he expect me to know that I had to don a special kind of footwear?

Realizing I was new to all this (after all, in the States I'd always had stoves that used gas), Francisco explained the other precautions I was to take in order to prepare the midday meal: If I were to stand on a board on the floor, use a wooden spoon instead of a metal one, and ensure that my hands were completely dry before attempting to stir, I would be sure to diminish the electric current running through my body to levels far below those used to get essential information out of prisoners of war.

In an effort to adapt to Colombian culture, I also tried to get over my cultural prejudices regarding food. In Cali, I sportingly sampled what I had formerly refused in Costa Rica—rubbery tripe and canned sardines—but chicken soup was what never failed to defeat me. It wasn't the broth per se that creeped me out. It was the little chicken feet with their little chicken claws that lined that bottom of my bowl that I was not too enthusiastic about. But Francisco took to these extremities the way I gobbled down Reese's peanut butter cups: licking off the outside and sucking on the yellow goo on the inside.

One day as I watched Francisco devour a suspiciously familiar piece of a cow's anatomy, my American breeding came through again and I couldn't help but comment on the disgusting nature of what he was putting into his mouth.

"It's delicious," he said, apparently completely oblivious to the fact that he was eating an animal's tongue. "Do you want some?"

I shivered in revulsion, looking at all the hairs lining my beau's meal. "You actually expect me to kiss those lips?"

"You'll like it," he said, pointing to his mouth. "Two tongues inside."

My first three weeks in Cali slipped by, day after day of domesticity in one of the most dangerous countries in the world. During that time, violence was something distant we just heard about on the news. There would be a guerrilla attack or a paramilitary massacre in some city with a foreign name far away from us, but this had as much direct impact on my life as gang violence in South Central Los Angeles.

A year or two earlier, I might have gone running off to the jungle in search of adventure, but now I wanted to revel in a quieter existence. My travels had been eventful and exhilarating but also emotionally draining. I wanted to sit back for a while and enjoy being part of a family—no prison escapes, no bombs, just a simple life with Francisco spiced up with a dose of Colombian flavor to keep it from being bland.

Melba's neighborhood of Jamundí seemed like the right place

for it. It was a planned community, which would have been mind numbing and depressing had it existed in Orange County, but located on the outskirts of Cali, suburban life was hardly sterile and dull. Even though the streets were nearly identical when looked at from a distance—each block consisted of one long rectangular building divided up into separate townhouses—when you moved in closer, you realized that the whole place was swimming in a flurry of activity, music, and commerce.

There wasn't a commercial property in the whole neighborhood so the residents of Jamundí had transformed their living rooms into stores, restaurants, and any other enterprise imaginable. With the addition of an oven and some glass-enclosed cases, a family was suddenly in business as a bakery. Fit the place with some shelves, dry goods, and vegetables, and they transformed their place into a small grocery store. Everyone was a budding entrepreneur. There were living room restaurants that dispensed soup and a different lunch every day. Other places specialized in nighttime snacks. On outdoor barbecues on the sidewalk, women grilled hot dogs and hamburgers or corn patties with melted cheese called *arepas*. Our neighborhood also included a video store (whose merchandise consisted of grainy movies recorded off of HBO), two arcades (a living room equipped with several Nintendos where kids sat down and rented the games by the hour), and a drugstore (staffed by a knowledgeable pharmacist who would diagnose your condition, sell you medication, and even inject you with your purchases in the back room). And there were several makeshift businesses as well. Sometimes there would just be a handmade sign outside of someone's home: Clothes for Sale or Homemade Ice Cream or Mechanic.

In Jamundí, the *arepas* came hot off the grill, the *papas rellenas* were prepared as you watched. Milk was lukewarm, fresh from the cow, and clothes were tailor-made. For the price of a pair of socks at The Gap, a professional dressmaker would create a garment from scratch made to fit your measurements.

Living there was peaceful and predictable in a comforting sort of way. Every morning began the same: Francisco and I would walk over to the "bakery" where we'd pick out breakfast, which varied depending on what was due to come out of the oven in our neighbor's living room. My favorite was the *pan de bono,* small doughnut-shaped breads made with fresh cheese that we'd gulp down with sweet cups of Colombian coffee. We'd bring enough home for Melba and the girls—their brother, fourteen-year-old Toño, was already at school by then and their father Eduardo had already gone to work.

I'd spend the morning reading or jotting down notes in my journal while Francisco hung out with his sister. Sometimes I'd cook. Other times it fell to Francisco or Melba. But by noon, the house took on a frenetic pace. The girls went to school from one to five in the afternoon, meaning that they swallowed down their lunches, grabbed their school bags, and raced out the door by twelve thirty.

In the afternoon, there were just four of us left in the house—Melba, her two-year-old son, Francisco, and me—so after Francisco and I had taken our "siesta," an hour of precious alone-time in our room that rarely resulted in actual sleep, the four of us would go for a walk or run some errands in town.

It was a simple life, the kind that would have bored me to exasperation two years earlier, but prison had put things in perspective for me. The six months I had spent not having Francisco made having him all the more poignant. So while I grumbled about the difficulties of squeezing us both into a cramped twin bed or voiced my opposition to the overcharged electric stove, the truth was, I didn't care where we lived or what our circumstances were.

We had waited so long to be together. And now that we were finally in Colombia, I couldn't help but think that everything was going to be okay, that the hard part really was finally over.

I figured that all I had to do was stick to my domestic existence and nothing terrible would occur. I simply had to avoid prisons, crime, drug cartels, and guerrilla war, and life would turn out just fine. But the problems plaguing Colombia crept in insidiously. They attached themselves like a virus to the poverty that flowed into most Colombian homes. And not even Jamundí was immune.

One day it occurred to me that Melba didn't seem like the kind of woman to get divorced. She loved flaunting her status as matron of the house, a devoted mother who looked after her son and two nieces and possessed a spotless home. But where was her husband?

"Is Melba separated?" I asked Francisco one afternoon in our bottom bunk, both of us semiclothed and still slightly out of breath after half an hour of tumbling and turning on the tiny bed.

He gave me a look that let me know I had struck a nerve.

"What?" I asked, suspiciously. "Where is he?"

"Miami."

This was disappointing. Miami was a perfectly reasonable place to be. "What's he do in Miami?"

"He's in prison there."

I was shocked. Melba was straight as an arrow, even prudish, certainly not the kind of woman to be married to a criminal.

While I tried to adjust my outlook to squeeze in this new information, it suddenly occurred to me that Melba's husband wasn't the only family member missing from the house. Where was Stephanie, Jenny, and Toño's mother? "What about Martha? Don't tell me your sister is in prison too."

Francisco nodded his head. And that was how I got my introduction to what typical family life was really like in Colombia.

Being a drug mule in Colombia was like playing the lottery. Everyone was doing it because everyone believed they could win. Most *mulas* were everyday people—teachers, mechanics, even doctors who saw this as their only chance at a better life. The ten or fifteen grand they stood to gain was more than a lawyer earned in a year. All it took was one successful trip carrying a few kilos of heroin or cocaine aboard an airplane to turn their lives around. And assuming the worst, that they didn't make it, what were they really giving up? They were already poor. They already dealt with violence on a daily basis.

In a country where the average citizen was forced into breaking the law on a daily basis just to get through life (bribes were standard practice for everything from getting a driver's license to getting out of being arrested if you were caught walking out of the house without ID), the idea of taking the next step wasn't such a big deal. Many people did it just once and returned to Colombia with the money for a house, a car, or a savings account and went back to their normal lives. And of course, there were the unlucky ones—like Francisco's family members who did it just once and got caught.

Melba's husband, Leonardo, a Mormon who wouldn't even go shopping on Sunday, had decided that slipping five kilos of cocaine in a suitcase was an acceptable thing to do. He had figured that if he could make just one successful trip to Miami, it would be a way out of poverty. So he bought a plane ticket (being sure to schedule it for a weekday—he didn't want to violate the Sabbath) and boarded the plane, his bags full of more than just Books of Mormon. He was caught at immigration and was now serving the second year of his three-year prison sentence.

Francisco's sister Martha had fared even worse, her punishment a year longer due to the nature of her crime. She had assumed they would never suspect a mother with her son so she had brought young Toño along. For him it was going to be the trip of a lifetime. He was eleven years old and he had finally arrived at the country that had created Disney World. And he was going to see Mickey Mouse and Donald Duck and look, wasn't that a pretty doggy racing over to welcome them to the airport? Unfortunately, this pretty doggy had been specially trained to sniff out little boys' feet, especially when their moms had hidden drugs in her little boy's shoes. From there, the rest of the day was a blur. His mother was dragged away in handcuffs and he was sent back to Colombia alone wearing a pair of flip-flops—the DEA agents had confiscated his shoes.

That afternoon, after becoming privy to Francisco's family members' darkest secrets, my relationship with them changed significantly. I had spent a month living in relative harmony with everyone, but ironically enough my new insider status damaged the connection I had with Melba. Upon learning about her situation, I had initially thought it would make me able to relate to her better— after all, I certainly knew what it was like to wait for a man in prison.

I did my best to console her, but she seemed to resent it. She was not like me—she believed in societal expectations I placed no stock in: "Be pretty, find a man to take care of you, get married and have kids, and everything will be okay." She followed rules that had betrayed her, but because they were all she had left, she clung to them for her survival, hiding behind a facade of sanctimonious respectability. And because I refused to accept this code, she failed to believe anything I had to say. So instead of bringing us closer, my attempt to offer her advice only strained our friendship.

Over the next month, she grew increasingly impatient with any attempt I made to engage her in conversation. Not wanting to exacerbate the tension that had bubbled up out of nowhere (I still wasn't sure exactly what to attribute it to), I tried to stay out of her way as much as possible, but every time Francisco and I prepared to leave the house, she grew friendly and enthusiastic and asked if she could come along. This change of attitude so surprised me that at first I wondered if I had been wrong about her antagonism toward me, but after a few trips into the city with her I understood the source of her fake cordiality: She was tagging along to take advantage of the fact that I paid for everything.

I had often wondered how Melba was supporting herself. She didn't have a job and her husband was in prison. All I knew was that anytime a bill arrived at our table, Melba conveniently disappeared. I'd been paying rent for a month now, which was really only fair, but now I was buying groceries for the entire household, picking up the tab for the girls' lunches when we ate takeout, even shelling out Melba's bus fare when we all went out together. She would glide innocently past the guy collecting the passengers' money as if she hadn't seen him, and Francisco would shrug his shoulders and dish out enough for all three of us.

Francisco and I were still living off of my savings and I didn't mind sharing my money with him until we got on our feet, but taking care of Melba seemed excessive. Every day, our money situation was becoming more and more of an issue. Nine months earlier, I had left the United States with sixteen thousand dollars. Now I was down to just over three grand.

For years, writing had been my sole means of economic support, but being a specialist in constructing English sentences (never mind that I ended a large percentage of them in prepositions) wasn't exactly in high demand in the Spanish-speaking country I was in. If Francisco and I were ever going to move out and get a place of our own, we would have to start seriously thinking about how to earn a living.

"I think we should start a raffle" was Francisco's first idea.

"A raffle?"

"Yeah, you know, we sell tickets to win something small—a ring or something and then we move on to something bigger—like my sister's house."

It was an interesting idea but it seemed like giving away Melba's house had the potential to create a few new family problems. I imagined her coming home one day and finding other people living there. Surely she'd figure out something was up.

"Okay, well, I have another thought," Francisco assured me. "But we're going to need a bulldozer."

I shook my head and pointed out that he knew nothing about construction. Not a problem, he explained—he was thinking more of destruction. "There's this bridge in the south of Colombia. We need to knock it down. See, I met this guy in prison and he told me he had hidden hundreds of thousands of dollars in the concrete—"

I shook my head.

"You're right. I'm sure the guerrillas already got to it."

As goofy as Francisco's ideas sounded, in reality, these were the ways you earned a living in Colombia. It was a surreal country. I kept hearing stories about people who bought houses from ex-drug dealers and later found millions of dollars hidden away behind the plaster of the wall. And there were cases of farmers innocently tilling up land who'd come across metal canisters in the dirt filled with thousands of hundred-dollar bills. It was the Colombian version of winning the Publishers Clearing House sweepstakes, inadvertently funded by the cocaine traffickers who kept running out of places to store their ever-accumulating wealth.

There were a few good jobs to be had, but this was not a merit-based society and any well-paying gig invariably went to those who had no need for the money. Latin America as a whole was almost feudal in its approach to social class. The household you were born into determined your entire future. Your last name said more about you than any other trait you would ever possess. You could even be forgiven for being broke as long as you were from the right family. A poor Santodomingo or Grajales (the U.S. equivalent of a Rockefeller or a Ford) was seen as a sort of dethroned king, a tragic figure who needed to be aided at any cost.

Francisco was lucky to have the light skin and blue eyes so prized by the upper class, but he nevertheless got gypped out of a good last name on a technicality. His family history read like a good soap opera. Francisco's father had been christened Sánchez instead of Restrepo because at the time of his conception, the baby's mother, Cecilia, had been involved with two men. In a rage of jealousy, Jaime, the man who had by now become her husband, refused to give the baby his prestigious last name, insisting in a rage of jealousy that there was no proof the child was his, even though the boy grew up blue-eyed and light-skinned, just like Jaime and unlike Cecilia's discarded beau.

A Restrepo by any other name simply did not smell as sweet. The difference between the Sánchez family and the Restrepos was staggering. Francisco, Melba, and all the other Sánchez relatives lived modest lives, in simple, box-shaped homes with small yards and cheap furniture. But Francisco's aunt, a Restrepo, lived in a palace, a penthouse apartment with three floors filled with servants. And I hadn't even visited "the big house" located out in the country.

Being a Sánchez wasn't always easy, especially when Francisco was growing up. When his mother passed away, Francisco's father became useless as a breadwinner, turning to alcohol to dull his sense of loss, and it fell to fifteen-year-old Francisco to pick up the pieces of what was left of the family: his drunken father who was often found passed out in the park and little Melba, who was just eight years old. (By this point, Martha had already moved out and was taking care of her own husband and kids.)

Francisco did his best to earn money selling clothes and toys door to door and taking any menial job that came his way. It was a depressing existence with no end in sight, until one day something completely unexpected happened. Francisco found himself face to face with one of the most powerful men in Colombia, a leader of the Cali drug cartel who had an idea. He proposed that Francisco, with his blue eyes and light complexion, would easily pass for an American citizen, and with a fake passport he would glide effortlessly past European immigration officials, even if he had a bunch of cocaine stashed in his suitcase.

He was a nineteen-year-old boy sitting at the desk of the richest man he'd ever met in his life and he didn't have the guts or even the desire to say no. In Colombia, this was as loud as opportunity would ever knock and it altered the course of the Sánchez family's life.

A young Colombian who had never traveled, Francisco's first trip out of the country was made as a *mula*. Trembling, with five kilos of cocaine duct-taped to his legs, Francisco walked up to the immigration counters in Madrid, and half an hour later he walked out of the airport a rich man. When he returned home two weeks later, it was as a hero, his arms burdened with gifts, clothes, and toys for his family, not to mention the ten thousand dollars in cash he carried in his suitcase.

From then on, it became a game. Francisco bought himself boots and a cowboy hat and went to Germany disguised as a Texan. He grew himself a beard, borrowed a guitar, and traveled to Holland as an American backpacker. And one time, he went with his cousin, the two of them posing as an American couple spending their vacation abroad.

The money changed Francisco's family's life. His cousin made the trip just once, so nervous she bit her nails down to the quick, but when she returned to Colombia, she had the money to buy the plot of land that she transformed into her dream house. Francisco made his own investments. Eventually, he bought himself three cabs. He rented one out, drove one himself, and handed the third over to his father so that his dad would have a way to earn a living.

It all worked wonderfully for a while, but selling drugs never went on forever. There was a saying in Colombia: "What flows *in* like water flows *out* like water." Those that didn't quit by choice were coerced by force, ending their vocation by either death or imprisonment, often leaving a family even worse off than before. Incarceration turned a breadwinner into a dependent. Not only was a jailed father unable to provide for his family, he suddenly became an expense. There were legal fees plus the cost of international plane tickets for the families that could afford to visit.

I saw these effects firsthand. Suddenly deprived of their mother's income, Stephanie, Jenny, and Toño were now surviving on what their father brought in from his small grocery store. They had lost their house, been forced to move in with Melba, and now lived an even more meager existence than before. Worst of all was the psychological effect of having watched their mother walk out the door one day and never come back.

They all dealt with this loss in their own way. Toño was angry, almost violent, hating anything remotely connected to the United States. Jenny would erupt in willful outbursts, challenging anyone to tell her what to do. But little Stephanie was just sad and lonely, seeking anyone who could take her mother's place. She often trailed me around the house, trying to convince me to let her participate in whatever activity I happened to be involved in: "What are you writing? Do you need any help?" or "What are you reading? Will you read it to me?"

At night, she liked to jump into bed with me and beg, "Can I sleep with you? I don't take up much room. Just this once, okay?" And every morning, there were the same questions: "Will you take a shower with me? Pleeeeaaase? I'll help you wash your hair."

She was so persistent and sweet that eventually she wore me down. I didn't let her into the tiny bed with Francisco and me (at least not at night), but eventually I started bathing with her because it made her so happy. She'd make me kneel down while she soaped up my hair and then she'd hand me the shampoo, expecting me to return the favor.

It wasn't really a maternal urge on my part. I didn't think of her as a daughter. It was more like hanging out with a younger version of myself. I had been a lonely kid too. I had felt like there had been no one to take care of me, so I sympathized with her plight. Besides, hanging out with Stephanie was actually a lot of fun. When she forgot how sad she was, she was charming, smart, and confident, and I appreciated the fact that she was always gracious every time I made another botched attempt to act like a grown-up. Once, I tried to teach her a song, but the only Spanish tune I remembered from my childhood was one she already knew, so she decided to teach me one instead. Francisco laughed as we performed it for him in the living room, hand motions and all, as Stephanie belted out the words with all her heart.

After another humiliating failure (a disastrous attempt to sew clothes for her dolls), one day, I sat both of the girls down at the dining room table to perform the one arts-and-crafts project guaranteed to be a success. I took a sheet of white paper, carefully folded it up, and began skillfully carving away at it with a pair of scissors. I extended the paper hopefully and sure enough, I had created a perfect snowflake.

"It's beautiful," Stephanie remarked, beaming up at me.

I tried to contain my pride. "Do you want me to teach you how to make one?" She nodded.

My exultation lasted all of two minutes. "So, what do you call it?" she asked.

What was she talking about? "You don't know what it is? It's a——" I paused, realizing I didn't know how to say snowflake. Francisco was watching a soccer game on TV (technically in the living room part of the house but in reality only two feet away). "Francisco, what do you call a piece of snow——you know, that individual grain of snow that's unlike any other?" I asked in Spanish.

Francisco shrugged without looking away from the screen. I took a sigh and reached for my dictionary. *"Copo de nieve.* That's what it is. A *copo de nieve."* Both of the girls gave me a blank stare. "Around Christmastime, you know, snowflakes?"

The game had gone into halftime and Francisco walked over. "Wow, that's really neat. What is it?"

"A *copo de nieve*," I announced.

"A what?"

And suddenly it occurred to me—it had never snowed in Cali. There was nothing wrong with my perfectly crafted snowflake— these people had just never seen one before. They didn't even know what the word meant.

This was the lesson that kept recurring in my travels: that the ideas I had been raised with, the truths that had formed my child-hood, my adolescence, and my early adulthood were limited by geography. They collapsed in on themselves when transferred to a foreign place. "The way things are" was rarely a true statement; it needed to be amended to "the way things are *here*." So much of what I had learned growing up was really just arbitrary.

In San José, I had once taken the wrong side of an argument with a cabdriver who had told me that Costa Rica had just two seasons. A country with two seasons? What a ridiculous notion. I kept insist-ing that there were actually four, but that Costa Ricans had chosen to lump them together differently. We could have done the same thing in the United States by insisting that we had six months of Sprimmer followed by half a year of Wintumn. Later, I realized how shortsighted I was being. Just because I grew up in a country that had four seasons didn't mean that every place did. Four seasons was a result of the latitude that the United States occupied. In the trop-ics where the temperature rarely varied, the only major change in the climate was whether it rained or not, resulting in two seasons: "wet" and "dry."

My father had been so right—memorization wasn't a type of learning; it was the opposite of learning. The minute you memo-rized a fact, you took it to be true. "There are four seasons" sounded like a pronouncement from God. But when you understood what caused the seasons—the tilt of the earth, a country's position rela-tive to the sun—you didn't fall quite so easily into the same trap.

It was one of the most difficult things to do—stepping outside of your own culture. In a different country, it wasn't enough to speak the language. You had to construct your world all over again, begin with the basics, learn the essential distinctions from scratch, redefine Good and Evil, Wrong and Right, Happiness and Pain.

This was why I did not judge Francisco for his past as a drug mule. Had he been from the States, I would have expected other things of him. But he wasn't an American, he was a Colombian. He had done what was acceptable (even prestigious) to accomplish in the place he had been born.

I accepted his past on the condition that it remain his past. My only request was that he never get involved in any illegal activity again. As I said to him jokingly, "It's one 'get out of prison free' card per customer."

Whether Francisco's actions had been wrong or right was irrelevant. It was merely a practical decision: I did not want fear and flight to be part of my life anymore.

Chapter Ten

The Road Less Traveled Is Usually the One with Guerrillas on It

Note to reader: *Hi, this is Wendy, the one who's been writing this book so far. Just wanted to let you know that the next five pages are kind of rough going, full of politics, ideas, and a few discerning conclusions about the state of humanity. Sorry for the inconvenience. If you can hold on for just a thousand or so words, I assure you that the plot will pick up again. (And not that you heard it from me, but a few really bad things are just about to occur.) Thanks for your attention. We now return you to your regularly scheduled book.*

There is something about politics that seems to get people riled up. It is the educated person's football. Saying you are a fan of Israel or Palestine or Cuba or the United States seems so much more significant and logical than being on the side of, say, the Dallas Cowboys. You get all the fun of cheering for your team ("Go guerrillas!") yet none of the arbitrariness. It's a game you can believe in—without all the commercials.

For a long time, I had been trying to pick my teams in the arena of world conflict, but the more I learned about politics, the more difficult siding with one group or the other had become. Before I went to Lebanon, I did a lot of research, figuring that I'd know what group to side with by the time I arrived, but every additional piece of information I gleaned only further complicated my understanding of the country. The Maronite Christians had a long list of offenses committed against them by the Muslims, the usual atrocities of war—terrorist acts, torture, rape. But for every indignity a Maronite could name, a Shiite or Sunni could match it with another equally horrific act perpetrated upon them by a Christian.

After a bit more investigation, I discovered that I hadn't been the only one with problems figuring it all out; it seemed that the Lebanese had had a tough time picking sides as well. It was a land of ever-changing alliances. At one point it had been Maronites against all Muslims. Then it changed to Sunni Muslims against their former brothers, the Shiites. Then it was Maronites on the side of Israel against the Palestine Liberation Organization. Then it was Maronites on the side of Lebanon against Israel.

It was difficult to imagine a more complicated situation, yet somehow Colombia still managed to provide the Middle East with some pretty tough competition. Now that I had been living in the country for two months, it had become even more important for me to be able to speak intelligently about politics (plus I would know who to root for when I watched the news), but the more I learned about guerrilla war and how it intersected with the drug trade, the fuzzier my understanding of the whole situation became.

As best I could tell, the country's first step in the wrong direction began when Colombians began trying to find an export that Americans were willing to shell out money for. They had dabbled in sugar, bananas, even petroleum, but they finally struck it big for the first time when Juan Valdez began gracing the breakfast tables of nearly every American home, and Colombia became synonymous with coffee.

It was only one logical step away to assume that if Americans were able to part with eight dollars a pound for something that woke them up in the morning, they'd be willing to pay much more for something that woke them up at night. And while mild-mannered Señor Valdez continued strolling through the commercials on network television, Pablo Escobar began to dominate the news—Pablo's advantage being that his publicity was free.

The great thing about this new Colombian export was that unlike coffee, which required very specific climatic conditions and obsessive care, the coca plant was a common bush that hedged nearly everybody's lawn. Discovering that money was literally growing on shrubs had two major effects: (1) Normal, everyday Colombians starting snipping off the profits and (2) their yards began looking pretty shabby.

Finding a stash of cocaine in a Colombian garage was about as likely as coming across a barbecue in a garage in the United States. The principal difference, however, was that in the States, your neighbor wasn't likely to come riding by on a motorcycle carrying an AK-47 and shooting your windows in just because you were a little late returning what you had borrowed—unless of course, you lived in Montana.

This new, nearly ubiquitous Colombian wealth kind of put a damper on the whole underground Marxist revolutionary movement. Communist rhetoric had worked well when the peasants were worried about the effect of rain on their crops; however, it was failing miserably now that the peasants were concerned about the effect of rain on their Mercedes.

The Marxist guerrillas weren't about to lose out when everyone else was making a profit. After all, the arms that they needed to forward their movement did *not* grow on trees. So when the leaders of the cocaine cartels began looking for guards to protect their laboratories, the guerrillas filled out job applications, figuring their experience trying to overthrow the government would be considered adequate employment crossover skills.

From there, things got a bit blurred. The guerrillas were working for the cartels, the government was trying to destroy both groups, and everybody was busy running for political office. (Even Pablo Escobar got himself elected to congress.) So everyone began attending the same cocktail parties; they were just shooting each other in the parking lot.

These days, the guerrilla groups that still espoused an ideology of creating a decent life for the poor masses (this would make them good guys, right?) funded their "revolution" through kidnapping, cocaine, and extortion (um, make that bad guys). Wealthy landowners became victims (good guys) and were forced to pay a *vacuna*, a monthly sum that they handed over just so that the guerrillas (bad guys) would leave them in peace. However, lots of wealthy landowners (good guys) got fed up and in order to defend their lands and protect their families, they hired private militia (rich guys become bad guys again). These private armies (bad guys) were a little too good at what they did—apparently, they'd been overachievers in paramilitary school—and instead of just protecting their employers they began massacring whole villages of innocent Colombians because guerrillas were rumored to be among them. So the guerrillas began protecting the villagers (making them good guys again). In the end, the Colombian government was making deals with the drug traffickers, the drug traffickers were making deals with the guerrillas, yet everyone managed to remain at war with one another. Try finding a team to root for in all of that.

I spent my first few months in Colombia, trying to sort it all out—and miraculously enough, I finally did. I wish I could claim that my epiphany was a result of intense research and exceptional insight. However, my conclusion came to me the easy way: I stole it from someone else.

The most invaluable clue for comprehending international conflict had landed in my lap six years earlier thanks to a woman named Marta, my mother's best buddy from college. Marta and I were so similar—at times it struck me that there'd been some sort of administrative mix-up in the spirit world and that I had wound up being born by mistake to Cathie Dale instead of to her. As my mother put it with a tinge of jealousy every time I mentioned her college friend's name, "No wonder you like Marta. She's a Thinker," with emphasis on the word "thinker," as if it were a nationality or race. "Rhoda is Irish, Amanda is Asian. Marta—she's a Thinker."

During one of our infrequent chats (I wanted to see her more often, but she lived in Tucson), Marta was discussing her intellectual obsession du jour, the conflict in the former Yugoslavia. She had spent months absorbing any information she could get her hands on, and her desk and shelves were stacked high with books and magazine articles tackling the issue from every possible angle.

"So what do *you* think?" I had asked her, figuring that her analysis would be pretty accurate and credible.

"After reading all about the history of the Muslims, the Croats, and the Serbs, comprehending the ethnic conflict that has plagued the area for centuries, understanding the religious differences and the main grievances cited by each group, I have finally come to understand exactly why it is they are fighting." She paused before sharing her conclusion, the words that would form the basis of my understanding of Colombia and any other world conflict for that matter: "They're fighting because they want to."

In spite of its disadvantages (kidnapping, guerrilla war, drug mafia violence, paramilitary massacres, etc.), Colombia was still the most breathtaking country I had ever seen, teeming with green tropical plants that took over the landscape like ebullient kudzu. From the moment I had set foot on the shores of Sapzurro, the place had gotten to me. Even then I had sensed it—my new country was bursting to the seams with optimism.

That was the thing about Colombia—it took away everything but hope. You *hoped* you wouldn't get kidnapped, you *hoped* the guerrillas wouldn't attack, you *hoped* the paramilitaries wouldn't get to you, you *hoped* you'd find a million dollars in the ground. Against all logic, you still convinced yourself you'd find a way. It was intoxicating. It was like religion. It was wonderful and inspiring and false. And it was the only explanation I could find for my irrational love of the place.

Granted, there were the warm tropical nights that lingered in my memory—evenings punctuated by the beat of the *cumbia* flavored with the taste of strong Colombian *aguardiente*. But these were just details. The real reason I loved Colombia defied explanation. The whole place was ancient and mystical in a way that only Gabriel García Márquez was able to portray. I had come to the conclusion that he was not a magic realist at all. He was a realist—he had just described Colombia the way it is.

I imagined myself settling into a quiet and contented existence with Francisco here. I envisioned the small house we would buy in the hills, the daily trip to the corner store to buy the strange fruits I was becoming accustomed to: *anonas, maracuyá, guayaba.* The only obstacle I could foresee was the issue of money. Below the surface of the enthusiasm I felt for my new home was the nagging worry that we wouldn't find a way to earn a living.

I'd had a couple of backup plans before I left the States, but my attempts to write for AFP and Hughes Aircraft had already fallen through. Francisco had gone back to all the travel agencies where he had worked a decade earlier, but they were never hiring. In this economy, they had already laid off everyone they could spare.

Getting a good job had proven impossible, so we both hoped to resort to the path favored by our neighbors: We would start up a home-based business. Fortunately, Melba had gone to Miami to be near her husband for an indefinite period of time, leaving us in charge of the house and providing me with a tremendous sense of relief, one that had come cheap at the price of two hundred dollars. Right before her departure, she'd stood glancing over at the American Airlines counter with a pathetic stare, explaining that she didn't have quite enough for the ticket for her son. I'd swallowed my anger, walked straight to the ATM, and come back with a stack of twenties that she pocketed with a cold "thank you."

Now that she was gone, not only was I calmer and happier, Francisco and I had taken over the master bedroom, which provided us with some much needed privacy. And since the only other adult in the household was Melba's brother-in-law who spent most of his time at his grocery store across town, Francisco and I basically had the house at our disposal. Every afternoon after we got Stephanie, Jenny, and Toño off to school, Francisco and I would settle in at the dining room table and brainstorm potential business ventures.

"How about we sell a trip ourselves?" Francisco asked one morning over breakfast, animatedly tossing aside the classifieds.

"What do you mean?"

"Every Colombian wants to visit the United States. We sell a trip to Disney World."

I could see him getting excited about the idea. "Do you really think it would work?" I asked.

"Most Colombians don't even think about taking their vacation in the United States because they can't get in. The visa restrictions are too tough. But if you go with a tour group, your admission to the country is practically guaranteed. At one of the travel agencies where I used to work, part of my job was helping tourists get American visas."

I'd never set foot in Florida (a layover at the Miami airport didn't count) and Francisco had never even visited the United States. I could just imagine the fiasco, both of us as disoriented tour guides, trying desperately to locate Disney World.

"Well, it's got to be around here somewhere, Francisco. For God's sake, pull the bus over at that gas station and ask how to get to the happiest place on Earth."

"No, no, we'll find it. I think we need to make a right at the next light."

"Francisco, this is really not the time to refuse to ask for directions."

"You distract the passengers. I'll pull out the map."

There had to be other businesses that we would be better suited for. "What about planning the trip?" I asked Francisco. "What about the logistics? What if we get trapped somewhere between Fantasyland and Tomorrowland and can't find our way out?"

"There are package deals already set up. We do the selling and then tack on a big commission for us."

I didn't hold out a lot of hope. In this economy, most people were struggling just to survive. Who had the money for an overseas vacation? But Francisco returned from the travel agency so enthusiastic, with his arms full of glossy brochures, that I didn't have the heart to spoil the plan. Besides, I believed in him. He was always so confident in his ability to take care of himself that it was hard not to trust him, and fortunately, our investment would be minimal. It was only ten dollars to put an ad in the paper: "Visit Disney World! U.S. visas arranged." And we got the girls to distribute flyers around the neighborhood by offering them two dollars a piece.

The first time the phone rang in response to our ad, I was pleasantly surprised. When Francisco hung up, I walked over to find out what had happened, but the phone rang again. Francisco gave me an excited smile and went to answer. And when he replaced the receiver five minutes later, the phone rang another time.

That day, I did not speak to my boyfriend. There was such a surge of interest in our trip to Florida that Francisco didn't even have time to eat. And when he finally couldn't hold it anymore and absolutely had to go to the bathroom, he handed the phone over to me so that I'd take over the incoming calls.

Frankly, I couldn't believe it. In Colombia, most people had even cut down on food—the other day our grocer had shaken his head and complained, "I don't understand why *my* business is suffering. In a bad economy, people still need to *eat*"—yet Francisco and I were having an incredible amount of success promoting a luxury trip abroad.

"Maybe they're bored," I said to Francisco, lying in bed later that night. "None of them have jobs so they look through the classifieds. And they call our number because they have nothing better to do."

Francisco shook his head and laughed.

"Well, how do *you* explain it?" I asked. "It doesn't make any sense."

"Well, we'll just see who shows up tomorrow."

We had told all of the interested callers to meet at the house the next evening at seven. By seven fifteen, the living room was packed. We had used up all the chairs, people were crammed onto the stairs, and latecomers were squeezing through the crowd trying to find a place to stand.

Meanwhile, I was going crazy in the kitchen. My job was to be a Proper Latina Hostess, which meant getting lemonade out to all the visitors. But we only had seven cups so as I squeezed lemons in the kitchen, Stephanie and Jenny would distribute drinks and then hover over the guests, waiting to snatch up an empty glass, which I would subsequently wash and refill for the next person.

Francisco was busy in the living room, charming the crowd that had gathered for the event. When he was in a good mood, Francisco could be eloquent and persuasive, and he talked about the trip in such compelling detail that he had managed to convince even me that we were headed to a tropical utopia, a place of happiness and sunshine that served as a model of peace and prosperity for the rest of the world. And the crowd was eating it up.

Everything was going great until he opened up the meeting to questions. I figured we'd get things like: "Does the hotel have a swimming pool?" "What meals are included?" "How much time will we have at the beach?" But the actual queries were nothing like this.

"So, no one's going to be following us around, right? Like, say at Disney World. We won't have a tour guide the whole time, right?"

"No, it's just a shuttle there and we meet up at the end of the day to return to the hotel."

"Okay, if we don't make the flight back home, no one's going to look for us, right?"

This was starting to get weird. "Well, if you want to extend your visit, I don't think it would be a problem."

"Right. So if we decided to stay, everyone else would go home. And no one would follow up on what happened to us, correct?"

And that was when I realized what was going on. No one cared about going to Disney World. They were looking for a way in to the United States. And our package deal provided them with a good shot at a visa, which was cheaper and safer than crossing the Mexican border illegally.

After the last one had shuffled out of the house, I shook my head and said to Francisco, "Oh my God! We've turned into coyotes!"*

$\mathcal{N}$ow that our big trip to Miami had ended in failure, Francisco and I were getting more and more desperate about earning a living.

"Well, what is it exactly *you* want to do?" Francisco asked, losing his patience. "Explain it to me one more time."

It had always been a difficult concept for anyone living outside of New York or Los Angeles to grasp. Whenever I said I was a writer, people would stare back at me with a puzzled expression. "People *do* that?" I would be asked. So I was prepared to give Francisco a bit more explanation. I told him that I wrote radio commercials, magazine articles, television scripts—but these jobs weren't exactly in overabundance in Cali.

"Well, you're just going to have to do something else here," Francisco insisted. "Unless your writing experience extends to doing ransom notes."

It was an interesting idea and there certainly was a market for it in Cali: "Give your kidnapping the image it deserves. Hollywood

---

*A coyote is a guide, generally Mexican, hired by Latin Americans to help them sneak across the border into the United States.

writer will let people know you mean business, increase your chances of success, and ensure high profits."

"I want to write for TV and film," I explained to Francisco.

Francisco was still frustrated with me, but I could tell I had just given him an idea. "What is it?" I asked, wanting him to tell me what he was thinking.

"You know, you can find just about anything you want in the Yellow Pages," he said mysteriously.

Francisco, who must have been a Hollywood agent in a past life, quickly took to the idea of having a job that involved getting paid when someone else worked. He hastily transformed himself into my unofficial manager, made a few calls to his new contacts picked from the pages of the phone book, jotted down some notes, and kept dialing. But by the fourth call, I realized that the case was pretty hopeless.

"Francisco, you have to accept the fact that we're in Colombia and you're not going to find a worthwhile film industry in a country where there isn't a significant Jewish population."

Francisco ignored my comment and spoke into the receiver. The conversation that followed wasn't exactly encouraging.

"Good afternoon. Is this Studio One?" There was a pause. "Oh, is there an adult there I could speak to?"

"Hang up," I insisted. "Give up."

But he continued undaunted. "Could you put your dad on the phone?"

By the time Francisco hung up, he informed me that we had a date to do coffee with a Colombian film director.

Two hours later, we rang the bell of a once luxurious Spanish-style home that was now in need of a new coat of paint. A short, blue-eyed man with white hair, a beard, and a round belly answered the door and for a minute I began to think we had arrived at the North Pole instead of northern Cali. But the address seemed to be correct and since the only short people running around turned out to be his children, I assumed we were at the right place.

"Please come in. I'm Manfred Hirsch," the man said, his eyes all a-twinkle.

"Colombian?" I asked.

"I'm Jewish," he said. "Colombian too."

I gave Francisco a knowing smirk and we made ourselves at home.

Colombian film was about as common as Alaskan oranges, meaning that neither one of them got a whole lot of press. If he really had wanted to make it big, Hollywood was where Manfred Hirsch should have been, though geography wasn't exactly his family's strong point. At least this is what I gathered when he told me that the reason his parents had wound up in Colombia in the 1930s was that they were trying to go to the North American continent.

"There seems to be some logical step I'm missing out on," I commented to our host, who had turned out to be an amiable and funny man.

"Well, their English wasn't very good and they thought they were headed to *British* Columbia."

Jewish exoduses always seemed to be riddled with problems: If it wasn't the Red Sea, then it was the Caribbean. I imagined the Hirsch family disembarking from the plane expecting to see maple trees and people who said "eh," and instead finding themselves surrounded by coca plants and people who said, "Give me all your money or I'll kill you." It must have been some shock.

Before meeting Manfred and his wife, Cristina, my biggest sense of personal accomplishment had come from leaving to buy bread in the morning and returning home without being kidnapped.

But now my days were spent with Francisco at the Hirsch house, mornings filled with mugs of steaming coffee and afternoons spent dreaming out loud of a burgeoning Colombian film market.

For the next four months, it seemed that every time I looked up, there was Manfred in front of me, grinning mischievously, smoking a cigarette, wearing cut-off shorts, an old T-shirt, and cheap flip-flops. He was a bit of an eccentric as far as wealthy Colombians went. Whenever he was invited to any social function, he meandered unselfconsciously among the overly dressed and overly jeweled socialites, never wearing anything more formal than faded jeans and the occasional long-sleeved shirt.

The four of us would sit in his living room filled with worn antiques, and although Cristina and Francisco did their part to contribute to the stories and ideas being shared, it was obvious that the group camaraderie centered around Manfred and me. He and I were a strange pair—he was more than thirty years my senior and had a wife and five kids—and I'm sure that anyone who ever saw us walking down the street struggled to figure out the nature of our relationship, but he wasn't a father figure or even a mentor to me. As bizarre as it may have seemed, Manfred and I had become best friends.

We simply couldn't get enough of each other. Practically every afternoon (never in the morning—Manfred and Cristina were night owls and never got up before noon), Francisco and I would head over to their house and spend the rest of the day engrossed in the kind of intense conversation I had rarely experienced since college: personal anecdotes, philosophical musings, and funny stories. When this had gone on for hours and the guilt started to set in, we'd finally buckle down and get some work done.

In addition to enjoying each other's company, Manfred and I had discovered that we were perfectly suited as creative partners. What Manfred's business lacked was a good writer and what my writing lacked was an income, so the two of us hoped to pool our experience in producing TV ads.

Manfred had never invested much effort into marketing himself and his production company had collapsed along with the economy, but we had a strategy to revive his flagging business: Francisco would be in charge of rounding up clients, I'd write the ads and come up with some cutting-edge promotional materials, Manfred would direct, and Cristina would oversee production.

We'd already invested months in the project and had yet to see any income—Manfred couldn't afford to pay us until we actually sold a commercial. My savings had dwindled down to just over a thousand dollars, but it was still okay. I guess I had been in the country long enough to let a little bit of Colombian optimism seep in.

December rolled around, which provided me with a unique problem: I really didn't want to go to Bolivia for Christmas. Why didn't other people have these kinds of dilemmas? As I lay in bed staring out the window (Francisco was still asleep), I searched my memory for any advice I might once have heard, but there simply wasn't any—not one time had a single friend of mine come up to me and complained: "My parents just don't get it. I don't want to visit the Andes."

I didn't want to go to Bolivia, but my reasons had nothing to do with what was surely a very nice country. Basically, I didn't want to be anywhere near my parents, two people who would require a lot of nice happy chatting from me in spite of the fact that I was jobless and nearly broke in Colombia.

Just a month earlier, I'd made a difficult attempt at self-revelation, trying to tell my parents the truth of what had been going on in my life. Through several e-mails and one long distance call, I had somehow managed to give them the condensed version of meeting Francisco, freeing him from prison, and fleeing to Colombia, but as usual news of my life seemed to fly right past them. I have no idea how my father took this information, but my mother (who was always the one to write or pick up the phone) was just interested in knowing if life in Colombia was like she had seen in the movies, and she asked hopefully if there was any chance that I was hanging out with CIA agents, drug traffickers, and hit men. The only thing she had to say on the topic of Francisco was that she was glad I finally had a boyfriend, and was there any chance that it was serious so that she could look forward to me settling down?

I had hung up the phone, even more convinced in my belief that my parents had never actually listened to me. Was there nothing I could do to get them to pay attention to *my life* instead of their own?

No, probably not. So I decided I wouldn't be bitter or ugly about it, I would just move on. We'd break up, the same way women and men did all the time. Our expectations didn't match so it was time to look for someone more compatible. It really was in everyone's best interest. Besides, they were young and attractive; they'd find themselves a new kid. And maybe after a little while, we could even be just friends.

Could it be as simple as that? No, of course not. Everyone needs to know *why* you're dumping them if they're going to move on. Should I pause before giving them the reason so they'd think I hadn't been dwelling on this for the past decade? Hmmmm, let's see, what could the reason be? Here we go, this is it, simple: "You never once said, 'What can I do to help?'" There's your reason, Mom and Dad. Happy now?

That was my reason, but I didn't have the guts to say it. I sucked at breaking up. So I'd see them and pretend that everything was okay, just like I had always done.

As if the thought of spending two weeks with my parents didn't distress me enough, there was also the troublesome issue of how I was going to get there. In my most recent phone conversation with my mother, she had explained the complicated logistics of my impending trip. The first step was to pick up my plane ticket, which she had arranged to have waiting for me at a nearby airport, conveniently located just three hundred miles away.

"It's very easy, Wendy. All you have to do is go to Bogotá and get it."

"Right. But Mom, I live in Cali."

"I know honey, but it was a hundred dollars cheaper this way."

This was all too typical of my mother's travel arrangements. Her children's personal comfort never stood a chance when competing with the allure of bargain air travel. I had spent my life on red-eye flights, with last-minute discount tickets and bizarre connections by land. And every protest of mine was always met with what she considered to be the irrefutable phrase in her favor: "But honey, you can sleep on the *plane*." She didn't expect me to stay awake on the journey over. That would be cruel. She only expected me to be up at 2 A.M., to catch the shuttle at 3 A.M., to arrive at the airport at 5 A.M. But 6 A.M. to 8 A.M. on the plane—this was all generously handed over to me as prime sleeping hours.

This time, I was supposed to take an overnight bus from Cali to Bogotá, grab a cab to the airport, and then hop on a flight to Cochabamba, Bolivia. Never mind that this trip was placing my life in jeopardy, that I was living in a country where travel by land was extremely dangerous and if it should occur to any of several armed guerrilla groups operating in the country to stop the bus, I was prime pickings for a kidnapping. My parents, nonworriers by nature, just assumed that natural calamity would somehow bypass anyone who happened to be a Dale.

When the Northridge earthquake devastated most of Los Angeles in 1993, I'd called my folks up two days afterward, once electricity had been restored and I'd been able to access a working line. "Don't worry, I'm fine," I had said in response to my mother's hello.

"Good, we're fine too, honey. What have you been up to?"

"Mom, the earthquake, didn't you hear?"

"Sure. Was that near *your* house? We just figured it was another part of Los Angeles."

But this time would be different. I would show them, I thought as I hugged Francisco good-bye and boarded the bus bound for Bogotá. I would get kidnapped, just to prove how negligent they were as parents.

Three hours into my journey, we had yet to run into any guerrillas, but the next best thing was happening. I took it as a positive sign when the driver got off the bus, returned five minutes later, and shouted out to the passengers, "Is anyone here a mechanic?"

Our bus had broken down, and if we could just remain stranded for at least four hours, I'd miss my plane. This wasn't too much to hope for. This was Latin America. Bus repairs were never accomplished in less than half a day.

I took my travel alarm clock out of my suitcase and set it on the seat next to mine. An hour slowly dragged by. Then another one. There was still a lot of banging on the underside of the bus, which buoyed my hopes. Just a couple of hours more, I thought to myself.

We started into the third hour and I allowed myself a measured bit of optimism. Then the fourth hour approached. Finally, the driver climbed aboard, shrugged his shoulders, and announced that the bus was irreparable, that we'd have to wait for another vehicle they were sending from Bogotá.

I couldn't believe my luck. Getting out of my trip to Bolivia couldn't have been simpler. I wasn't going to have to endure an unpleasant confrontation with my parents, the guilt-inducing silence at the other end of the line that would have followed my confession that I wanted to spend the holidays with Francisco instead of them. I just called them up from the bus station and tried to contain my glee.

"Yes, Mom, bad news, you're not going to believe this, but our bus broke down. We were stranded for six hours and I missed my plane. I wanted to hop right aboard the next flight but it's not leaving for another three days and, well, I don't have the money for a hotel, so I guess we'll just have to do this next year. Sorry about that. But these are the kinds of things that happen when you travel by land in Colombia. Hey, there's good news though—at least I didn't get kidnapped."

I could tell my mom was disappointed, but what could she say? "Well, I guess there's nothing you can do. Have a Merry Christmas, sweetheart."

Hours later, I was aboard a bus headed back to Cali, convinced it was a sign. Through no effort on my part, my trip to Bolivia had fallen through. This had to be a message sent to me from above. I was done trying to please my parents. I was done holding out hope that they would someday come through for me. It was over. Our relationship had come to an end.

My siblings and I would form a new family. I'd convince my sisters that there would be no more Christmases at my folks'. We'd find a new place to meet up every year. And when my brother was old enough, he could come too. We didn't need parents. After all, *we* had always been there for each other.

Besides, I had Francisco. When my siblings were far away, I would rely on him. It would be Francisco and Wendy, both of us clinging together like a lighthouse (wait, did lighthouses cling?) or, better yet, like Velcro. That was it—he and I clinging together like Velcro against the world. He was an orphan and I would be too. We didn't need any parents to complicate the picture. We'd be fine— we'd be better off on our own.

The list of Colombian superstitions supposed to guarantee luck in the new year was longer than most restaurant menus. Two days after Christmas, Francisco explained that all we had to do was adhere to a few simple rituals to ensure our good fortune.

"Say, you want love. Well, you have to wear red underwear on New Year's Eve. If you want money, you wear yellow ones."

This was easy: "I would like an order of prosperity with a side of success, please." After all, if he was really dishing up wishes, money was the only thing missing from our lives. We had each other—no need for red underwear. And we were happy together. Over the past few months, I had grown even more certain that I had made the right decision in leaving everything behind to be with Francisco.

Of course, I had my bad days too. Occasionally, in a fit of weakness, I'd yell out to him, "I got you out of prison. What have you ever done for me?" And if I was in an especially bad mood, I might think silently to myself that this hadn't turned out the way I had planned at all. We were getting poorer by the day and there wasn't any solution in sight. Getting him out of jail was supposed to be the end of our problems, not just one in a series of never-ending obstacles. I had sort of imagined that once he was free, my job would be over, and he'd begin to take care of me. So far, this hadn't happened, but I blamed our circumstances more than him.

I had never said it out loud, but I had made a silent commitment never to abandon Francisco just because times were tough. I would never do to Francisco what my parents had done to me. Besides, things were going to get better. We had a brand-new year to look forward to.

"How about travel?" Francisco asked. "People who want to travel walk around the block at the stroke of midnight carrying a suitcase."

I laughed at the image of the entire neighborhood going out for a stroll dragging a bunch of empty luggage behind. "No, I think we definitely need to stick with asking for money."

"Right. So, we need to take what's left of the cash, carry it with us, and wish as hard as we can when the new year strikes."

Whether this was going to work or not was questionable, but it was starting to become a fun game. Yellow underwear, walking around with hundred-dollar bills plastered on our bodies—at least it was an entertaining way to spend the last day of the year.

On December 31, both of us with new underclothes and four one-hundred-dollar bills in our pockets, we stepped outside onto the tiny balcony outside the master bedroom and waited for the countdown to begin. Neighbors swarmed on the grass below us, some of them dancing to music, others drinking licorice-flavored *aguardiente* and swaying uncertainly. It was a huge unorganized block party and suddenly everyone began chanting in unison: *"Cinco, cuatro, tres, dos, uno."*

Beneath us, the crowd was welcoming in the new year. People were shouting and screaming, hugging, and kissing. They threw confetti and blew into squawking toy horns. I looked at Francisco and thought, The worst year of my life is finally over. It's done.

I don't know how it happened that we both started to cry at exactly the same moment. Looking back, I imagine that they had been tears of relief. At least, I think that was why *Francisco* was crying. In my case, I suspect that deep down, somehow I knew that not even yellow underwear would work enough magic to save me.

The new year brought about change just as we had hoped, but not all of it was good. Melba returned from the United States with nothing more than a day's notice, making it pretty obvious that she was ready for Francisco and me to find another place to live. She came by to pick up the bed Francisco and I had been sleeping in, letting us know we had twenty-four hours to get the rest of our things and leave, and went to spend the night at her cousin Helena's, but not before informing me that she had decided she didn't really owe me two hundred dollars. Due to some sort of new math they must have been teaching in Colombia, she had arrived at the sum of just seventy-one bucks.

"Fine," I said, "I'll gladly take seventy-one dollars." At that, she stuck her nose up in the air indignantly and stormed off without handing me a penny.

Francisco and I had nowhere to go and showed up on Manfred's front steps nearly in tears. He invited us in, calmed us with encouraging words and warm drinks and proposed a handful of potential solutions: his camper, a place on his living room floor—there was even a vacant apartment for rent that was owned by a friend.

One look at the place and Francisco knew there was no way he could talk me out of moving there. The moment we walked in, my outlook on our bleak situation changed entirely. I jumped up and down like a five year old and squealed, "Oh my God! We'd be living in a *tree house!*"

The apartment was like the Disney version of where Tarzan and Jane would have lived. There was electricity and running water, but a good portion of the place was actually made of bamboo. The kitchen and dining room were quite normal—white plaster with exposed beams—but to get to the bedroom, you had to climb a twelve-foot ladder that led to a huge wooden loft. And the living room was even more exotic, a combination of bamboo supports and mats woven from palm fronds. There weren't any windows—just cutouts in the walls covered by wooden shutters, much like the openings in a barn. And the view was spectacular. We were on top of a towering hill that looked out over the entire city.

Of course, we didn't have anything to fill the place with, but the lack of furnishings seemed to go with the place. It was like *Gilligan's Island;* we would make something out of nothing. Bamboo, a few sticks, some rocks—who needed Ikea when you could forage for your furniture?

The day we moved in, Francisco hauled in three tree stumps from outside, set them down in the living room, and informed me proudly that now we had chairs. We also had a hot plate that Manfred had loaned us, a few pans, a set of silverware, two glasses, and a twin mattress. Manfred hadn't had an extra TV, but he offered us a monitor left over from his film days that doubled as a tiny nine-inch television as well as a radio.

I wanted to buy furniture (more important, a fridge), but our financial situation was steadily growing worse. Our new apartment wasn't an extravagance—it was only costing us fifty dollars more than we had paid to Melba each month, but my dwindling savings had yet to be augmented by any actual income. We had been working steadily with Manfred for four months, but so far we had yet to see any actual return on our investment.

We were all doing our best to make our new business venture a success. Francisco spent his mornings going from office to office, trying to drum up business. Anyone who expressed interest got a free script for their product, which was where Manfred and I came in. The second meeting consisted of the two of us acting out the commercial I had written and explaining details such as costs and production times.

The people whose offices we visited were enthusiastic and amazed—visualizing their product on TV had the tantalizing effect of seeing their name in lights—but after a few weeks of "deliberation and discussion" they always came back with the same chagrined and apologetic answer: Given the poor economy, it just wasn't the right time.

Nevertheless, we refused to give up. As soon as we'd get another "no," there'd be a new client who expressed interest, buoying our hopes yet again. Like a chain-smoking grandmother in polyester playing the slots at Vegas, we kept convincing ourselves that the more losses we stacked up, the sooner our win was about to occur. All it took was one lucky pull of the lever to obliterate the memory of all the quarters we had dumped into the machine. So we kept at it, hoping one of our clients would finally come through.

I was beginning to get scared. Not having money in the United States was bad enough, but being poor in another country brought out an entirely new level of fear. In the United States, there were always possibilities, always temporary work as a last resort, but there was nothing to fall back on here. Worse yet, I'd recently overstayed my visa, not having the money it would have cost to petition for an extension of my stay.

As our funds diminished down to the two-hundred-dollar mark, my efforts to round up money grew more and more intense. I suddenly recalled every person who owed me money and made every attempt to collect. I got a few hundred bucks out of a friend in Los Angeles, remembered a commission check I was owed by my printer. For a fleeting moment, I even considered asking my parents, but knew what the answer would be in advance: "It's just not a good time for us right now, Wendy."

My biggest fear was reaching the zero point and not having enough to even eat, so we began rationing our intake. We were always hungry, spent our nights dreaming about food, and waking up in the morning to the familiar shout of the fifteen-year-old bread seller hawking his products made breakfast the happiest time of day. *"Pan de bono, arepas,"* he'd cry out, reminding us that sustenance was only minutes away. I'd put the water on for coffee while Francisco raced out of the house halfway clothed, chasing after our meal.

We had come up with a plan to subsist on just over a dollar a day, meaning that our midday meal consisted of lentils and rice, with a grated up carrot added for flavor and vitamins. It was cheap, provided protein, and most important, it didn't require refrigeration.

At dinner, using the hot plate Manfred had loaned us, one of us would chop up and fry two green plantains, sprinkle on salt, and eat them with ketchup. Long ago, I had quit draining off the oil, figuring we could use the extra calories. And when we were able to sneak a few oranges off of a nearby tree, we'd squeeze the juice out and mix it with sugar and water.

We augmented our diet with occasional visits to homes that had refrigerators, accepting any invitation (Francisco's distant relatives, the kind neighbor downstairs) and tried not to make a scene as we gorged ourselves on tender meats and fresh salads. Any time we were asked over for lunch by Francisco's wealthy aunt (a Restrepo), we were always overjoyed at the thought of eating a square meal, an enthusiasm that was slightly tempered by the knowledge that the cab ride there would consume our budget for two days' worth of food.

Sitting in front of the hearty stews and sumptuous entrées that the maid brought around, we would try to cram in as much as possible, eating enough to fill us for that day as well as the next.

The only time I lost my appetite was when Francisco's aunt refused him a small loan. Sitting at the table in her three-story penthouse apartment filled with servants, I couldn't help but look at the silverware in front of me and enviously think that a single place setting would buy Francisco and me food for a month. It was the only time in my life that I ever struggled with the temptation to steal.

My relationship with material things had changed. I had become practical now. The ridiculously expensive Coach wallet, the Bally shoes I'd bought myself at a duty-free shop in London, my collection of pearls—these things were completely useless to me now. These luxuries from my past seemed like relics, anthropological clues to a life lived long ago.

As our money grew sparser, so too did our visits with Manfred. After four months of failed attempts and a bank balance of less than a hundred dollars, we finally resigned ourselves to the fact that we'd have to look for a source of income elsewhere. I knew Manfred would have offered us money had he had any to spare, but his own financial situation was nearly as precarious as our own.

Francisco had tried asking all of his relatives for a loan and I'd already spent the money so generously offered up by my closest friends. I wasn't about to endure another refusal from my parents, which just left my sisters, but they were both struggling to pay their way through college. I couldn't possibly impose on them.

The shift from optimism to resignation to despair was so gradual that I didn't even notice the decline. It seemed like one day we were full of hope and patience and the next, we were on the brink of starvation. But the realization that I could not survive this way any longer came on what Francisco and I would later come to refer to as the Day of the Maracuyá.

We had been walking down the hill, treading carefully down the fifty or so irregular stone steps that led to the bus stop. Usually, I kept my gaze on the ground to watch my footing—the steps ranged in size from a few inches to several feet (one massive stair actually reached up to my midthigh and I had to sit on it and scoot down like a little girl). But this time, while taking a short rest, I happened to glance overhead for a second. In the vine above us was something that looked suspiciously edible.

I couldn't have been more excited had I discovered a hundred-dollar bill on the ground. This was something for nothing, a gift from the universe. And it was fruit, part of the food group that had been missing from our diet for months (not counting the three occasions that we had "borrowed" oranges off our neighbor's tree).

"What is it?" I asked Francisco, jumping up and down in excitement on one of the teetering steps. "Can we eat it?"

"*Maracuyá*," Francisco said in awe.

"It's maracooties? Can we eat it? Can we?"

Francisco nodded without taking his eyes off of my discovery.

The fruit was a good four feet above Francisco's outstretched arm but the fact that our potential meal was tough to reach did little to deter us. This was our reward for all we had endured. Now we just had to find a way to retrieve it.

I began looking around for a stick, but the only one that was long enough was nearly four inches in diameter and every time I swung it overhead, the weight of the club nearly toppled me over, making my aim completely random.

After a wider search of the immediate area, Francisco spotted a thin stick that was long enough, but because it was so slender, it was blown easily in the wind and the one time the switch did manage to make contact, it didn't have the weight the knock the fruit from its hold.

We refused to give up. We gathered up a pile of rocks and took turns taking aim. It looked easy, like a carnival game, and it lured us in like unsuspecting children with pockets full of quarters. The fruit was barely out of our reach—but when standing directly under it, we had to fight gravity. It was impossible to toss a rock straight up in the air, so we were forced to resort to moving farther away from our target, attempting to nick the fruit with the downward arc of our stone.

The first one to knock down a fruit was Francisco. Like hunters after freshly killed prey, we both ran to retrieve the fallen fruit. There was no need to fight over it. There was another one waiting. Francisco generously handed the *maracuyá* to me and I cradled it in my hands, holding it patiently as Francisco continued tossing stone after stone.

It took us forty-five minutes and nearly two dozen rocks, but finally—exhausted, filthy, and jubilant—we sat down on a log to enjoy the literal fruits of our labor. We cracked open the thick green skins in unison, ready to devour the contents in one large gulp, but instead of fleshy seeds swimming in reddish-orange juice, we were met with nearly empty shells, a few white unformed seeds inside. The fruit was unripe, useless, devoid of smell or flavor.

There was nothing to be said. We had invested nearly an hour and who knew how many calories in a pointless endeavor all in the sake of getting something to eat. We let the shells fall to the ground and sat looking down in silence.

The depression that ensued was only partly due to the fact that we had been outwitted by an egg-shaped piece of fruit. It was intensified by the realization of what I had become. I had joked in the past about being a starving student and then a starving artist, but never before had I been on the verge of actually starving.

Once we finally found the energy to make our way down the rest of the hill, I rashly squandered one-tenth of what was left of our money on a trip to the Internet café. For five dollars, I had a computer for an hour and I used my time to write a desperate plea to my sister, Heather. She was staying with my aunt and uncle at their house in West Virginia for the summer and I hated to ask her for help—she had just graduated from Vassar and was trying to figure out what her plans were. But I didn't know where else to turn. Hunger had made me desperate.

I got an e-mail back two days later with good news. Heather informed me that she had just won a Fulbright to Peru and that there was a chance she'd be able to visit. Plus, she wired me two hundred dollars, which Francisco and I happily invested in juicy steaks and a day's supply of *maracuyá,* purchased this time at the market.

And all of a sudden things started looking up. I had sent out a bunch of résumés to every potential employer imaginable, and one day I got an unexpected phone call from the creative director at McCann-Erickson. He wasn't offering a lot of money, but the ad copywriting job would buy us food on a daily basis. Days later Francisco got himself a job as a cabdriver, which wasn't glamorous, but it was an income. We would make it. We hadn't come this far to stop trying.

That was when I got the phone call.

"Heather was visiting us," my uncle explained, calling me at my home in Colombia. "She's had an accident in the Miata. It's bad. We're not sure how much time she has left."

There was a ticket waiting for me at the American Airlines office, he explained. I needed to pick it up and fly to D.C. before my sister's time ran out.

Chapter Eleven

Kidnapped
in the United States

I have never understood the concept of fulfilling someone's last wishes after they have passed away. I mean, it's not like that person is ever going to find out or anything. I try to keep my word when it comes to living people, but once you've crossed over to the other side, all commitments are null and void as far as I'm concerned.

Personally, I don't have any special requests when it comes to my own burial. Although I admit that the idea of having my ashes scattered over the Caribbean or the Amazon does have a certain romantic appeal, for me to appreciate this ritual I would have to be around to witness it. And other than burning myself alive, I have yet to figure out a way to do this. So when it comes to my own death, my last wishes are going to be a shot of good whiskey and a strong cigarette.

This same reasoning has gotten me very frustrated when it comes to eulogies. I figure that if I wait until my friends are gone, they'll never get the chance to appreciate the fine prose I have crafted in their honor—which seemed to offer a simple solution: A few years ago, I started writing homages for the people I cared about while they were still alive. Needless to say, this hasn't gone over as well as I might have hoped. In my well-meaning attempt to provide a present for my friend Lisa, I remember the shocked look on her face when I gleefully handed her a typed piece of paper and said, "Look, Lis, I wrote your eulogy."

What Lisa and my other friends have failed to understand is that my eulogies are not moribund prophecies—quite the opposite. I have always written them in the superstitious belief that the things you appreciate are never taken away from you. It is one of the few irrational beliefs I can't seem to shake: If I could value what I had, remember to care about the people who surrounded me while they were alive, losing them would have nothing to teach me, would be unnecessary, and therefore would not occur. At least, I always hoped the powers-that-be would see it that way.

But this time, I wondered if I was too late. As I sat down to write a tribute to my sister, I was frantically racing against time, hoping that a silly eulogy would have some magical power to cheat death and most of all timidly wishing that if I could just love her enough, there wouldn't be any real reason that she would have to die.

Over the next week as Francisco half-dragged, half-carried me to the offices I had to visit to get the stamp necessary to leave the country, the memories of her came to mind. I had known her her whole life, from the very first day of her existence. She'd been the funny one, the goofy kid, and I had been her big sister. I was five years older—enough of a gap to have a headstart on all of life's essential first lessons. I was the one who taught her right from left, who made sure she knew how to tie her shoes, who improved her pronunciation on all the essential bad words in Spanish. I informed her of the dangers of allowing llamas to spit in her eyes (living in Peru made this information essential). I even explained the safe way to cross the road.

By all accounts, my training had sunk in. By the age of four, she cursed like a Latino, avoided llamas like a Peruvian, and crossed the road like a chicken, meaning that she always got to the other side. Or so it seemed at first. After a bit more studied observation, I began to notice that my baby sister had a minor problem with her technique. Although she had gotten the stop, look, listen part down, she didn't quite grasp the fact that these steps had to be performed *before* stepping off the curb. In the midst of crossing, I would ask if she had remembered to check for traffic. Not wanting to disappoint me with a negative answer, she would set her things down on the double yellow line, dramatically look left and then to her right, and from the middle of the road, she would assure me that, yes, she had indeed made sure it was safe to cross the street.

This had all happened so long ago——to end in what? Now it was twenty years later and my little sis was dying in a hospital bed, and I was far away, unable to change the outcome. I fell to my knees and sobbed, clinging to hope and regret and wishing that just one more time I could have been there to remind her to look both ways.

"There's danger everywhere," my friends in Cali said, upon hearing the news of my sister's accident, taking a bit of solace in the fact that there was an impending death and for once it had nothing to do with Colombia.

My biggest concern now was getting to her as quickly as possible and the only thing keeping me from it was a large pregnant woman called Esperanza. She was a Colombian immigration officer whose job was to ensure that foreigners with no money weren't going to stick around Colombia for long, taking away jobs from the country's citizens. Needless to say, the fact that I showed up every month begging that she extend my visa for free because I was unemployed and therefore broke was not going over so well.

Every visit was the same with Esperanza (whose name in Spanish ironically enough means "hope"). I would timidly step into her drab dilapidated office and begin a lengthy explanation of what I needed and she would listen to me with a pained expression that I wasn't sure whether to attribute to my presence or the fact that she was knocked up and probably experiencing morning sickness.

Esperanza was now the only thing standing between me and an exit visa, but she wasn't about to hand one over until I paid the hundred-dollar-plus fine I owed for having overstayed the legal time limit twice already. Since I didn't have the money, my only hope was to outwit Hope with a bit of psychology. Her thought processes were like those of an army drill sergeant, meaning that she considered it her job to make my life as painful as possible (yes, it did worry me that she was multiplying), so I figured I would start by begging for what I absolutely didn't want.

"Esperanza, I need to stay in the country."

"I see," she said, leaning back in her chair and giving me a malicious grin. "Then you'll have to go to Bogotá and request a visa." And then trying to contain her sadistic glee, she added, "It's around four hundred dollars."

"Well, here's the thing—I don't have any money."

She grinned from ear to ear. "Well, then, I guess you'll just have to leave."

"Okay, I'll leave."

This threw her for a minute. She wasn't quite sure how to handle people who weren't fighting with her, and here I was being agreeable. But to her relief, she remembered the fine I owed just in time.

"Well, you can't leave. Not until you pay the $120 you owe."

"Then, I'll just stay."

"Okay. I mean, no," she said, losing her composure for the first time. "You can't stay unless you pay the four hundred dollars in Bogotá."

"Considering that I don't have four hundred dollars or one hundred dollars or even fifty cents to part with, it seems to me that you have two choices: You can let me stay for free or you can let me go for free, but I don't have any money to give you."

The look on her face was all I needed. I knew that I had stood up to immigration and won. And with my $120 exit stamp in my hand that I had gotten for free, I stepped momentarily out of the depression weighing me down, realizing that I had accomplished something great and miraculous, knowing that it was a triumphant day for illegals all over the world.

There was nothing left to take care of, but my flight didn't leave for five more days because my uncle had failed to find me a vacant seat on an earlier flight. I was in a painful state of limbo—between two countries and two possibilities: I didn't know whether to begin grieving for my sister or cling to hope. I wavered drastically between the two emotions. At unexpected times, in the middle of a walk to the small corner store or simply while watching our tiny TV, I would suddenly burst into tears. Other times, I was positive that she was still alive, that she would at least hold on long enough for me to see her one more time.

I couldn't wait to get to her as quickly as possible, but on the day of my departure it was painful to leave Colombia. I had said good-bye to Manfred and Cristina the previous day and it had been hard, but it was nothing like the scene at the airport when I parted with Francisco. Tears came easy to me that week. I cried at the entrance, I cried at the gate, I cried when the woman at the ticket counter asked if any persons unknown to me had left a suspicious-looking article in my care.

It wasn't like I was going away on vacation. I didn't know when I would see Francisco again. Our separation was to be just temporary, but there was no definite date for my return. Nothing was certain. The rest of my life was on hold, pending the outcome of the unsure future that awaited me in West Virginia.

Francisco stayed with me until the last possible minute, which given the ultra-secure measures that characterized the Cali airport, wasn't very long. The first of three X-ray scans my bags would go through was immediately upon entering the airport. Then, at the ticket counter, the place was swarming with guards, and since Francisco wasn't in possession of a ticket, they wouldn't even let him walk up to the counter with me. He had to wait behind a bright yellow line painted on the floor while I got my boarding pass.

However, it was the final line that was the hardest. As I took my place among the hordes of passengers waiting to clear immigration, I began to realize that this was it, that these were our last few minutes together. Other couples stuck it out through money problems, minor jealousies, and arguments over the position of the toilet seat; Francisco and I had loved each other through near starvation, guerrilla war, and false imprisonment.

I had vowed not to leave him just because things got too tough, but this time my sister needed me more. It was like a game of paper-scissors-rock, Heather against Francisco. Death trumps poverty. Heather wins.

Francisco would have to find a way to make it on his own for a while. His new cabdriving job didn't start for a few more days, which meant he had yet to see any income. And I had reluctantly taken out thirty-five dollars from the ATM machine so that I'd have something in my pocket while in the United States, leaving just enough in our account for Francisco to survive on for a week.

"Take care of your sister and come back to me," he whispered into my ear. "You're going to be okay. It'll all work itself out. God may squeeze you a little bit, but He never strangles you."

We stretched out our good-bye as long as the security guards would allow. The line moved on without us as we hugged, then kissed, then reluctantly separated. It was as far as Francisco was permitted to go.

There was a partition made of tinted glass that I was forced to walk around alone. But after all the time Francisco had spent in prison, we laughed at the notion that something like a wall could separate us. Although I couldn't view Francisco through the smoky glass, I spotted the glow of his lighter, which he held aloft for me to see, so I would know he was still there, waiting.

It was the memory of that small flickering flame that would help me get through the three months that were to come.

• • • •

The realization that I had arrived in the most powerful country in the world came to me by way of my senses. The unnatural white of the fluorescent lights, the crisp chill of the air-conditioning, the ubiquitous presence of blandly inoffensive music—the sudden appearance of these things jolted my fragile system. I had forgotten what it was like to be in an environment where everything was so carefully controlled.

In Colombia, you were subject to the whims of nature. When it was cold outside, you felt a chill. When it was hot, you sweated it out. When it was dark and the electricity was down, you went to bed. But here, we had overcome climate and seasons. We were even more powerful than the sun.

Walking through National airport, I felt the grandeur and simultaneous sterility of the country I had been born into. Colombia was harsh, even cruel, but it was this very unpredictability that gave it its flavor. In the United States, everything was always perfect, ordered, improved.

I felt out of place. I didn't know if this was due to the contrast between what I was feeling and what I was seeing—I felt so out of control yet I was walking through a meticulously planned environment—or was it simply that I had been gone so long that this no longer seemed like home?

I made my way through the crowd trying to find my aunt and uncle, hoping that a familiar face would make the whole experience less jarring. As I scanned the group in front of me, I suddenly spotted someone I recognized, but it didn't bring about the desired reassurance. Instead, I went through a moment of pure terror and confusion when I realized that the person who had come to pick me up at the airport was the same as the one who was supposed to be wasting away in a hospital.

I hugged her, I pinched her, I cried over her, and when I was convinced that I truly was standing in front of my sister, that she was living and breathing, it suddenly dawned on me that something was terribly wrong with this picture.

"What the hell is going on? What about the accident?" I shouted. I have generally saved the word "fuck" for very special occasions but this one seemed to merit it. "What the fuck am I doing in the United States?"

"Uncle Bob wanted to see you," she responded. "And he didn't think you'd come if he just asked."

(Fuck.)

On the drive over to my aunt and uncle's house, my sister helped me piece together how I had wound up in the United States. She had wanted to help me out of my dire financial circumstances but hadn't had any money to send so she had gone to my aunt and uncle for help. Somehow the phrase "boyfriend freed from prison followed by starvation in war-torn Colombia" had sort of slipped out of my sister's mouth, and my uncle had readily handed her two hundred dollars and then secretly plotted to get me back to the United States. Knowing I would never willingly leave Francisco behind, he had found my Achilles' heel, an unwavering devotion to my siblings.

Heather, for her part, remained innocent of the lie perpetrated upon me, mostly because she had been completely unaware of what was going on. She had been in Arizona visiting our sister, Catherine, when Bob called her up with a message consisting of limited information: "Wendy is coming home. You have to get back here." And once she had arrived in West Virginia, the damage by then had already been done.

Looking back, the fact that my uncle was capable of this should have come as no tremendous surprise. He had always gone out of his way to make everyone in his family feel insignificant in order to make his own sense of self-loathing seem small in comparison. He had once been a respected photojournalist, but his best days were behind him and my aunt Trish's lucrative corporate law position was now the primary source of income in their family. My sisters and I never understood how such an educated and determined woman could become so submissive in his presence. He criticized the way she drove, her sense of direction—even her ability to make the right purchases at the grocery store.

He had a wardrobe full of Dockers and Polo shirts, knew a few gourmet cooking tips, and engaged in a constant stream of yuppie activities to cover up the fact that he was born unsophisticated and provincial—which was only interrupted by his outbursts of acting unsophisticated and provincial. Over the stove as he stirred pots of *coq au vin, canard aux champignons,* and *spaghetti alla puttanesca,* he would rant about how women should never be allowed to drive, how niggers were destroying the city.

I wondered how my sister was able to spend so much time in his presence, but they were the only relatives living anywhere near Vassar. Based on the other coast, I had been forced to endure Bob only on three visits (he had married into our family and was Trish's second husband). Each time he had made my skin crawl. On one especially trying visit, he had regaled my sisters and me with the shocking tales of his sexual exploits—knowing that my uncle gave great oral sex was a detail I would have been happier not knowing.

However, when I had first heard about my sister's "accident," my dislike for him had taken a backseat to Heather's well-being. I was so distraught with grief that I had nearly forgotten how I felt about him.

In Cali, I had been forced to wait helplessly for nearly a week believing that all earlier flights were booked. The truth was that my uncle had been stalling until he and my aunt could leave town, hoping that a few days in Heather's presence would calm me down a bit. However, entrusting this responsibility to a person I had expected to be dead wasn't exactly great planning on their part.

My first few days at their house, they kept calling up Heather and asking if it was safe to come home yet. My sister would tell them the good news that I was getting calmer and calmer and the bad news that their wine collection was growing smaller and smaller.

A day after my arrival, I had been poking around an uninteresting-looking storage room packed with boxes and old clothes, not expecting to find anything of note. I was simply bored and had run out of places to rummage in the rest of the house. I don't know why I chose to peek into the carton in the middle of the room. But when I did, it was as if I had been witness to a miracle. I could actually hear the ta-dah music in my head (the same sound my Macintosh makes when I start it up) as a ray of white light shot its way through the window, illuminating the green glass bottles filled with red and white wines. Happily hauling one of each flavor with me upstairs, I concluded that if someone had to kidnap me, at least it had been accomplished by the only members of my family who purchased their alcohol in bulk.

That day and on every day to follow, the only escape I had from the misery of my daily reality were the drinks I began pouring for myself at ten in the morning, which sped to my bloodstream even quicker with the aid of a pack of cigarettes. My muscles constantly ached, my throat was hoarse, and my stomach burned, but in a strange way the pain pleased me. It felt oddly appropriate.

I was pretty satisfied with the quantity of my drinking, but after a period of seven days of sustained inebriation, the blurred figure in front of me with my sister's voice was starting to get a bit worried.

"Wendy, alcohol has turned into your reason to get out of bed in the morning."

"That's not true," I said, defending myself. "At least not since I keep my tequila on my nightstand."

My sister (who was, after all, a Fulbright scholar and felt the need to adhere to some standard of societal decency) took a deep sigh and insisted on trying to get me to see the light (and unfortunately she wasn't referring to the ray of light shining down on the Chardonnay in the basement). "Wendy, I think you need to take a good look at the situation you're in," she insisted.

"Okay, this is what is happening: I free an innocent man from prison and then Bob comes along and kidnaps me. Wait a minute— aren't you supposed to be dead? Ghost Heather, would you please bring me another margarita?"

I thought that summed up the situation rather nicely.

9 was desperate to make contact with Francisco. After days of failed attempts, he finally picked up the phone. I had planned to tell him everything, but once I heard the reassuring sound of his voice, I decided against it. In a long distance relationship, you never bring up any subject that can't be completely covered in one phone call. Waiting to continue a conversation at a later time is too painful. I didn't want Francisco to worry. So I sketched the barest outline of the plan my uncle had managed to carry out and assured Francisco that my sister was fine. Once I had laid out the basics, the only thing left to talk about was my desperation so I hung up the phone as quickly as possible, in order to keep Francisco from hearing the fear in my voice.

I would figure something out, but in the meantime I needed Francisco to focus on his own problems: surviving in Colombia without resorting to anything illegal. I had a nagging fear that the only thing preventing him from making a drug run had been my presence, and I couldn't bear the thought of losing him again to another prison.

Francisco's biggest character flaw was that he had an incessant need to please. He wasn't firm in his beliefs; he shifted his opinion to mesh with that of whomever he happened to be hanging out with at the time. When I had been with him, this had worked in my favor (perhaps I had even taken advantage), but now that he was deprived of my influence, I worried about what he could get himself mixed up in. I needed him to be patient the same way he had held out when we had been separated before.

Over the next week, we sent e-mails frantically back and forth, and the continual contact helped to reassure me. Francisco's letters were filled with affection and encouragement, and it appeared that things were going relatively well for him. He had begun work as a cabdriver and was barely earning any money, but he had taken in a roommate in order to augment his income. I wasn't sure how I felt about a stranger living in our house, but at least he was finding a way to manage for a while without me.

How I would face my aunt and uncle was a stress that constantly weighed down on me. I didn't really blame Trish—Bob constantly manipulated her to get his own way—but I wasn't sure how to react when I saw my uncle. I was filled with violent fantasies of punching him in the face, but I knew I would never actually carry them out.

When my aunt and uncle finally did walk through the door a week after my arrival, I repressed the urge to be aggressive and dif-ficult and resorted to being diplomatic (any foreign-service agent will tell you this means behaving well and drinking as much as pos-sible). Had I been dealing with a rational man, I might have tried to talk things out, but I planned to flee Bob's house as soon as possible and knew I would never speak to him again—ours was a relation-ship that didn't merit saving.

In silence, I wondered what my relatives' plans for me were. I had no money. I had left my belongings behind in Colombia: my clothes, my computer, my irreplaceable writing samples. Did they really expect me to simply forget about these things and my boyfriend and live happily ever after with them?

Having never fully thought through the consequences of their actions, now they found themselves bewildered by a situation they didn't begin to know how to handle. They tiptoed around me, hoping that not mentioning the issue would make it disappear on its own. In the meantime, I was acting as if everything were fine in order to keep conflict to a minimum—but the pretense weighed down on me and I longed to escape. I had arrived in the country with just thirty-five dollars, which had now dwindled down to less than twenty (spent mostly on cigarettes), which meant that the only way back to Cali was to find myself a job.

I spent several days scanning the want ads and then called up a temp agency that specialized in bilingual positions, figuring it would be a relatively easy and commitment-free way to make a quick buck. After polishing up my résumé and tailoring my experience to make it look like I'd spent my entire professional life as a Spanish-speaking secretary (screenplay writing with Manfred became "skill at writing bilingual documents"; conversations with Francisco became "translation experience"), I informed my aunt and uncle of my plans to go in for an interview. They seemed relieved at the prospect of my gainful employment: Getting a job was surely a sign of my nascent sense of responsibility—though my uncle couldn't resist slipping in a dig: "Oooooh, twelve dollars an hour. That would be quite a step up for you."

On the subway into D.C. with my sister (she knew the city much better than I did and I was relying on her to get me around), I rehearsed the upcoming meeting in my head. It had been years since I'd gone in for an interview for an office job and I was trying to remember the helpful tips guidance counselors had imparted to me so long ago. There was something about being immaculately dressed, showing a positive attitude, and being sure to leave your chewing tobacco at home. (I went to high school in the Midwest, okay? This was the kind of stuff you had to tell kids over there.)

As we got closer and closer to our stop, it occurred to me that my answers still needed a bit of fine-tuning. For example, in response to the query, "So, what is your least favorite part about working in an office?" my gut instinct would choose to say: "The working part." Interviewing wasn't like that word-association game where you mentioned the first thing that popped into your head—or even the fourth or fifth thing. The trick to getting a job was simply to lie shamelessly.

In spite of my preparations, there turned out to be a few obstacles at Telesec Temporary Services that I just hadn't been expecting. As I walked through the glass doors of the twelfth-floor office adorned with potted plants, the receptionist oh-so-cheerily handed me a stack of forms to fill out, apparently trying to set an example of the courteous demeanor and optimistic outlook characteristic of all the company's temps.

"Did you need a pen?"

I knew this was a trick question. Showing up without a writing implement would count as the first strike against me, a sure indication that I was unprepared for secretarial work and pen ownership in general. Luckily, I had thought of this minutes before when I had spotted the broken-off tip of a number two pencil on the floor in the corner of the women's rest room.

"I have a pencil, thanks," I said, clinging to my tiny stub of lead.

What followed was a grueling two hours of filling out forms, taking computer software tests, and watching industrial videos in which nonprofessional actors with Colgate smiles explained what a bright future awaited me in my new temporary life. Finally, I was ushered into another room for my oral interview, where I was joined by the office manager.

After a few preliminary easily answered questions, I came upon my first real roadblock when I was expected to explain the unaccounted time on my résumé. Not having a pat answer prepared, I resorted to the truth: I was still trying to account for it but it had something to do with living in Colombia.

At this point, had the woman conducting my interview been

your typical temp-agency employee, I probably would have been ushered out with a suspicious smile, a handshake, and a plastic "thank you for your time." But there were several things I had going for me: I typed seventy words per minute, I was one of the all-time high scorers on the English grammar test (and the woman seemed so excited by this that I just didn't have the heart to tell her that I ended a large percentage of my sentences in prepositions), and when my interviewer found out that I had spent time in South America, she nearly hugged me, asked if I knew her home country of Venezuela, and insisted on conducting the rest of the interview in Spanish. So two days later when she called me up to proudly announce that she had a position for me, it wasn't going to be at a boring insurance company or telemarketing firm as I had feared. I was to begin work at the prestigious Inter-American Development Bank (basically the Latin American version of the International Monetary Fund).

The job turned out to be as much as I could have hoped for. It was mostly South and Central Americans working there and the whole place had a Latin atmosphere, which meant I spoke Spanish all day and wasn't expected to get a whole lot accomplished. Besides, it was the finals of the World Cup, and since in Latin America all development work takes a backseat to soccer, my biggest responsibility was screaming "Brazil!" every time "our team" scored.

So for the next two weeks, I managed to put on panty hose, a guise of respectability, and a fake smile. In return, I got a paycheck—not enough to get me back to Colombia—but enough to help me flee the house that had become my prison.

Gainesville, Florida was famous on several counts: It was the birthplace of Gatorade, it was the home of the University of Florida Gators, and it even once boasted a well-known serial murderer. However, I wasn't really a big fan of fluorescent drinks, reptiles, or people out to kill me, so there didn't seem to be a lot drawing me to the place.

My friend Michael begged to differ. He was one of my oldest friends and the best thing I'd gotten out of a miserable year of high school in Montana. Over the course of a week's worth of lengthy phone chats made secretly from my aunt and uncle's balcony (drinking had a way of making me indifferent to the financial consequences of long-distance calls), he had been insisting I come stay with him and his wife for a while. Their home was small but it had an extra bedroom. I could stay months if necessary—whatever it took until I got the money to return to Cali.

It was a simple matter to quickly pack my bags, wish my sister all the best in Peru, and manage a disingenuous but cordial-seeming farewell with my relatives. Then it was a quick flight to Jacksonville and a slightly longer shuttle ride to Gainesville, and by the end of the day I had arrived in a humid, tree-filled city where everything was named Gator. There was Gator Gasoline, Gator Books, Gator Car Wash, Gator Insurance, and of course lots of Gatorade. And there was my friend Michael sporting a blue-and-orange Gator T-shirt, the same as I had remembered him: warm and funny with a smile that had a way of erasing all the years.

It had been a long time since I had last seen Michael. After graduating from college, he had moved to some remote country in Africa so I had been forced to content myself with the occasional postcard or news from secondhand sources about what was going on with his life. I hadn't heard anything from him for several years when an envelope covered in stamps from Namibia arrived at my apartment in Los Angeles. Michael was asking me to be his "best man" at his wedding. I desperately wanted to fly out to Africa for the ceremony, but the announcement had arrived too late—I had already purchased a nonrefundable ticket to visit my parents in Honduras.

Michael and his new wife, Sharon, a slender and graceful black South African, had returned to the United States a year later and had settled on Gainesville practically at random. They had wanted to live in a university town—both of them eventually hoped to complete their master's degrees—and Gainesville offered the added advantage of humidity. Having spent the past few years in arid Namibia, Sharon wanted to experience the rain.

I arrived on their front steps pretty much resigned to being miserable until I saw Francisco again, but goodwill diffused its way through their tiny home, infecting me in the process. I settled in to the sky-blue room they had painted in anticipation of my arrival and was amazed at how far out of their way they went to make me feel welcome. Over the next few weeks Michael raced ahead of me every time there was a cash register in sight, paying for any purchase even when I was picking up personal items at the drugstore. Sharon started showing up with small gifts for me—on different occasions, I received a shirt, a purse, shorts, lotion, and sweet-smelling shampoos. Apparently, the idea of two lovers being separated by a continent was a story that struck a cord with her, and as we huddled around the kitchen table over her exotic homemade curries, she would press me for information about my relationship, reveling in all the romantic details of my meeting Francisco in a prison. On a few occasions, she even dragged me down to the Western Union office and handed over a handful of twenty-dollar bills to be wired to Colombia to ensure Francisco's survival.

I was embarrassed at their generosity, but reluctantly accepted the money. By now Francisco's precarious situation had become a source of continual worry. Instead of earning a salary, cabdrivers lived off of the money handed over by passengers. Unfortunately, the rental fee Francisco paid to the owner of the vehicle often exceeded what he made in a day. Day after day, I could feel him losing hope. I kept reassuring him that there was an end in sight, that I'd be returning to Cali with money, that we'd move to Bogotá where the economy was better and we'd quickly find work. He just had to hold out a little while longer.

My plan was to get a quick job and make the money I needed to return to my boyfriend, and Michael and Sharon's plan was to get me to Colombia in as sober a state as possible. My current lifestyle that included drinking before noon was not exactly gelling too well with their lifestyle that included eating a well-balanced nutritious breakfast, so I figured I could at least make an effort, and I started adding orange juice to my vodka in the morning.

Trying to get a handle on all of my vices and please the friends who were being so kind to me, I decided to also cut down on my cigarette use, limiting my smoking to the time I was drinking. It was a good plan in theory, but now according to my own rules every time I wanted a dose of nicotine, I also had to pour myself a cocktail—so instead of cutting back on smoking, the result was just an increase in my alcohol consumption.

Realizing that this couldn't go on much longer, I decided to resort to drastic measures. With a great deal of effort, I finally threw out my pack of cigarettes, slept through my last hangover, and fit myself with a new pair of running shoes.

I liked the track where I had chosen to go jogging. It was just four blocks from Sharon and Michael's house, was usually uncrowded, and partially shaded by trees. The only problem was that it was next to a mental institution. Unfortunately the lunatics liked to use the track during their free time (which people living in asylums seemed to have a little too much of).

Now had it been the personality-less catatonics who were accustomed to head out for a nice leisurely stroll, there wouldn't have been much of a problem (other than the getting-them-to-move issue), but for some reason my running track seemed to attract every loudmouthed patient with Tourette's syndrome. Each time I passed them, they would bark "woof woof woof" at me like angry German shepherds.

Then there were the people who didn't quite understand the purpose of the white lines painted onto the asphalt. Instead of seeing them as friendly guides to help them stay in one lane, the patients viewed them as obstacles to be jumped over. Every time they heard my footsteps behind them, they would begin hopscotching over the lines, determined to keep me from getting past. I'd go to the right, they'd go to the right. I'd move to the left; they'd do the same. The only way around them was to head onto the grass, which for some strange crazy reason they seemed to have an aversion to.

But the most unsettling patient was the "I want some of that ass" guy. Each time I would sprint on ahead of him (I wouldn't have had nearly as many problems had the lunatics been in better shape and run a bit faster than me), he would launch into a lengthy monologue on the quality of all of my most private physical features (most of which were described as "juicy") and remind his companion that he was gonna get himself some of that juicy ass.

The bright side was, I ran extra fast on lunatic days.

I still missed Francisco terribly, but somehow over the next two and a half months, I managed to settle into a simple routine that was pretty close to being happy. The change was physical as well as mental. The healthy food and exercise were having their effect and my body was turning into a mass of hard muscle that I no longer recognized. I'd run my hand over my newly flat stomach, my toned limbs, amazed that with all the experience I had owning arms and legs (twenty-seven years), not once had it occurred to me that they could ever look like this.

In the past, my muscles had been like petulant children, doing my bidding only at the prospect of a reward. "Come on, if you take me to the fridge, I promise you'll get a beer." "Just a few laps around the track and we'll have some nice chocolate, the kind you like from Switzerland." But now, there was every indication that my little limbs had finally grown up. Getting them to move no longer required guilt trips or pleading. They did my bidding simply because I asked them to. Now I could run five miles a day without struggling. Even when I was simply strolling across the room, there was an agility I had never experienced before.

The improvement I was making to my physical self began spilling over into the rest of my life. With a bolt of confidence, I had whizzed my way through an interview at a nearby temporary agency and was now a full-time secretary at the City Attorney's Office, which sounded dull but was actually a mellow job working with nice people. My boss was a well-meaning, slightly timid lawyer just a few years older than me, who treated me as his equal, enthusiastically accepted my edits to his dictated letters, and cheerfully tolerated the misspellings I inserted into his correspondence, a result of having written exclusively in a foreign language for the past two years.

For the first time in my life, I didn't mind the routine of going into work every day. This was partly because I realized how important my job was to my future—it was my only means of returning to Francisco—but there was something else as well. Now when I looked outside the window of the office, the world looked different, in a way that had nothing to do with the view. In the past, having a job had meant missing out on something. But now, instead of longing to be out there, instead of wondering what lay beyond the window—now I knew.

This realization was almost spiritual. For someone without religion, whose actions weren't centered around earning brownie points to be redeemed in the next world, my creed had long been an attempt to get the most out of the life I had, the existence I was sure of. I had been striving to avoid the destiny that plagued so many of the people I knew. Growing up, I had gotten the same advice repeated to me—sometimes it had been from a teacher, other times from a friend of my parents, a woman in line at the post office, or a man selling shoes at the mall—the faces were different but they all had the same thing to say: Don't marry prematurely. Don't have kids early. Travel as soon as possible. You're only young once.

I had done exactly as they had advised, but without the end result they had anticipated. They believed that if you managed to cram enough happiness in by the time you were thirty, it would last you for the rest of your life. You'd always have a pleasing memory to call up from the reserve tank when times got tough. I was free of children, I had yet to get married, I had traveled, but my attempt to avoid responsibility had been fleeting. Travel didn't protect you from the dark side as I had once hoped. It merely allowed you to experience everything—the good with the bad—more fully.

When I relived the memories of the past two years of my life, I recalled terrible things: hunger, fear, sorrow, and loss. I had seen prisons and war, crime, and injustice. I hadn't found lightheartedness; I had discovered intensity, which probably served me better. The people who had populated my childhood still looked out the window holding on to the illusion that happiness was out there. I looked outside, content for once to be where I was, aware of the fact that I wasn't missing out on anything.

Of course, just when you think you've got it all figured out, just when you're sure the foundation for your life is sturdy, one new piece of information can shift the continental plate of your existence, making your whole worldview come tumbling down in an instant.

When I opened the e-mail from Francisco and read the introduction, I knew to expect the worst.

Dear Wendy,
    Something has weighed down on me for weeks. I thought I would tell you about it when you got here, but I can't stand the guilt.

This was not my favorite e-mail greeting. As far as good open-ings went, I tended to prefer the romantic "You are the best thing that has ever happened to me," "My darling dearest," or even the trite "How are you? I am fine" to the heavy "There's something I have to tell you" bit. This was not good, not good at all.

The e-mail confirmed what I had feared all along. Out of hunger, fear, and a desire to take action instead of idly sitting by, Francisco had gotten himself a fake passport in the hopes of scoring a trip to transport drugs abroad. He regretted it, he was sorry, he promised he wouldn't go through with it. It was the only solution that had oc-curred to him on a day when he hadn't had anything to eat.

The e-mail terrified me, but I forced myself to see his side of the situation. After all, I knew the power that hunger could wield. Francisco hadn't carried his plan out; he had confessed. I would have to forgive him. I would be there in just three weeks. Twenty-one short days to go.

Just for the sake of argument, let's imagine for a minute that Francisco wasn't a part of my life. Let's say that something happened to him, something painless and relatively benign—he got abducted by aliens (the nice kind, not the cavity-probing variety) and they de-cided to take him off to their home of Politak, a planet where they spoke a slightly modified version of Portuguese and (in what turned out to be an incredibly strange intergalactic coincidence) spent their days preparing for Carnavalak, a holiday that consisted of wearing elaborate costumes, a festive parade, and the consumption of Tumorak, the planet's most popular beverage (a success it had achieved in spite of the unfortunate double-entrendre of its market-ing tag line, which roughly translated meant "This tumor's for you.")

Okay, so let's imagine that Francisco is out of the picture, resid-ing far away on a bucolic planet drinking lots of *cocteles do tumor,* and I'm in Gainesville, Florida, living a relatively contented existence now that all the city's known serial killers have been rounded up and prosecuted. What would I do? How would my life change if I didn't have to consider Francisco's welfare?

Okay, so maybe these weren't the nicest kinds of thoughts to be having, but it could have been worse—I could have had Francisco stranded on Ort, a place without festivities of any kind where the only variety to be experienced in this homogenously boring planet covered completely in sand was the ingestion of a drug called *plob,* which was the earthly equivalent of getting shot up with novocaine. I had the decency to get Francisco exiled to an intergalactic paradise, which I actually considered pretty generous on my part. On second thought, after learning what Francisco had recently done, perhaps Ort was a better place for him.

It wasn't just that Francisco had purchased a fake passport. Based on his most recent e-mail, I had learned that he had accomplished this with the aid of my checkbook. Granted, the five-hundred-dollar check he had forged belonged to an account I had closed long ago, so I wasn't out any money, but who knew what this would do to my credit—and I especially didn't relish the idea of having any document with my name on it in the hands of people who made illegal passports. To do something stupid was one thing; to do something stupid that screwed me in the process—well, this was what got me to thinking about Francisco's hypothetical interstellar disappearance in the first place.

Had I been just a few years younger, I might have looked on it as a challenge to start over again, to go back to Los Angeles and build myself up from nothing, but I was too drained to even contemplate this idea. For once, I wanted to follow the easy path. Returning to Colombia had been my goal for three months now. I didn't have the energy to start looking for someplace new. I had no choice but to move on with what we had planned.

· · ·

W**hen** it comes to relationships, the lesson that has come hard to me is that you'll never get anyone to do anything they don't want to do. Oh, you may do okay at getting your way for a little while, but every tiny success you get is on credit—the bill comes later—and it's itemized.

For me, this lesson occurred four days before I was supposed to leave for Cali. I had my ticket in hand, my bags halfway packed. I had been sorting and re-sorting clothes and bath products into three equal piles so that my suitcases would be evenly weighted—this was when the phone rang.

"*Hola, mi amor,*" I said, happy to hear the sound of Francisco's voice. "Can you believe it? Just four days till I see you." I thought it odd that he didn't answer immediately. After all, I hadn't said anything that required much reflection. "Francisco, are you there?"

It's ironic that I asked if he was there, because he literally wasn't.

"I've left Cali. I'm headed to Europe in the morning." It was a tone of voice I had never heard him use before. He was so cold and clinical with me, like a doctor detaching himself emotionally in order to break the bad news to the patient.

"Where are you?"

There were over a hundred right answers to this question. I could have forgiven him for being nearly anywhere, in any nation except one. "Costa Rica," he said.

It was the worst kind of infidelity—he had cheated on me with a country. I had given up everything to get him out of Costa Rica yet he had risked his freedom to go straight back there. I didn't know how he managed to get in, but it didn't matter. Everything we had been through suddenly didn't count anymore—he had wound up exactly where I had first met him, a year and a half of my life in vain.

"I had a layover here. I'm delivering a shipment of shoes to Italy."

I knew this was code for making a drug run. "Why?" I needed to know.

"I need to earn a living."

Not the Italy part. "No, I mean, why Costa Rica?"

He took a deep sigh. "I thought I'd stay for a day or two and ask Laura why."

I couldn't believe it. He said the word Laura with real affection. The bastard. After all that she had done to him, I didn't know how he could stand to even be in the same room with her. He had gone all the way to Costa Rica to see his ex after all that I had endured for him?

I needed to say something. I knew it was the last moment I would ever have to convince him to love me again. It was my last hope to get him back. But nothing occurred to me.

"So, well, take care. I won't bother you again," he said.

And the line went dead. The man I was never going to leave had dumped me just like that.

This is the lowest point—the nadir, to use a nice literary word. This is as bad as it gets. I have to go through it because we all have to live with the consequences of the decisions we make, as much as we may try to avoid responsibility. We all have to grow up, as painful as it is. But I'm thinking, this is *my* coming of age story. You're completely innocent of the stupid decisions I made. And you're probably a very nice person who has shelled out good money for this book. You don't deserve to have to go through this with me. So if you want to skip on ahead, I won't hold it against you.

Life is hard enough. Come on, avoid the pain, take what happiness you can get.

All I saw was beige. The beige of the carpet. I was lying face down in it and for a minute, I couldn't remember why. I had this nagging feeling that there was something I'd forgotten, but I had no idea what it was. I was staring at each little strand of carpet, marveling at the tiny curl of the fibers.

And suddenly it came back to me. The phone conversation. Francisco. Gone forever. The thought made me want to cry. I touched my face, but it was already all wet. I realized that I had been crying all along. I'd been examining the strands of the carpet and sobbing.

I tried to focus on the carpet again because it seemed less painful than the other topic on my mind, but it didn't work this time. I would never feel his arms around me again, I realized. I would never touch his face. I would never see him walk through the door again. I curled up in a fetal position and shook with sobs.

For a brief moment, I remembered the carpet again. Yes, the carpet. I was able to focus on the rug under my body, but suddenly I hated it. As if the carpet were to blame for everything I was going through, I could no longer stand the sight of it. I hated the feel of it on my skin. I didn't want to see beige anymore. I needed to see black.

I crawled the four feet from Michael and Sharon's living room into my bed and covered myself with a blanket, hoping that by shutting out sound and light I could turn off my brain. It worked for a few seconds. It was quiet and still. Black and calm. I took a deep breath. Oh fuck! It's just not fair. I rolled over onto my stomach and pounded my fists into the mattress.

"You fucker! You bastard! You asshole! You shitface! You—" I had run out of expletives. "Fucking expletives!" I screamed.

Now what? Should I yell some more? Would it help? "Aaaaaaah!" I shouted. "Grauphhhhht!" I added.

I suddenly felt exhausted. I needed to rest. I rolled over onto my back. I was going to sleep. Just for a little while. I would fall asleep and then I would figure things out. I closed my eyes. It was hot. The comforter was too thick. I could barely breathe. Who bought such thick blankets in Florida? I poked my head out.

I sat up in bed and pulled aside the curtain in front of the window. A cricket was in the grass, hopping around just like nothing had happened. How could he be so callous? I wondered. Fucking cricket acting like everything was okay. I hated that cricket.

I felt a sudden surge of energy. I stormed out of bed, marched through the living room and out the front door. There he was, the cricket that had been taunting me. He reminded me of a hornet—he was shiny yellow and black—but he was nearly six inches long and practically as big around as a quarter. I tried to step on him but he just soared into the air and landed a few feet away. He looked evil. Maybe it was a she. No, I hated him—it was definitely a he.

I took a step forward, but ready this time, he wouldn't let me get too close. He jumped a few feet away.

I took off my shoe and aimed, but I was too slow. My shoe landed with a thump. I removed the other one and raised it over my head.

I was ready to fling it at my nemesis when I heard my name being called. "Wendy! Wendy, what are you doing?" It was Sharon. Sharon and Michael had come home. Suddenly I realized that I looked mad—I was barefoot standing in the grass. If anyone attempted to charge me for the attempted murder of an arthropod, I would be exonerated on the grounds of temporary insanity.

I looked at my friends and lowered the shoe. "I hate crickets," I said. And I hugged Sharon and began to sob.

At first I hated myself, hated how stubborn I was and stupid I was and unlovable I was. I wanted to be a different person, the kind of woman a man would never abandon. That was what I had expected of Francisco. I thought that if I could do enough, if I could stand by him during the worst times of his life when everyone else walked away, he couldn't help but love me. He would be the one person who would never leave. He would fill the void left by my parents. He wouldn't be like them. He would always be there for me, spending the rest of his life trying to make it all up to me.

If it had been me, I would never have deserted someone who had gotten me out of a prison. I would have thought, This person really loves me. I really owe this person one. But then again, I would never have wound up in jail in the first place—and maybe that was the point. I had thought that having an interesting life would be what Francisco and I had in common—when all along the common ground I should have been looking for was someone who had never been incarcerated.

I wasn't sure who I hated more—Francisco for never having taken care of me or myself for being so stupid, for thinking that giving was the same as receiving. I told myself that now at least the only person I would have to take care of was myself, but I missed him in spite of myself. Missing someone I hated—it didn't make a lot of sense, but I didn't care. Neither did my emotions.

Over the next week, each hour that went by was excruciating. All I wanted to do was lie in bed and think about how terrible my life was. I had nothing, no place to go. I had lost the man I loved. I had given up my home, my freelance writing business, my savings. I suddenly understood what the beige carpet must feel. I had been stepped on and sullied and squashed, and then I had been ripped up and replaced without a second's thought.

Anyone else would have gone home. That's what people did when they got in trouble. They went back to the house they grew up in, to the town where everyone knew their name. They went back to homemade dinners made by Mom. They recuperated in the bedroom they had grown up in, slept in a bed still surrounded by trophies and out-of-date posters that had remained in the exact same spot since high school. Subsisting on a steady diet of love and homemade baked goods, a person could recover. It just took enough time, enough hugs, enough chocolate-chip cookies.

I wanted to go back to my childhood home and rest, but to which one? There had been so many. There had been my parents' married student housing dorm in Tucson, the little house out in the desert near Palm Springs, the Victorian home in South Carolina, the Tudor-style structure in Minnesota, even the "station wagon house" in Tennessee, the only time I had been required to share a "room" with my two sisters.

Which house would I go back to? It didn't matter. I'd take any of them. I had the strangest urge to go and knock on the doors of all the places I had lived. I imagined a kindly older couple opening the door and asking me in. Maybe they would have lost a daughter who would have been just about my age and they'd beg me, please, wouldn't I think of staying with them for just a little while? It would be such a comfort to them. I would wake in the morning to fresh orange juice and toast. She would teach me how to quilt and he would proudly show me his prize daffodils, which had won him three blue ribbons at the state fair.

One day, while making fresh bread, I would be inspired to confide in her and I would tell her my history in the house, how I had nursed wounded animals back to health here, how I had collected fireflies in a jar. I would thank her for keeping the bedroom just as her daughter had left it and I would tell her that I knew it meant a lot to her girl. I would lower my voice and confess my dirty secret. Trying to hold back the emotion, I would tell her my parents had disassembled my room before I had even left home. I would explain that I had gone to Germany for my senior year as an exchange student (the old woman would be impressed by that), but when I came back, my posters, my trophies, my clothes, my tapes, my books—all of these things were gone. My sister Heather had taken over my room.

The kindly older woman would look at me with eyes full of

compassion, clasp my hand, and ask what I had done. I would lower my gaze and admit: "The basement. They made me sleep in the basement."

And then I would feel better because I had finally said it out loud. It would all be okay. They were going to take care of me. I was home.

Chapter Twelve

Livin' Bolivian

What I needed was a miracle. Was this too much to ask? It didn't seem like an entirely unrealistic request. After all, the past two and a half years had been full of serendipitous twists. I had defied incredible odds when I had run into Saúl in Costa Rica. There had been Francisco's brush with Fabiola at the prison when we had needed an attorney. And the day that Francisco had walked out of the gates of La Reforma would always be a miraculous occurrence for me, no matter what had happened afterward.

All I needed was one more tiny dose of magic. Not an excessively large miracle. Just your everyday standard-sized supernatural occurrence—a good job offer, for instance, or a friend who was going abroad and needed someone to housesit for a year. There were lots of possibilities.

But nothing happened. I was still working at my temp job at the City Attorney's Office wondering what to do next. I was sending out a stream of résumés for local jobs I was overqualified for but so far had received no response. And I had been calling up everybody I knew, but no one had an extra house they were looking to fill.

If this were a fictitious story, I could have concocted a miracle. I would have made up some fabulous ending: Ed McMahon shows up with a one-million-dollar check, I use the money to go to Spain, and then fall in love with a matador who has a penchant for sequins and overly tight clothing but is otherwise perfect in every way. It would be the granddaddy of all finales. But I can't invent the facts here. This is all true. And what really happened was the smallest most unassuming miracle of all. It was no bigger than a thought.

I had been running at the track (which was now a standard part of my daily routine) while pondering the nature of war. It was a subject that occupied a good portion of my thoughts these days—thinking about conflicts plaguing the countries I had visited was so much more pleasant than dwelling on my own problems. But a neuron must have misfired or a cerebral connection got crossed, because somehow these two disparate subjects got interconnected.

"They're fighting because they want to." It was such an easy phrase, such a simple yet effective philosophy when trying to understand world events, yet I had never applied it to my own life.

As I thought it over, my relationship with my parents actually did have a lot in common with guerrilla war. Here I was, hiding out from them, depriving them of information of my whereabouts, and reappearing whenever it suited me to deliver a deliberate attack. What was more guerrilla-like than that? I had figured this was normal behavior for a daughter-parent relationship, but now I was starting to suspect that maybe this was normal behavior only for a person intent on overthrowing a right-wing dictatorship.

I was angry and full of resentment, fighting a battle against the people who had raised me. And if I was incapable of getting along with my own family—my own flesh and blood, people who shared the same race, nationality, and genetic makeup—what chance did Muslims have of understanding Jews? What were the odds that the United States would sit down with Castro, that Colombia would achieve peace? If I couldn't resolve my personal issues, how could I expect entire nations to come to an agreement? With people like me, what chance was there for world peace?

What followed was a brilliant moment of clarity, in which I suddenly grasped the answer that could change my life as well as the world. It was this:

War is like chocolate ice cream.

(I know, I know. It sounds more like a Ben & Jerry's tag line than a recipe for world peace, but just bear with me for a minute.) My life experiences had led me to a simple conclusion: There were lots of people running around stressing the virtues of chocolate ice cream and I would never see eye to eye with them. I was a cookies-and-cream, butter-pecan, mint-chocolate-chip girl myself. You could try to convince me that chocolate ice cream was a worthy cause, that it had never done anything to hurt me, that it was a well-meaning and virtuous flavor, but still you'd never get me to come out in favor of it.

Now, if you couldn't persuade me to give a frozen dairy-based dessert a chance, what was the likelihood that you'd get me to change my religion, alter my political stance, diminish my attachment to a certain disputed piece of land? About as probable as the sudden popularity of salmon-flavored ice milk.

What I suddenly grasped was that peace didn't come about by convincing someone to see a conflict from your point of view. Getting along with someone else didn't necessarily mean agreeing with them. Disputes ceased when you were able to view the other's person's opinion as wrong yet accept their privilege to cling to it anyway.

I finally understood that a war ended when being at peace became more important than being right.

Any story can be constructed in many ways. Any conflict has at least two different viewpoints. Take the facts and reorder them and you can come up with a handful of contradictory conclusions.

I had used this reasoning to get Francisco released on bail. The judge had seen a criminal and a flight-risk; I showed him a family man with a long history in Costa Rica. All I had done was present the other side of the story.

And if I had been able to do this for Francisco, perhaps my mother also deserved this same PR makeover. I needed to review the evidence, see the conflict from her point of view. I would reconstruct the story, build my image of her from scratch.

That horrible night so many years ago when I had called my mother from a pay phone to tell her I had become suddenly homeless, what had really happened? Thinking it over, I hadn't really been looking for help. The truth was, I had just called to rub the situation in her face, to let her know how much I was suffering to go to college as a result of the fact that she and my father wouldn't pay for it. I wouldn't have gone home had she begged me to. It would have meant the end of my studies at UCLA. But I had wanted her to ask me anyway. I had been seeking just a smidgen of security, any small sign that my parents would come through for me, not necessarily that night but in the future, that if the time ever came when I was really desperate, if I really had nowhere left to go, that they wouldn't let me down. But no, nothing.

I had carried that night in my mind for so many years now, evidence that I would always have to face my problems alone, but maybe my conclusion had been premature. Maybe my mother had meant something else. It wasn't that she hadn't wanted to help. She just hadn't known how.

Unlike my uncle who felt the need to control everyone around him, my relationship with my mother had always been based on her faith in my ability to make my own decisions. She had never second-guessed me. She believed in me. If I didn't want to go to Arizona, she wasn't going to force me.

Standing alone and afraid at a pay phone in front of my nine-hundred-dollar Mazda parked in the bad part of La Cienega, I hadn't wanted to go to Arizona, I just wanted the invitation. "I'm homeless" meant "Tell me that you'll be there for me." But my mother hadn't understood this—nuance had never been her strong point. All these years I had blamed my mother for not caring about me when the only thing she was really guilty of was an inability to read between the lines.

Could it possibly be as simple as that? All this time, it was just a misunderstanding? I needed to find out. Trembling, I picked up the phone in Michael and Sharon's living room, dialed my parents' extremely long number, and after a few rings there was my mother's voice, the same way it had sounded so long ago. It had taken me eight years to finally tell her what was on my mind, yet I accomplished it in only five words. I took a deep breath and asked, "Mom, can I come home?"

The road home is never easy. There are always enchanted forests to be crossed, yellow-brick roads to be taken, Greyhound bus rides to be endured. Getting to Cochabamba was going to require a long international flight plus two trips by land, one of which was going to be made on a rickety bus winding its way down through the arid and cold mountainous terrain around La Paz—at thirteen thousand feet, it was the highest capital city in the world. But I didn't mind. Even when our bus was forced to pull off to the shoulder somewhere in the Bolivian *altiplano* and wait idle in the chilly air for four hours while road workers made repairs to the pavement (a process that occurred every day from noon to six), I remained in a good mood. It had taken me nearly a decade to find my way home—what were a few hours more?

Thirty-one hours after I had left Gainesville, I was finally in a cab headed toward my parents' house. The movement of the taxi swirled up a cloud of dust (I was beginning to feel like a Charles Schultz character), but through the haze I could still make out the lofty peak of Mount Tunari in the distance. I scanned the outskirts of the city, and curiously enough, the whole area reminded me of southern California. It was all blue skies and green towering mountains.

The city itself was quaint. It was filled with colonial architecture, artsy cafés, and airy plazas. And how could you not love a place with cobblestone streets! As we bumped our way along the irregular path (I couldn't refuse the childish urge to make the sound "aaaaah," which came out in staccato bursts as a result of all the bouncing), I decided that no one in their right mind would ever give up a cobblestone street in exchange for a smooth ride. Sometimes beauty had to outweigh convenience.

I assumed we were heading the right way, but my directions had been given to me by my mother. Instead of consisting of useful information, they contained entertaining tidbits such as "We live on the street with the video store that's owned by the communist." However, as we drove around the perimeter of the newly constructed Mariscal Park, the cabdriver and I weren't having any luck spotting either video stores or Marxists.

"According to my directions, it's on the north side of the park. Is this the north side?"

The cabdriver nodded.

"Wait a minute. Up ahead. What does that sign say?"

Sure enough, it was a video store. This had to be the street. We made a right and followed the road. Just two more blocks and we'd be there.

Seated in my parents' living room, everyone wanted to talk first. I felt like the prodigal son, only instead of being welcomed back with a fattened calf, I was being showered with attention and funny stories. In fact, there was so much chatter going on, I became convinced that my family members had spent the past two years taking notes of the important things they wanted to tell their eldest daughter whenever they saw her next. I could just imagine the journal entries made by my father:

• *The history of Bolivia, especially the part about Patiño's tin mines. She'll need to know about that to lead a fulfilling life.*

- *Mining practices of Croatian immigrants to Bolivia in the early twentieth century. Don't forget to mention early smelting practices, which should provide Wendy with lots of funny stories, not to mention a solid background in the melting temperatures of alloys.*
- *An explanation of Bolivian vegetation broken down by climate zone. She'll need this in case she wants to make a salad.*

My father had gotten the first half hour practically to himself, a rare opportunity since most conversations were dominated by my talkative mother. My brother had added a few quips here and there, but my mother had remained surprisingly silent, apparently at a loss to add anything to the esoteric subjects my father insisted on tackling. However, the restraint finally proved too much for her and she suggested a change of topic. "Hey Wendy, you want to hear about how we found our maid?"

"Sure. Why not?" I said. I wanted to hear about everything that I'd missed.

"Well, they've really simplified the process of finding good help here," she said enthusiastically, sitting up in her chair. "It's all very well organized. See, they have a maid market. You go there and they all line up and you check them out—you can ask them any questions you want. I chose Vicenta. She looked very well groomed and has proven to be a good cook."

My father, the intellectual. My mother, the aspiring slave master. These were the people I had been born to. They spent the rest of that evening cracking me up, filling my head with strange and funny images of my new home, painting a picture of all there was to do and look forward to in the months to come. It was going to be a vacation of sorts—I was in a foreign country with no obligations and no job.

There was a sense of poetic justice to this. I had found irresponsibility at my parents' house. After all, I had tried to use travel as a stand-in for the childhood I had never had, which, looking back, hadn't been such a far-fetched idea. When you're a child, everything is bright and new and amazing, and that's what going to an unfamiliar place is like—foreign places are always new. All of a sudden you are transported to an infantile state, unable to speak the language and unaware of the rules.

Travel is like the high drama of youth. It's the best and worst at the same time. One minute you are flung to the depths of despair, the next, you feel the giddy, exaggerated joy of an adolescent. For me, it had been a chance to make rash decisions, to take wild risks, to lose everything knowing I'd still have plenty of time to earn it all back.

Of course, even foreign places grow familiar given enough time; even novelty grows old. Some would argue that this is what makes travel pointless. And in a sense, it's true—childhoods never last. But everyone deserves one.

Even if they have to wait until they are twenty-seven years old.

I spent the next eight months in relative happiness, living out the carefree adolescence I had never had. I slept in. I ate rich new foods. I left a trail of crumbs in the living room, and since I had a maid following behind me with a dust cloth, I never had to clean anything up.

I read books in Spanish and in English. I walked around the center of town with my brother. I learned the names of a half-dozen different kinds of potato while shopping in the open-air market with my mother. I made friends with an amazing group of artists who threw extravagant parties with live music in a nineteenth-century adobe structure that looked like an ancient church. Occasionally when I felt restless, I'd take a long-distance bus ride up into the mountains and stare out the window at my old friends the llamas, which always brought back memories of my childhood.

As the months ticked by and I felt myself getting stronger and happier, even the pain that Francisco had caused me began to subside. I recalled him from time to time but no longer wished to have him physically present. In person, he was capable of weighing down my life, but I was the one in control of my memories. I could play them again in my head, picking out the details that I felt like remembering, rolling out the story the way I saw fit. In time, I suspected that I would be able to focus on what I had gained from him instead of dwelling on what he had taken.

I also knew that at some point, I would have to be heading back to Los Angeles. I had put off my return for nearly a year. The thought of starting over again—sleeping on a friend's floor for a time, getting a temporary job—these things weren't appealing, but after all that I had been through, they were really just minor inconveniences. I had tackled prisons and guerrilla war. I had become fearless.

Besides, I knew I could always call up my parents if things got too bad. For so many years, I had had nowhere to turn during the tough times. Although I still didn't know what country my parents would wind up in, I now knew that help would always be just one overseas plane ticket away. My parents had never provided me with a stable home, but now I realized they had given me something better: the ability to make any place in the world my home.

Besides, my folks had their problems too. Their money situation was beginning to get precarious and they were thinking of heading back to the United States in the next few months, in the hopes of starting over again in middle age. My dad who had decades of experience as a well-paid mining engineer knew exactly what kind of job to get: He wanted to become a chef. My mother (who had never had a job and thought that working sounded like a fun, novel way to spend forty hours a week) began mulling over exactly what she was qualified for. The week following Christmas, since all of her children were in Bolivia for the holidays, she came to my sisters and me for advice.

"I'll do anything as long as I don't have to wear panty hose," she informed us, asking us to look over a list of potential jobs that she had come up with.

Heather, Catherine, and I handed back a significantly shortened list, but my mother refused to get discouraged. Two days later, she came up with another idea. Inspired by an action adventure movie on cable in which Jean Claude Van Damme single-handedly defeats a dozen well-armed trained mercenaries, Mom came rushing into the kitchen to inform us of the message that Hollywood was sending. "I finally understand what pays well in America," she informed us. "I need to find a job that's in high demand and requires specialized skills."

My mother was set on the idea of becoming a CIA agent—especially as it seemed that Jean Claude Van Damme was never required to wear tights.

My sisters and I knew that secrets stuck around our house about as long as my mother's lemon squares, and we began to think about the fate of our nation depending on Cathie Dale. I could just imagine the day when Rich would stroll into the room and announce, "Mom said not to tell anyone, but we're going to war."

But my mother seemed pretty happy about the idea. She gleefully walked around the house practicing strange accents, fitting herself for trench coats, and trying to solve the mystery of why all of the vegetables in our house were turning into decorative rosebud shapes and where the balsamic vinegar and goat cheese had come from. My father, meanwhile, had narrowed his culinary school choices down to two academies.

My sisters and I watched the spectacle with detached interest, at times cracking up at the unique family we were all a part of.

"And you, Wend, what are you going to do?" Catherine asked.

The details for me were still kind of fuzzy. What exactly was I going to do? How would I start over again? It was the kind of situation that would have driven me crazy three years earlier, but I had been in Latin America long enough to let a little bit of wisdom seep in. There was a saying around here: "There are only two types of problems, those you can do something about and those you can't. If you can do something about your problem, why worry about it? And if you can't do something about your problem, why worry about it?"

In Latin America there were so many things that were out of your control. The check you were expecting might arrive or the bank could go bankrupt, wiping out your life savings in an hour. The bus you were expecting might come in an hour, or it might not come at all—which meant that you could stand in line freaking out, checking your watch, and asking everyone where the bus was, or you could set your bags down and start up an impromptu party with the people around you. Either way, the bus was either going to come or it wouldn't. There was nothing worrying would do to make it come any faster.

This attitude was the only way to survive Latin America and it had taken a lot of time to make it finally sink in. After all, I had been trained from birth that everything was within my control. I had to be accountable, be responsible, make things happen. But now I understood that responsibility was only part of the equation—life was the process of finding the delicate balance between responsibility and spontaneity, adulthood and innocence, duty and joy.

In the United States, we placed so much stock in responsibility, because we held on to an illusory notion that we were completely in control of our lives. Any bad event was an aberration, an act that needed to be remedied. We believed in order: The movie was supposed to start on time, the ATM machine was expected to work, the mechanic would never be out to lunch when we needed a repair. Bad things weren't supposed to happen, but when they did, someone had to be punished. If I slipped in a restaurant, it was the owner's fault. If I got in a car accident, someone was always to blame. In the United States, there was an incessant need to control a world it was often impossible to control. Because the truth was, sometimes the plate simply slipped out of your hands.

I wanted to explain this to my sisters but I didn't know where to start. How did I condense the past three years of my life into a simple response? So I just shrugged my shoulders and said I didn't know what my plans were. I had no idea what would come next.

My sisters seemed to understand. After all, they had been raised by the same two crazy parents. Heather nodded sympathetically and insightfully commented, "You know, for our lives to get any weirder, we'd have to start hanging out with circus people."

I laughed and said, "The bearded lady—I just bet she's waiting for us outside."

About the Author

For a person who has spent most of her life trying to avoid working, Wendy Dale has held an impressive number of jobs. She's been a corporate writer, a public relations consultant, a speechwriter, a desktop publisher, an ad copywriter, a screenwriter, and there was even a brief stint as a celebrity journalist. Among her many accomplishments: the television special she co-scripted, *The New Adventures of Mother Goose,* was nominated for an Emmy. She lives in Los Angeles with a pet cockatiel, a guy she picked up in Bolivia, and a massive caffeine habit. This is her first book.